changing the way the world learns[SM]

To get extra value from this book for no additional cost, go to:

http://www.thomson.com/wadsworth.html

thomson.com is the World Wide Web site for Wadsworth/ITP
and is your direct source to dozens of on-line resources.
thomson.com helps you find out about supplements,
experiment with demonstration software, search for a job,
and send e-mail to many of our authors. You can even
preview new publications and exciting new technologies.

thomson.com: *It's where you'll find us in the future.*

The Wadsworth Special Educator Series

The following Special Education titles are new for 1998 from Wadsworth Publishing:

- *Special Education Issues Within the Context of American Society*
  Susan McLean Benner, Ed.D., University of Tennessee, Knoxville
  ISBN: 0-534-25230-3
- *Promoting Learning for Culturally and Linguistically Diverse Students*
  Russell M. Gersten, Ph.D., Eugene Research Institute
  Robert T. Jiménez, Ph.D., University of Illinois, Champaign
  ISBN: 0-534-34417-8
- *Beyond High School: Transition from School to Work*
  Frank R. Rusch, Ph.D., University of Illinois
  Janis G. Chadsey, Ph.D., University of Illinois
  ISBN: 0-534-34432-1

Promoting Learning for Culturally and Linguistically Diverse Students

Classroom Applications from Contemporary Research

Russell M. Gersten
Robert T. Jiménez

Wadsworth Publishing Company

IⓉP® An International Thomson Publishing Company

Belmont, CA • Albany, NY • Bonn • Boston • Cincinnati • Detroit • Johannesburg
London • Madrid • Melbourne • Mexico City • New York • Paris • Singapore
Tokyo • Toronto • Washington

Education Editor: John Gill
Assistant Editor: Valerie Morrison
Marketing Manager: Jay Hu
Project Editor: John Walker
Print Buyer: Barbara Britton
Permissions Editor: Veronica Oliva
Copy Editor: Lachina Publishing Services
Illustrator: Lachina Publishing Services
Cover: Jeanne Calabrese
Compositor: Lachina Publishing Services
Printer: The Maple-Vail Book Manufacturing Group

Printed in the United States of America
1 2 3 4 5 6 7 8 9 10

For more information, contact Wadsworth Publishing Company, 10 Davis Drive, Belmont, CA 94002, or electronica
at http:// www.thomson.com / wadsworth.html

International Thomson Publishing Europe
Berkshire House 168-173
High Holborn
London, WC1V 7AA, England

International Thomson Editores
Campos Eliseos 385, Piso 7
Col. Polanco
11560 México D.F. México

Thomas Nelson Australia
102 Dodds Street
South Melbourne 3205
Victoria, Australia

International Thomson Publishing Asia
221 Henderson Road
#05-10 Henderson Building
Singapore 0315

Nelson Canada
1120 Birchmount Road
Scarborough, Ontario
Canada M1K 5G4

International Thomson Publishing Japan
Hirakawacho Kyowa Building, 3F
2-2-1 Hirakawacho
Chiyoda-ku, Tokyo 102, Japan

International Thomson Publishing GmbH
Königswinterer Strasse 418
53227 Bonn, Germany

International Thompson Publishing Southern Africa
Building 18, Constantia Park
240 Old Pretoria Road
Halfway House, 1685 South Africa

Library of Congress Cataloging-in-Publication Data

Promoting learning for culturally and linguistically diverse students
    : classroom applications from contemporary research / [edited by
    Russell M. Gersten, Robert T. Jiménez.]
            p. cm. — (The Wadsworth special educator series)
        Includes bibliographical references and index.
        ISBN 0-534-34417-8 (pbk. : alk. paper)
        1. Language arts (Secondary)—Social aspects. 2. Literacy—Social
    aspects. 3. Multicultural education. 4. Critical pedagogy.
    I. Gersten, Russell Monroe, 1947– . II. Jiménez, Robert T.
    III. Series.
    LB1631.P76 1998   97-30575
    428'.0071'2—dc21   CIP

 This book is printed on acid-free recycled paper.

Dedication

This book is dedicated to the memories of Valerie Anderson, one of the great action researchers in the field of reading, who had deep insights into productive ways to teach English language learners; Eric Hedges, who died before he could reach his potential; and Sydney Gersten, who immigrated to this country in 1927, but didn't tell his son for many years.

Contents

PART II: THE TRANSITION YEARS: INTERMEDIATE SCHOOL GRADES

PART III: MIDDLE AND HIGH SCHOOL GRADES

Preface

Are there any underlying principles of good education that can help teachers of culturally and linguistically diverse students sort through the flood of new instructional practices and programs that all claim to be "good education"? What about literature-based instruction, sheltered English instruction, native language instruction, multicultural education, cooperative learning, instructional conversations, community-based education, and explicit and direct instruction? Are they all valid? What are their similarities and differences? Are there ways to combine them so that students are provided with optimal opportunities to learn content-specific information while they simultaneously learn English? And perhaps most perplexing of all, for teachers, is the question, How and in what ways should instruction be adapted or modulated so that all the components of an effective curriculum for native English speakers are also accessible to culturally and linguistically diverse students?

The answers to these and other questions demand information that goes beyond merely identifying, describing, and expounding on the dilemmas faced by those who serve culturally and linguistically diverse students. Focusing on dilemmas too often seduces policy makers into thinking that good education consists of nothing more than simply abandoning that which is inadequate or problematic. We believe that it makes more sense to synthesize research from the fields of bilingual education and cognitive strategy instruction and from the general knowledge base on effective instruction as a prelude to improving teaching.

Two general principles, agreed on by the authors, underlie their contributions to this book. First, children for whom English is a second language require a unified educational experience from kindergarten through high school—that is, something more than a patchwork quilt of disparate and, at times, incompatible programs.

Second, programs characterized by native language or sheltered English instructional techniques, in and of themselves, are not enough to ensure academic success. The authors also share a general distress at the overwhelming trend toward providing no services to English language learners beyond those extant in the general education classroom.

The first section of the book comprises three chapters that focus on issues related to supporting early literacy development for English language learners. Claude Goldenberg integrates a conceptually driven model of leadership with a balanced approach to early literacy development that has been proven effective in increasing student learning. He describes efforts to combine an emphasis on skill building with meaningful communication.

Jozi De León and Catherine Medina delineate classroom characteristics that build on and are compatible with students' home experiences. They identify some key concerns for early childhood educators and then discuss several concrete, specific suggestions for improving instructional practice.

Valerie Anderson and Marsha Roit's chapter focuses on early literacy issues and provides a range of instructional principles useful for creating a reciprocity between learning to read and oral language development for English language learners. Their chapter provides some specific and helpful ideas for building language fluency and comprehension via a range of literacy activities.

The second section of the book focuses on issues related to the transition years, when students' instructional day is increasingly in a second language (English). A major premise of this section is a belief that instruction for English language learners needs at a minimum to provide access to the same curriculum presented to native English-speaking students and to ensure that when exiting a program, students will continue to receive instruction that takes into account their transitional status. In other words, English language learners should be truly transitioned and not unceremoniously terminated from specially designed instruction.

Russell Gersten, Susan Marks, Thomas Keating, and Scott Baker present factors leading to successful second language instruction. These factors are presented through research data that delineate a range of effective teaching practices to support comprehensible instruction for English language learners.

Carmen Arreaga-Mayer's chapter describes effective instructional grouping strategies that incorporate peer-mediated learning procedures. Russell Gersten's chapter further describes the instructional practices of an expert teacher who successfully attends to both language development and learning in academic content areas.

William Saunders and his colleagues in the Los Angeles Unified School District have put together step-by-step directions for helping students respond to literature in a three-year transitional program. At the heart of the program are procedures that help students make connections between their own experiences and a specific piece of literature.

Elba Reyes and Candace Bos provide crucial information for implementing a process called semantic mapping, which provides English language learners with some very important learning scaffolds, making it easier for them to organize and understand key concepts in a story.

The third section of the book focuses on issues pertaining to English language learners in the middle and high school grades.

Robert T. Jiménez and Arturo Gámez look at the situation faced by teachers of recently arrived middle-school-age Latino students who have very low levels of literacy and prior schooling. Their chapter describes the foundation for an approach to teaching literacy that provides multiple opportunities for students to build reading fluency, makes use of culturally relevant and familiar texts, and focuses on comprehension.

Anne Graves presents various ways to make connections with students' communities and families. She also explains how instructional strategies can make language comprehensible while conveying important conceptual material.

Anna Uhl Chamot's chapter presents a set of principles for integrating content area instruction for English language learners, particularly for those students at the high school level. She presents these principles within an instructional approach, called Cognitive Academic Language Learning Approach (CALLA). This approach is based on a cognitive model of learning, with a specific goal of developing higher-order thinking skills. Her chapter presents the crucial steps for teachers interested in implementing such a model in planning and delivering instruction to English language learners while teaching content material.

Jana Echevarria describes strategies and techniques for adapting curriculum in middle schools and high schools. She provides numerous examples of ways to adapt science, social studies, and math lessons for culturally and linguistically diverse students, and she includes lists of curricular resources and materials to assist teachers in this endeavor.

As a summary chapter, Sharon Vaughn and Russell Gersten present an overview of the major themes raised in the book as a whole and link these to issues in the field of education for English language learners.

Teachers and others who work in the schools should find many useful suggestions in this book. We hope that it provides important benchmarks for teachers, program coordinators, and directors as they evaluate programs, curricula, instruction, the mix of instructional techniques, and the use of languages. We especially believe that focusing on the goals and objectives of programs designed for culturally and linguistically diverse students can only benefit all involved. Perhaps most importantly, we hope to make available specific approaches, at times accompanied by step-by-step directions, for teaching students who are all too often forgotten and ignored.

This book was supported in part by the Division of Innovations and Development of the Office of Special Education, U.S. Department of Education, grants HO23A40035 and HO23E50013. The editors wish to thank Jane Williams, Louis Danielson, and the other members of the Language Minority Research Task Force (Robert Rueda, Janice Chavez, Ji–Mei Chang, Carolyn Adger, Marie Hughes, and Kathleen Harris) for their support and assistance with helping to conceive and then providing important feedback on this book.

Promoting Learning for Culturally and Linguistically Diverse Students

Classroom Applications from Contemporary Research

PART I

The Primary Grades

1

A Balanced Approach to Early Spanish Literacy Instruction

Claude Goldenberg
California State University, Long Beach

INTRODUCTION: BALANCING
SKILLS AND WHOLES

Once upon a time, basketball coaches around the country were involved in a furious debate over how to coach. There were two groups of coaches, each openly contemptuous of the other. Both sides felt the other had ulterior motives and political agendas, didn't care about players, had misguided philosophies, or were simply ignorant. The basketball-loving public was confused and could not understand why professionals seemed to be so divided along basic issues. Basketball lovers were particularly concerned since the overall level and quality of basketball playing seemed to be, if anything, deteriorating. While the coaches argued and sometimes insulted each other, generations of basketball players were being lost.

On one side were those—called the fundamentals-first coaches—who were convinced that you got better at basketball by isolating and then focusing on the basics of the game. During practices, these coaches stressed the fundamentals. Players went through practice and drill routines for basic aspects of the game—shooting, passing, dribbling, rebounding, and playing defense. They practiced everything except actually playing basketball. The only time players got to play was during official league or tournament games. When things went poorly in the games, the coaches' response was, "These kids are just not getting the fundamentals," and they would intensify their drills and their practice routines. Many players improved in their skills, but they were not very good basketball players, nor were the teams very good basketball teams.

A different group of coaches took a very different approach. These coaches believed that you learn to play by playing and not by breaking the game down into skills or subskills. These coaches—who called themselves whole-basketball coaches—thought that learning to play basketball should be a natural process. They advocated having players play real games all the time. Players chose up sides and played among themselves during practice. These teams hardly ever received explicit instruction or practice in shooting, passing, dribbling, rebounding, or playing defense. Even if individual players or whole teams were noticeably weak in some aspect of the game, coaches did not work explicitly on these weaknesses. Instead, they looked for or tried to create coachable moments during games when they could help players work out the rough spots. Individual skills were never singled out for work and practice outside the context of a game. Some players became frustrated; others enjoyed and benefitted from large amounts of playing time. But team play did not really improve.

Disagreements in the field of literacy instruction sometimes resemble this fractious basketball debate. Just as the fundamentals-first coaches stressed game fundamentals nearly to the exclusion of actually playing the game, early literacy instruction sometimes runs the risk of stressing the basics of letters, sounds, and decoding to the near exclusion of having students engage in actual reading and writing. Similarly, educators who stress the importance of making literacy highly meaningful or authentic from the beginning are reluctant, as were the whole-game coaches, to break reading and writing down into skills and provide students with instruction and practice to improve performance overall.

Although the terms have changed over the years, the phonics (or skills) versus meaning debate in literacy instruction has raged for much of this century. Indeed, the debates sometimes sound more like "wars" (Stanovich, 1993/94). Only highly charged topics with explicit political or social implications, such as bilingual education, school desegregation, or sex education, attract more fervid partisanship than the debate over how children should be taught to read. The reasons are many and complex and the subject of many academic, professional, and popular works.[1] But the partisans sometimes act and sound like the coaches in our tale.

Over the past decade, however, there have been increased calls for balance in early literacy education (e.g., Adams, 1990; Anderson, Hiebert, Scott, & Wilkinson, 1985; Delpit, 1986; Goldenberg, 1991; Honig, 1995; Spiegel, 1992). Condemarín (1991) and Goldenberg (1990, 1994) have made analogous arguments for a balanced approach in Spanish reading. A balanced approach is based on an interactive view of reading, which suggests that both skills and meaning are important for literacy development. Instead of exclusively emphasizing letters and sounds or meaning and purpose, a balanced approach involves a mix. It provides children with instruction and learning opportunities that promote both development of phonological processes (i.e., the sounds letters make and how those letters and sounds combine to form words) and attention to authentic communication via the written word—the use of literature, journals, diaries, and other meaningful print forms. Learning about letters and sounds as well as learning about the meaningful and purposeful aspects of literacy complement and reinforce each other, just as learning the fundamentals of basketball and learning to play in real games complement and reinforce each other. They are not in competition.

The idea here is not to reach a compromise or strike a deal for the sake of making everyone happy. Rather, the reasoning behind appeals for a balanced approach is that both perspectives in this debate have much to offer in the search for a comprehensive and unified approach to early literacy education that makes the most sense for students. Learners generally benefit both from explicit guidance in how to recognize words efficiently (the phonological approach) and from a wide range of opportunities to use print for authentic communication (the meaning-based approach).

Such a blend, or balance, underlies the approach to literacy education adopted in a schoolwide project that has improved academic achievement for low-income, mostly Hispanic students (Goldenberg & Sullivan, 1994). In this chapter, I will describe this approach to early literacy development (grades K–2). The framework for this approach consists of a set of goals and expectations for students' reading and writing development. The goals and expectations were purposefully designed to incorporate both perspectives (the phonics, or skills, perspective and the meaning and communication perspective) into a unified and comprehensive view of how children learn to become literate.

It is important to note that the balanced early literacy curriculum described here was developed and used in a larger context of schoolwide change and improvement (briefly described later). In other words, this project did not focus on early literacy exclusively; rather, a balanced approach to early literacy was but one aspect of a larger effort to improve achievement at the school. Reading and writing goals and expectations were developed at each grade level; various means for assessing students' achievement were also developed and used; achievement at the school indeed improved overall. Thus it is impossible to say whether improvements in the early grades are due specifically to a balanced early literacy program or to the larger change process at the school, which included having clear and supported goals and expectations for student learning at each grade level. The operating assumption of the educators and researchers who worked on this project was that both were involved—a substantive and balanced approach to literacy education was supported by an effective change process. Both substance and process are fundamental for successful school change (Fullan, 1991). Each is necessary; neither is alone sufficient.

THE NEED TO IMPROVE SPANISH LITERACY ACHIEVEMENT

The National Clearinghouse for Bilingual Education (1995) estimates that nearly 2 million students in U.S. schools speak Spanish as their primary language. Many of these students—although by no means all—are in bilingual education programs where they learn to read and write in Spanish before making the transition to learning to read and write in English. But even when taught and tested in their primary language, Spanish-speaking students often experience low levels of literacy attainment. First-grade children tested in Spanish score on average at the 32nd percentile on national norms; second- and third-grade students, still taught and tested in Spanish, drop to the 27th percentile (CTB/McGraw-Hill, 1988). Even students who receive intensive tutoring in Spanish reading (a Spanish version of Reading Recovery; Clay, 1985) still score at the 41st percentile. Students not eligible for this intervention, because they were above the bottom fifth of their class, scored on average at only the 31st percentile (Escamilla, 1994), nearly identical to the national sample of the late 1980s (CTB/McGraw-Hill, 1988).

Many bilingual programs are clearly failing to help Spanish-speaking children achieve at grade-level norms in their native language. This failure undoubtedly compromises the effectiveness of bilingual programs. According to bilingual education theory (e.g., California State Department of Education, 1981), students will ultimately achieve at higher levels in English if they first achieve at high levels in their native language. High levels of Spanish literacy do not guarantee high levels of English literacy, but poor achievement in Spanish augurs little success in English.

How should educators approach the challenge of promoting high levels of native language literacy for Spanish-speaking children? The project described here, as well as other recent successful ventures (e.g., Dianda & Flaherty, 1995), suggest that Spanish-speaking children, no less than English-speaking children, benefit from a balanced literacy program that teaches phonological skills while also providing meaning- and language-rich opportunities to interact with print.

A SCHOOL CHANGE PROJECT

The school where this project has been located—Freeman Avenue School (a pseudonym)—is one of five elementary schools in a small, heavily Latino school district in Southern California. Freeman's demographics reflect those of the district overall: 95% of the school's 800+ students are Hispanic; 93% come from homes where Spanish is predominantly spoken; 86% of students are limited-English proficient; 89% qualify for free school meals; and another 7% qualify for reduced-priced meals. Hispanic parents—mostly from Mexico—average around seven years of formal schooling.

When the project began in 1990–91, average achievement at the school was well below state, national, and district norms. In the final year of the administration of the California Assessment Project (1990), for example, students at Freeman scored between the 7th and 15th statewide percentiles on reading, writing, and mathematics. Within three years, however, achievement at the school had surpassed that in the rest of the district and in some respects had matched or surpassed state and national norms. In 1990, only 31% of

Freeman's first-grade students who were learning to read in Spanish were on grade level according to national norms; around the district, the figure was 41%. But by the time this group of students reached third grade, students at Freeman outperformed other Spanish-speaking third graders in the district and around the nation—61% were reading at or above grade level at Freeman, in contrast to 49% on grade level around the district (students had been at their respective schools since the beginning of first grade).[2]

Fourth graders tested in English reading, many of whom were limited-English proficient students who had first learned to read and write in Spanish, also improved. Before 1990, Freeman students scored below state and district students on tests administered by the California State Department of Education. By 1993, Freeman students' achievement was superior to that of the rest of the district and nearly equivalent to the state average: 28% of Freeman's fourth graders scored at the highest levels (4 and up on a 6-point scale) on the California Learning Assessment System (CLAS) reading test. In contrast, 17% of the fourth graders in the rest of the district and 30% of the fourth graders around the state scored at levels 4 and above.

A Model to Guide Change

The goal of this project has been unambiguous: To work with faculty, administrators, parents, and students at the school to improve academic achievement, primarily in the language arts. We were guided in our work by a four-element change model developed in collaboration with the school's principal (Goldenberg & Sullivan, 1994; Sullivan, 1994). The function of the change model was to help provide overall coherence to the school's change efforts, something often missing in the patchwork of disparate efforts that too often characterizes attempts to reform or restructure schools. As Fullan, Bennett, and Rolheiser-Bennett (1990) have pointed out, "The greatest problem faced by school districts is not resistance to innovation, but the fragmentation, overload, and incoherence resulting from the uncritical acceptance of too many different innovations which are not coordinated" (p. 19).

The model is derived from research in educational change and our own experience working in particular school settings. It consists of four sets of factors, or change elements:

- *goals* that are set and shared
- *indicators* that measure success
- *assistance* by capable others
- *leadership* that supports and pressures

Versions of three of these change elements—goals, indicators of achievement, and leadership—have long been associated with efforts to improve school effectiveness. A fourth factor—assistance—has recently begun to receive attention (see Fullan, 1985, 1991; Loucks-Horsley & Mundry, 1991; Tharp & Gallimore, 1989). We predicted that these four factors would influence teacher attitudes (e.g., expectations, sense of efficacy, attributions) and behaviors (e.g., teaching practices, parent contacts, interactions with students) known to influence important student outcomes, such as achievement and attitudes.[3] We expected the model to help create a school community where teachers would have regular and consistent opportunities for professional growth and development specifically aimed at helping them help their students achieve at higher academic levels. Figure 1.1 depicts our school change model.

There are of course many ways to operationalize the model in Figure 1.1. The important point, however, is that attempts to improve achievement or to improve any aspect of a school's operation cannot take place in a vacuum. There is a context—or culture—within which school personnel operate, and school improvement is as much a matter of shifting the context as of changing the specifics of instruction and curriculum (Fullan, 1991). Indeed, the premise of our work is that shifting the context (or culture) and changing the instructional and curricular specifics are inextricably linked—one cannot be done without the other. Space does not permit a full explanation of how the model was used at Freeman (interested readers are referred to Goldenberg & Sullivan, 1994). For purposes of this chapter, the origins and development of two particular change elements are most relevant—student goals and indicators of achievement. These two best embodied the balanced approach to literacy development described earlier.

Goals for Student Learning. Over a period of two years, a committee made up of teachers, administrators, and a researcher conceptualized and put into practice reading and writing goals and expectations (described later in more detail). Goals and expectations were informed by teachers' professional judgments, curricular materials in use, and key documents in the professional and research literature (e.g., Calkins, 1986; Chall, 1983a; Clay, 1985). Monthly full-day meetings of the Academic Expectations Committee were made possible one year by a restructuring planning grant from the California State Department of Education (SB 1274). Developing and finalizing the goals involved committee meetings, meetings with grade-level colleagues, meetings with the school's governing council (the principal and representatives from each grade level), and a meeting with parents. The goals and expectations went through numerous drafts and changes, as we strove to develop a comprehensive framework for the school's literacy curriculum that the entire school community would support.

Parents were also extremely positive, and when shown an earlier version of the goals, they urged us to write more-parent-friendly versions. One parent suggested that we make them "mas claro y en pocas palabras" (clearer and in fewer words) and that we distribute them to parents at the beginning of each school year. Another parent suggested putting the highlights on an overhead and showing that at back-to-school night as well. This parent was particularly pleased with the whole idea, saying that she thought "our standards are a lot

FIGURE 1. School Change Model

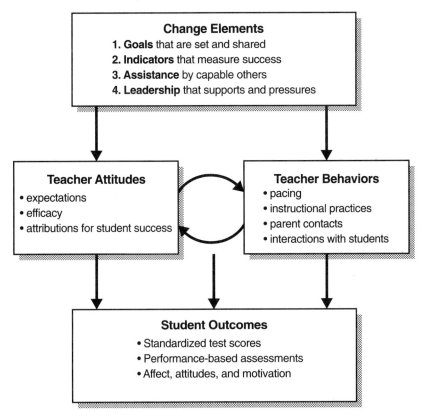

Note. From *Making Change Happen in a Language-Minority School: A Search for Coherence* by C. Goldenberg and J. Sullivan, 1994, Washington, DC: Center for Applied Linguistics.

lower" than they should be and that we "really need to push our children." She saw these expectations as going in exactly the right direction. At back-to-school night in September 1992, we did as these parents suggested. Overheads gave the highlights of our goals and expectations; hard copies of the overheads were also available. When the parents visited their child's classroom, they got complete parent-friendly versions for that grade level. Several teachers commented that parents came into their rooms that evening more enthusiastic than they had ever seen them.

Indicators of Student Learning. Indicators gauge individual student achievement but also provide an overall picture of whether goals are being attained. Indicators answer the questions, Is what we're doing working? and Where are the data? At Freeman, we have used several indicators, including student book placement, to gauge progress. We found in an earlier study that when reading achievement improves, students are more likely to be on grade level in their book placement (Goldenberg & Gallimore, 1991).

Perhaps the most important set of indicators we used consisted of performance assessments we have developed based on our language arts goals and expectations.[4] In the spring, a 20% random sample of students who have been at the school at least two academic years (or the entire year for kindergartners) are given two-day assessments. Students are asked about independent reading they have done and their attitudes toward reading and writing. They are asked to summarize and explain things they have read and to write original story endings. They are also assessed on their use of written conventions. In kindergarten and first grade, children are assessed individually on their knowledge of letters and sounds, beginning decoding skills, word and letter writing, comprehension of stories they either hear or read, oral and written comprehension, and oral reading skills. The assessments have been developed in collaboration with the Academic Assessment Committee, the immediate descendent of the Academic Expectations Committee. After school ends in the summer, teachers from Freeman and other schools participate in scoring sessions where they are trained to use rubrics to analyze and score student work. Results of the spring assessments are shared the following fall with the entire faculty.

Goals and indicators have helped provide focus for the change process by helping teachers prioritize areas of instruction that need emphasis or improvement (Saunders, 1995, April). By concretely representing the project's unambiguous goal—helping students achieve specific high-level learning goals—these goals and indicators serve as common, tangible representations of the collective enterprise. They also encourage active articulation and discussion among the faculty about whether student achievement is in fact improving. At the beginning of the school year, teachers hear a report about student performance on the spring assessments and plan areas to focus on in the current year, based on these results. In addition, at monthly grade-level meetings, teachers discuss and score (using rubrics) sample student products from each others' classrooms. This type of ongoing professional discussion is critical if meaningful and substantive change is to take place in schools.

LEARNING LITERACY
IN SPANISH AND ENGLISH

As just described, the backbone of our efforts to improve academic achievement at Freeman Elementary comprised grade-level academic goals and expectations in language arts. The goals and expectations for grades K–2 are shown in Tables 1.1–1.6. Tables 1.1–1.3 list the reading goals, Tables 1.4–1.6 the writing goals.[5]

Several features of the goals and expectations deserve specific mention.

Table 1.1. Reading Goals and Expectations: Kindergarten

READINESS BOOKS		CORE LITERATURE	
Spanish	**English**	**Spanish**	**English**
Cuéntame Siempre felices	The Cat in the Fiddle; The Mouse in the House; Happily Ever After	Tortillitas para Mamá Caperucita Roja La liebre y la tortuga	The Little Engine That Could The Three Little Pigs The Three Bears
WHOLE-TEXT/PREDICTABLE BOOKS		Nadarín Había una vez La Cucarachita Martina El gato con botas Cuando los borregos no pueden dormir	The Very Hungry Caterpillar Favorite Nursery Tales
Libros Palmas, palmitas (PP₁) New Zealand and other predictable read-along books	Yellow Fish, Blue Fish (PP₁) New Zealand and other predictable read-along books (e.g., Brown Bear, Spot)		

Readiness
Readiness skills on report cards and *Happily Ever After/Siempre felices*

A. Word recognition
- reads the names of 5 to 8 children in class/group
- reads 20 to 30 sight words—can be 50/50 mixture of words everyone is taught (e.g., from PALMAS or other books) and words in personal vocabulary list)
- recognizes signs and labels at school (and at home and in community)

B. Letters/phonics
- names and recognizes letters in name
- names and recognizes the 5 vowels, in and out of order
- names and recognizes letters in alphabet (uppercase and lowercase), in order
- names and recognizes letters in alphabet (uppercase and lowercase), out of order
- recognizes beginning sounds of words
- uses knowledge of letter sounds to begin to decode words
- hears rhymes in words, distinguishes between words that rhyme and words that do not, and produces a word that rhymes with a given word
- writes letters, as dictated
- writes words and short sentences, as dictated

C. Comprehension/literature/whole-text reading
- reads or pseudoreads for pleasure age- and grade-appropriate books and materials (ongoing)
- reads or pseudoreads 3 to 6 favorite picture books
- makes reasonable predictions about story content, based on a key illustration
- orally answers questions about story read aloud, even without picture cues
- uses 3 or more sentences to describe a picture
- answers oral questions about books
- answers questions about familiar books by choosing correct sight word
- selects from group of sight words the word missing from sentence read aloud (auditory cloze)
- is familiar with and can retell 3 to 6 favorite stories from children's literature

Table 1.2. Reading Goals and Expectations: First Grade

	READING BOOKS		CORE LITERATURE	
	Spanish	**English**	**Spanish**	**English**
PP$_1$	Palmas, palmi-tas	Yellow Fish, Blue Fish	Había una vez	My Favorite Good-night Stories
PP$_2$	Osito, osito	My Friends the Frogs	Cenicienta	Rumpelstiltskin
PP$_3$	Matarile-rile-ró	Grab That Dog!	Juanita y Margarita	Sleeping Beauty
Primer	Tara, tara, la guitara	Little Duck Dance	Sapo y Sepo son amigos	Snow White
1st rdr.	El sol y la luna	My Best Bear Hug	Osito	Beauty and the Beast
			Los zapatos de Munia	The Ugly Duckling
			La luna de Juan	Cinderella
			Donde viven los monstruos	The Tale of Peter Rabbit
			Las dos cabritas	Little Red Riding Hood

A. Word recognition
- has reading vocabulary of approximately 300 to 500 words (sight words and words easily sounded out)
- uses *both* context and phonic cues when encountering unknown (but familiar) words during reading of simple texts

B. Letters/phonics
- knows all letters and corresponding sounds (Span.)
- knows all letters and most common corresponding sounds (Eng.)
- uses knowledge of letter sounds to decode familiar words (Span.)
- uses knowledge of letter sounds to decode familiar 1-syllable, phonetically regular words (Eng.)
- writes words and sentences as dictated

C. Comprehension/literature/whole-text reading
- reads for pleasure age- and grade-appropriate books and materials
- independently reads books with high-frequency words, e.g., *The Cat in the Hat* and other Dr. Seuss books; *Brown Bear, Brown Bear; Will You Be My Mother?*
- reads simple texts at primer/first-reader level (about 50 to 100 high-frequency, sight and phonetically regular words) and answers questions asking for literal understanding, inference, and main idea
- answers written comprehension questions in simple sentences
- retells a story that has been read aloud, using correct sequence and appropriate narrative form
- describes a picture using more-complex language and making inferences about characters, motivation, etc.
- answers oral questions about books read aloud, imparting new information
- engages in oral discussion with teacher and classmates about texts read
- infers meaning of unfamiliar words from context
- is familiar with, and can retell, a large number of favorite stories from children's literature

D. Study skills
- uses book's cover and table of contents to gain information about title, author, chapters, and pages
- alphabetizes words by first letter
- uses a simple glossary to locate words and meanings
- follows simple written directions

Table 1.3. Reading Goals and Expectations: Second Grade

READING BOOKS		CORE LITERATURE	
Spanish	English	Spanish	English
2.1 *A ver, a ver, a ver*	*Cats Sleep Anywhere*	*China, China Capuchina*	*Frog and Toad are Friends*
2.2 *Pluma, tintero y papel*	*Come Back Here, Crocodile*	*Historia de una manzana roja*	*The Tortoise and the Hare*
		El patito feo	*Jack and the Beanstalk*
		Historia de Dragolina	*Alexander and the Terrible*
		El maíz	. . .
		El libro de las adivinanzas	*Ira Sleeps Over*

A. Word recognition and word skills

- has reading vocabulary of about 1,000 words
- uses knowledge of letter sounds to decode most words
- reading fluency is increased by coordinating the basic decoding elements, sight vocabulary, and intelligent guessing to figure out new words
- reads and identifies the meaning of words with prefixes and suffixes (Eng.)
- distinguishes among words that sound alike but have different meanings (homonyms) (Eng.)
- identifies synonyms (the same as) and antonyms (opposite from)
- writes words, sentences, and short paragraphs as dictated

B. Comprehension/literature/whole-text reading

- reads for pleasure age- and grade-appropriate books and materials
- independently reads—with increased fluency and comprehension—simple books and stories
- reads passages at second-grade level (about 150 words) and answers questions asking for inference, main idea, topic, literal details, and sequence
- answers written comprehension questions in complete sentences
- predicts the outcome of a story read to self
- engages in oral discussion with teacher and classmates about stories read or heard
- has these specific comprehension skills:
  —can identify the cause of an event, feeling, or situation
  —can identify the sequence of events in a story
  —can distinguish between what could really happen and what is make-believe
  —can identify the setting of a story
  —can infer meaning of unfamiliar word from context
  —can read question mark and exclamation mark correctly
  —knows quotation marks signify someone is speaking
- has begun to acquire these skills:
  —can paraphrase sentences
  —can state the main idea of a story
- is familiar with and can retell at least 4 core literature stories

C. Study skills

- uses parts of a book (contents, glossary) to locate information
- alphabetizes words by the second letter
- follows written directions
- uses key and grid on map to locate objects and identify them

Table 1.4. Writing Goals and Expectations: Kindergarten

General

- prints own name (first and last) using capitals and lowercase letters appropriately
- prints about 10 to 40 other favorite words
- uses some letter sounds to "estimate" word spellings
- uses the following *forms* to accomplish one or more *purposes* (recount a personal experience; tell/create a story; convey/explain factual information; persuade/influence):
    - picture story with accompanying oral narrative
    - rudimentary written story or narrative
    - journal entry
    - language experience story (dictates a story written down by someone else)

Handwriting

- begins to use correct manuscript writing
- copies short language experience story legibly and neatly

Table 1.5. Writing Goals and Expectations: First Grade

General

- prints words by sounding them out or from visual memory
- can "estimate" spellings of most words, at least to some degree
- writes simple story or narrative comprising a number of connected sentences
- uses the following *forms* to accomplish one or more *purposes* (recount a personal experience; tell/create a story; convey/explain factual information; persuade/influence):
    - letter to a friend or relative
    - story (original or a retelling)
    - recounting of a personal experience
    - daily journal entry
- uses a word processor to write stories or personal accounts
- begins to use capitals and ending punctuation (e.g., period, exclamation point, question mark) as appropriate to level of writing (relatively simple sentences and texts)

Handwriting

- continues to improve printing mechanics and correct manuscript writing
- uses correct manuscript writing when recopying own text (e.g., for publication, for final draft, to prepare for an audience)

A Balanced Approach to Literacy Development

First and most fundamental, the goals shown in Tables 1.1–1.6 represent a balanced approach to early literacy development in whichever language a child is learning to read and write.

Table 1.6. Writing Goals and Expectations: Second Grade

General

- writes phrases/sentences making comparisons and contrasts
- writes new endings for familiar stories
- writes more complex story or narrative comprising a number of connected sentences, organized coherently
- uses the following *forms* to accomplish one or more *purposes* (recount a personal experience; tell/create a story; convey/explain factual information; persuade/influence):
  - original story
  - simple letter
  - daily journal entry
  - relating of one or more facts about an event or area of interest
  - simple story summary
  - personal invitation
- demonstrates progress in use of capital letters at beginning of sentences and proper names
- demonstrates progress in appropriate use of capitals and periods
- begins to use question mark and exclamation point correctly

Handwriting

- continues to improve printing mechanics
- uses correct manuscript writing when recopying own text (e.g., for publication, for final draft, to prepare for an audience)

On the one hand, there is emphasis on bottom-up processes, reflected by skills-oriented goals such as word recognition, knowledge of letters and sounds, and printing. In kindergarten, children are expected to name and recognize letters, recognize the sounds in words, and discriminate between words that rhyme and words that do not (see Table 1.1, "B. Letters/phonics"). They should also be able to print their own name and begin using some letter sounds to estimate word spellings (Table 1.4). By second grade, children are expected to have a reading vocabulary of approximately 1,000 words (Chall, 1983a), be able to use knowledge of letters and sounds to decode most words, and read with increased fluency (Table 1.3, "A. Word recognition and word skills"). They are also expected to have essentially mastered the mechanics of getting spoken speech onto paper and to be able to use writing functionally (Table 1.6).

Several goals also speak directly to the development of phonemic awareness, the understanding that words are made up of smaller units of sound that can be segmented and identified. Phonemic awareness is considered one of the most important understandings children must develop if they are to become successful readers in an alphabetic language (Adams, 1990; Adams & Bruck, 1995; Jiménez & Ortiz, 1993). Kindergarten and first-grade goals that promote phonemic awareness include naming and recognizing letters, recognizing beginning sounds of words, hearing and discriminating rhymes, writing letters and words from dictation, and "estimating" the spellings of words when writing. In addition, several of the books listed for kindergarten and first grade contain rhymes and chants that also contribute to phonemic awareness.

On the other hand, the goals and expectations also emphasize top-down processes. These are reflected in meaning-oriented goals such as reading or pseudoreading for pleasure, talking about books, and encouraging attempts at communicative writing. In kindergarten, children should be reading (or pseudoreading; Chall, 1983a) books appropriate for young children, listening and comprehending when books and stories are read aloud, and retelling favorite stories (Table 1.6, "C. Comprehension/literature/whole-text reading"). They should also be making rudimentary attempts to write narratives or journal entries, including the use of pictures to accompany narrative, and be dictating language experience stories to someone who can transform them into written text (Table 1.4).

By second grade, children should be reading age-appropriate books and stories independently, with increasing fluency and comprehension, be able to discuss what they read or hear, and further develop comprehension skills such as identifying the sequence of a story and distinguishing cause and effect (Table 1.3, "B. Comprehension/literature/whole-text reading"). They should also be able use a variety of written forms (e.g., letters, original stories, summaries, invitations) to accomplish a range of purposes in writing (e.g., recount a personal experience, convey or explain information; see Table 1.6). Goals and activities that help children develop insights into the nature and functions of print are an important part of the literacy framework developed at the school.

A Developmental Approach to Literacy

A second general characteristic of the grade-level goals is that they reflect the developmental nature of learning to read and write. Children acquire increased knowledge and skills as they progress through the grades, and the understandings they construct change qualitatively and grow in complexity and sophistication.

For example, kindergartners are expected to be able to read or pseudoread at least a half-dozen favorite story or picture books, know the letters and sounds of the alphabet, begin making rudimentary attempts to write or dictate narratives, and ask and answer questions about favorite children's books. As they get older, the expectation is not simply that students will read and know more books, know more letters, and be able to write more. They are also expected to have a more complex understanding of how to read and derive meaning from what they read, of the purposes of reading and writing, and of the various meanings and purposes authors have. In addition, they should have increased skill and sophistication in accomplishing and interpreting these purposes.

Thus, second-grade students should be increasingly adept at improving reading fluency by coordinating their knowledge of basic decoding, their sight vocabulary, and their increased ability to figure out new words. They should be able to discuss, summarize, make inferences, and state the main idea of stories. They should be able to write original stories, simple letters, journal entries, and personal invitations. By fifth grade (goals and expectations for this grade are not included here), students should be able to pronounce virtually any written word they see. They should understand, appreciate, and be able to discuss works from different literary genres, read for pleasure a range of books and other materials, have extensive reading vocabularies (particularly in areas of personal interest), compose (drafting and redrafting as needed) original stories with conflicts and resolutions, and keep daily journals to record personal experiences. The nature of literacy and its demands change qualitatively and become more complex as students themselves grow and develop (see Chall, 1983a).

A Common Framework for Spanish and English

Students at the school, as is typical of students in bilingual programs, learn to read in either Spanish or English. Most of the limited-English-proficient students learn to read in Spanish then and transition into English sometime in third, fourth, or fifth grade; a small number of limited-English-proficient students learn in English from the outset. A third feature of the goals and expectations shown in Tables 1.1–1.6 is that they represent a common framework for literacy development in both English and Spanish. Of course, there are accommodations for the different spelling systems of the two languages (Spanish is syllabic and much more regular phonetically than English) and for the titles and languages of the books students are reading, but essentially the framework is the same for both.

Despite differences between the English and Spanish writing systems, both are alphabetic languages. As such, there is a systematic—in the case of Spanish, a highly systematic—relationship between letters and sounds. Although many teachers argue that the basic building block of Spanish reading is the syllable (in contrast to the letter or phoneme in English), it is likely that similar underlying processes help children decode and read words in English and in Spanish (Jiménez & Haro, 1995).[6] If so, much of what we know about learning to read in English can be assumed to be true about learning to read in Spanish.[7] And certainly the functional and communicative uses to which English and Spanish are put have much in common. Both languages draw on rich literary traditions that comprise a wide range of genres serving numerous purposes and goals. Both languages are used for communication that ranges from the fleeting and casual to the literary and stylistic to the academic and formal. Thus in our project we have assumed generally similar models of literacy use and literacy education for English and Spanish.

Traditional Features of Reading and Writing Instruction

A fourth feature is the number of fairly traditional items that teachers felt play an important role in literacy development and that are therefore represented in the goals and expectations. In addition to teaching phonics and comprehension skills, teachers also place emphasis on children's learning of reading and writing conventions, for example, how to use a book's cover, table of contents, and glossary to gain information; alphabetization to the first and second letters (Table 1.2, "D. Study skills"; Table 1.3, "C. Study skills"); understanding synonyms and antonyms (Table 1.3, "A. Word recognition and word skills"); using correct and legible manuscript (Tables 1.4–1.6, "Handwriting"); and the use of punctuation and capitalization (Tables 1.5 and 1.6).

We have also made dictation a part of our language arts programs, beginning with dictation of single letters in kindergarten and eventually leading to dictation of short paragraphs in second grade. Dictation is an excellent diagnostic tool, since in the early stages of literacy development it provides evidence of emerging phonological understandings (Clay, 1985). As children grow in their literacy understandings, dictations also reveal whether they are gaining in fluency and automaticity. Dictation can also play an instructional role, although I know of no study that has actually demonstrated dictation's effects on literacy development. Dictation is a common instructional tool worldwide, and several potential benefits have been suggested. According to Stotsky (1977), dictation enables students to practice grammatical constructions, spelling, punctuation, and capitalization while writing the sustained thoughts of others. Stotsky argues that use of literary passages for dictation enables students to develop language arts skills "in an interesting context, not in isolation," thereby "helping students acquire a greater 'feel' for the language of literature" (p. 4).

Basals and Core Literature

Finally, we have not rejected the use of basal readers, but we have also made core literature and authentic reading (both independent and assigned) just as much a part of the goals and expectations (see "Core Literature" listing and various items under "Comprehension/literature/whole-text reading" in Tables 1.1–1.3). Basal readers evoke harsh responses from many critics (e.g., Goodman, Shannon, Freeman, & Murphy, 1988). Yet there is evidence that they can provide students—and teachers—with useful structure to guide reading instruction and reading development (Chall, Jacobs, & Baldwin, 1990). Teachers at the school felt that the basal series offered many useful resources for the literacy program, resources that included excerpts from children's literature, workbooks and other instructional materials, charts, posters, and suggestions for integrating reading and literature with other curricular areas.

One issue that did come up repeatedly was the cumbersome end-of-book tests that were part of the basal series. Many teachers felt they took up far too much in preparation and administration time, and in many instances they provided little useful information about students' literacy development. As a result, the year after the Academic Expectations Committee finished formulating the academic goals and expectations, its successor committee—the Academic Assessment Committee—developed a set of procedures for teachers wishing to eliminate portions of the end-of-book tests from their classroom programs. Teachers had the option of replacing parts of the end-of-book tests with the authentic literacy assessments developed as part of this project.

IMPACT ON TEACHING AND TEACHERS

The goals and expectations shown in Tables 1.1–1.6 comprise the curricular framework for early literacy. They do not specify particular instructional strategies nor approaches. In general, reading is taught during a reading/language arts block that might last from one to two hours, depending on teacher and grade level. This in itself does not represent a significant change from previous practices, but we have seen instructional changes at Freeman as a result of the goals and of the larger overall project.

In kindergarten, teachers are explicitly teaching letters and sounds of the entire alphabet, not just the vowels and a handful of consonants. They use alphabet books developed as part of an earlier research project in early Spanish literacy (Goldenberg, 1994) as well as other materials they have (e.g., flash cards). Kindergartners are also receiving extended opportunities to "read" or otherwise interact with simple beginning texts, either commercially available or those developed for a previous research project. Children hear stories, are encouraged to become independent readers, and take books home to share with parents and other family members. Kindergartners and first graders are also learning explicitly how print functions, and how print and speech relate—individual and groups of letters represent sounds; aggregations of sounds comprise words that have meaning. These lessons are taught at school and reinforced through homework, which has also received emphasis schoolwide. Students at all grade levels are also engaged in far more writing than ever before. Teachers use writing-as-a-process approaches or otherwise encourage and show students how to represent thoughts, ideas, and stories on paper.

Here is what one teacher said about the changes in teaching at the school:

> In the writing group that I'm in[8] . . . every single meeting we discuss what we've done in our classroom, we discuss how to make it better, we discuss where we want our kids to go after that, we discuss so we know what the teachers are working on, and we can see— we pick up new ways to get across skills, we pick up new types of lessons to do, to address what our goals are in a particular subject area. So that alone has been better. I'm sure that [the other work groups] *have contributed to [those teachers'] classroom environment and their classroom teaching* [italics added].

Another had this to say about a quite traditional, but still useful and powerful, strategy:

> The upper-grade teachers have always given homework, but now they give more of it, and they give it more consistently. Less of it is busywork, although there's a wide variety in the kind of homework they give. I think the students respond positively—they're more serious and responsible about schoolwork when they have homework regularly. The homework in-service reminded teachers how homework fits into classroom lessons, how valuable homework is for the kids.

As mentioned previously, it is perhaps impossible to separate the effects of a more balanced and comprehensive approach to literacy instruction from the effects of our larger schoolwide efforts to improve achievement. One was inextricably a part of the other. There is no question that the changes in the early literacy program at the school were accompanied by many other changes that would be expected to influence student learning. That, indeed, was the whole point of the project. Our intent was never to isolate and manipulate specific, narrow features of the school's program. Instead, we assumed at the outset that many things would have to change to produce an impact on achievement.

Here is what a veteran teacher in the district, teaching first grade at the time, said at the end of the fourth year of the project:

> I think a lot of things have changed [at the school] in the past four years. . . . First of all, we as teachers, we're looking for common goals and directions for the curriculum. We want [our curriculum to be more] defined, and so when a group of teachers went to the principal and asked that this happen, that we define what were goals at different grade levels, she responded to this by starting a group that worked on that and continued to work on it for I think three years. . . .
>
> [D]efining these goals has made a difference in two things. One is our expectations have [become] higher and more the same across the school. [They have also become] more defined, so I think that that in turn has affected positively [what] the students are able to [achieve] academically. I think we probably have better reading instruction going on and probably more kids becoming fluent readers faster. . . . Certainly in writing, that we have defined the expectations and the way that we assess. It has all made a difference in what the kids are actually able to do. First graders, for instance, are able to write. Kids are able to write better and more, and reading comprehension for those of us that have worked on [that] specifically, I think it's made a difference for them.

A younger teacher, who was teaching kindergarten, echoed her more senior colleague's sentiments:

Back four years ago most teachers didn't know what other teachers were doing, especially new teachers. They didn't know the pacing, the direction on how to base their student's achievement, how to make it better. They basically were all in their own rooms and doing their own thing. And then the Academic Expectations Committee came around about four years ago and came up with the goals and expectations, and after that the teachers would come together and discuss them and said, well, how can we make this better for the students to make their achievement higher? And after I'd say about two years after that got started, the achievement was higher because of what the teachers were doing. Talking about it, getting together, trying to make it all come together.

The precise instructional impact of the goals and expectations is difficult to gauge. Yet it is clear that teachers' classroom efforts have galvanized around a shared and balanced set of learning goals to promote students' literacy development. Students receive instruction and learning opportunities that range from practicing and reciting letter names and sounds to participating in writers' workshops. Moreover, teachers have various forums in which they share and learn about instructional strategies to help them help their students accomplish the academic goals the faculty has established.

Whether they are learning in English or in Spanish, young readers and writers at Freeman Elementary stand a greater chance of becoming literate than ever before. A second-grade teacher captured the sentiments of most of the faculty:

From the children I've seen coming in here from other districts similar to ours, I don't think that a lot of places put such an emphasis on academic achievement [as we do]. [They just assume] the LEP [limited-English-proficient] child may be an economically disadvantaged child. There's more of an acceptance . . . [that] they're just going to be a year or two behind. [The principal at this school] doesn't accept that or just give up. There's no surrendering. We keep trying. We keep trying. And I think we've been pretty successful, so far.

ACKNOWLEDGMENTS

Funding has been provided by the U.S. Department of Education Office of Educational Research and Improvement, the Spencer Foundation, and the California State Department of Education. No endorsement from any source is implied nor should be inferred. Portions of this chapter have appeared in Goldenberg and Sullivan (1994). My thanks to the many colleagues, teachers, administrators, students, and parents who have made this work possible.

REFERENCES

Aaron, I., Chall, J., Durkin, D., Goodman, K., & Strickland, D. (1990). The past, present, and future of literacy education: Comments from a panel of distinguished educators, Part I. *The Reading Teacher, 43*, 302–311.

Adams, M. (1990). *Beginning to read: Thinking and learning about print.* Cambridge, MA: MIT Press.

Adams, M., & Bruck, M. (1995). Resolving the "Great Debate." *American Educator, 19*(2), 7–20.

Anderson, R. B., Hiebert, E. H., Scott, J. A., & Wilkinson, I. A. G. (1985). *Becoming a nation of readers: The report of the Commission on Reading.* Champaign, IL: The Center for the Study of Reading.

Ashton, P. T., Webb, R. B., and Doda, N. (1983). *A study of teachers' sense of efficacy: Final report, executive summary.* Gainesville, FL. (ERIC Documentation Reproduction Service No. ED 231 833)

Barr, R. (1973/74). Instructional pace differences and their effects on reading acquisition. *Reading Research Quarterly, 9*, 526–554.

Barr, R., & Dreeben, R. (1983). *How schools work.* Chicago: University of Chicago Press.

Brophy, J. (1983). Research on the self-fulfilling prophecy and teacher expectations. *Journal of Educational Psychology, 75*, 631–661.

Brophy, J., & Good, T. (1986). Teacher behavior and student achievement. In M. Wittrock (Ed.), *Handbook of research on teaching* (3rd ed., pp. 328–375). New York: Macmillan.

California State Department of Education (1981). *Schooling and language minority children.* Los Angeles: Evaluation, Dissemination and Assessment Center, CSU Los Angeles.

Calkins, L. M. (1986). *The art of teaching writing.* Portsmouth, NH: Heinemann.

Carbo, M. (1988). Debunking the great phonics myth. *Phi Delta Kappan, 70*, 226–240.

Chall, J. (1983a). *Stages of reading development.* New York: McGraw-Hill.

Chall, J. (1983b). *Learning to read: The great debate* (updated ed.). New York: McGraw-Hill.

Chall, J. (1989). 'Learning to read: The great debate' 20 years later—A response to 'Debunking the great phonics myth.' *Phi Delta Kappan, 70*, 521–538.

Chall, J., Jacobs, V., & Baldwin, L. (1990). *The reading crisis: Why poor children fall behind.* Cambridge, MA: Harvard University Press.

Clark, C. M., & Peterson, P. L. (1986). Teachers' thought processes. In M. C. Wittrock (Ed.), *Handbook of research on teaching* (pp. 255–296). New York: Macmillan.

Clay, M. (1985). *The early detection of reading difficulties* (3rd ed.). Portsmouth, NH: Heinemann.

Condemarín, M. (1991). *Integración de dos modelos en el desarrollo del lenguaje oral y escrito* [Integration of two models of oral and written language development]. *Lectura y Vida, 12*(4), 13–22.

Cooper, H., & Burger, J. (1980). How teachers explain students' academic performance: A categorization of free response academic attributions. *American Educational Research Journal, 17*, 95–109.

CTB/McGraw-Hill (1988). *SABE: Spanish Assessment of Basic Education, Technical Report.* Monterey, CA: CTB/McGraw-Hill.

Delpit, L. (1986). Skills and other dilemmas of a progressive black educator. *Harvard Educational Review, 56.* 379–385.

Edelsky, C. (1990). Whose agenda is this anyway? A response to McKenna, Robinson, and Miller. *Educational Researcher, 19*(8), 7–11.

Escamilla, K. (1994). Descubriendo la lectura: An early intervention literacy program in Spanish. *Literacy, Teaching and Learning, 1,* 57–70.

Frieze, I. (1976). Causal attributions and information-seeking to explain success and failure. *Journal of Research in Personality, 10,* 293–305.

Fullan, M. (1985). Change processes and strategies at the local level. *Elementary School Journal, 85,* 391–420.

Fullan, M. (1991). *The new meaning of educational change.* N.Y.:Teachers College Press.

Fullan, M., Bennett, B., & Rolheiser-Bennett, C. (1990). Linking classroom and school improvement. *Educational Leadership, 47*(8), 13–19.

Goldenberg, C. (1990). Beginning literacy instruction for Spanish-speaking children. *Language Arts, 67,* 590–598.

Goldenberg, C. (1991). Learning to read in New Zealand: The balance of skills and meaning. *Language Arts, 68,* 555–562.

Goldenberg, C. (1994). Promoting early literacy achievement among Spanish-speaking children: Lessons from two studies. In E. Hiebert (Ed.), *Getting reading right from the start: Effective early literacy interventions* (pp. 171–199). Boston: Allyn and Bacon.

Goldenberg, C. (1995). *The literacy attainment of students in "Writing to Read/VALE" and "Stories and More."* "Lawson," CA: "Lawson" School District.

Goldenberg, C., & Gallimore, R. (1991). Local knowledge, research knowledge, and educational change: A case study of first-grade Spanish reading improvement. *Educational Researcher, 20*(8), 2–14.

Goldenberg, C., & Sullivan, J. (1994). *Making change happen in a language-minority school: A search for coherence* (EPR No. 13). Washington, DC: Center for Applied Linguistics.

Goodman, K., Shannon, P., Freeman, Y., & Murphy, S. (1988). *Report card on basal readers.* New York: Richard C. Owen.

Honig, B. (1995). *How should we teach our children to read? A balanced approach.* Unpublished manuscript.

Jiménez, J., & Haro, C. (1995). Effects of word linguistic properties on phonological awareness in Spanish children. *Journal of Educational Psychology, 87,* 193–201.

Jiménez, J., & Ortiz, M. (1993). Phonological awareness in learning literacy. *Cognitiva, 5,* 153–170.

Koehler, V. R. (1988, April). *Teachers' beliefs about at-risk students.* Paper presented at the annual meeting of the American Educational Research Association, New Orleans, LA. (ERIC Documentation Reproduction Service No. ED 312 359)

Levine, A. (1994, December). The great debate revisited. *The Atlantic Monthly,* pp. 38–44.

Loucks-Horsley, S., & Mundry, S. (1991). Assisting change from without: The technical assistance function. In J. Bliss, W. Firestone, & C. Richards (Eds.), *Rethinking effective schools: Research and practice* (pp. 112–127). Englewood Cliffs, NJ: Prentice Hall.

McKenna, M., Robinson, R., & Miller, J. (1990a). Whole language: A research agenda for the nineties. *Educational Researcher, 19*(8), 3–6.

McKenna, M., Robinson, R., & Miller, J. (1990b). Whole language and the need for open inquiry: A rejoinder to Edelsky. *Educational Researcher, 19*(8), 12–13.

National Clearinghouse for Bilingual Education. (1995). *How many school-aged limited English proficient students are there in the U.S.?* (AskNCBE Paper, 1/20/95). Washington, DC: Author.

Rosenshine, B. (1986). Synthesis of research on explicit teaching. *Educational Leadership, 43,* 60–69.

Rosenshine, B., & Stevens, R. (1986). Teaching functions. In M. Wittrock (Ed.), *Handbook of research on teaching* (3rd ed., pp. 376–391). New York: Macmillan.

Saunders, W. (1995, April). *Making change happen: Teachers' views on the contribution of goals and indicators.* Paper presented at the annual meeting of the American Educational Research Association, San Francisco, CA.

Smith, F. (1992). Learning to read: The never-ending debate. *Phi Delta Kappan, 73,* 432–441.

Smith, K., Reyna, V., & Brainerd, C. (1993). The debate continues. *Phi Delta Kappan, 74,* 407–410.

Smith, L. (1993, September 29). A new reading on U.S. literacy. *Los Angeles Times,* pp. E1, E6.

Spiegel, D. (1992). Blending whole language and systematic direct instruction. *The Reading Teacher, 46,* 38–44.

Stanovich, K. (1993/94). Romance and reality. *The Reading Teacher, 47,* 280–291.

Stotsky, S. (1977). *Dictating literature in the language arts class.* (ERIC Document Reproduction Service No. ED 143 006).

Sullivan, J. (1994). *Producing change in an urban, second-language, elementary school.* Unpublished doctoral dissertation, Graduate School of Education, UCLA.

Tharp, R., and Gallimore, R. (1988). *Rousing minds to life: Teaching, learning and schooling in social context.* Cambridge, Eng.: Cambridge University Press.

Walberg, H. (1984). Improving the productivity of America's schools. *Educational Leadership, 41*(8), 19–27.

Walberg, H. (1986). Synthesis of research on teaching. In M. Wittrock (Ed.), *Handbook of research on teaching* (3rd ed., pp. 214–229). New York: Macmillan.

Walberg, H. (1990). Productive teaching and instruction: Assessing the knowledge base. *Phi Delta Kappan, 71,* 470–478.

Wang, M., Haertel, G., & Walberg, H. (1993). Toward a knowledge base for school learning. *Review of Educational Research, 63,* 249–294.

Winfield, L. F. (1986). Teacher beliefs toward academically at risk students in inner urban schools. *The Urban Review, 18,* 253–268.

CHAPTER NOTES

1. The many aspects of this debate are beyond the scope of this chapter. The interested reader is urged to consult, for example, Aaron, Chall, Durkin, Goodman, and Strickland (1990); Adams (1990); Adams and Bruck (1995); Anderson, Hiebert, Scott, and Wilkinson (1985); Carbo (1988); Chall (1983b, 1989); Edelsky (1990); Levine (1994, December); McKenna, Robinson, and Miller (1990a, 1990b); F. Smith (1992); K. Smith, Reyna, and Brainerd (1993); L. Smith (1993, September 29); and Stanovich (1993/94).

2. During the time this project was underway, the school district implemented Writing to Read™ labs in all elementary schools. Although there was some evidence that the labs helped boost early literacy scores districtwide (Goldenberg, 1995), improvement at Freeman was more marked than at the rest of the schools.

3. For the relationship between teacher attitudes and student achievement, see Ashton, Webb, and Doda (1983); Brophy (1983); Clark and Peterson (1986); Cooper and Burger (1980); Frieze (1976); Koehler (1988, April); and Winfield (1986). For teacher behaviors and student achievement, see Barr (1973/74); Barr and Dreeben (1983); Brophy and Good (1986); Rosenshine (1986); Rosenshine and Stevens (1986); Walberg (1984, 1986, 1990); and Wang, Haertel, and Walberg (1993).

4. Bill Saunders took to the lead in developing the language arts assessments used in this project. I am indebted to him for this and for his many other contributions to the project.

5. The division into reading goals and writing goals is in many respects arbitrary, and in some cases—such as with dictation—it is not clear why an item is in one rather than the other. Originally, we had thought of developing language arts goals as a whole, but the committee decided to divide them into reading and writing for greater clarity. The goals and expectations are included here as they evolved and were finalized at Freeman.

6. There is some controversy over the relative importance of *syllabic* versus *phonemic* awareness in learning to read Spanish (see, e.g., the discussion in Jiménez & Haro, 1995).

7. This, in fact, is an area in great need of basic and applied research. Such a research agenda exists in Spanish-speaking countries, but there has been virtually no such research with Spanish-speaking populations in the United States.

8. As part of the larger project, teachers participated in work groups where they focused on various curricular and instructional topics, such as writing, general language arts, instructional conversations, and thematic teaching.

2

Language and Preliteracy Development of English as a Second Language Learners in Early Childhood Special Education

Jozi De León, Ph.D.
New Mexico State University

Catherine Medina, Ph.D.
Northern Arizona University

I n a research study examining early childhood special education classrooms with at least a 70% Hispanic (Mexican American) student population, the authors interviewed five teachers and observed instructional practices in their classrooms to arrive at the conclusions included in this chapter. Several dilemmas emerged from the process of the investigation. The authors combine insights and research literature in making recommendations for providing optimal language- and preliteracy-related instructional opportunities for young language-minority students with exceptionalities. It is the intent of the authors to provide a qualitative understanding of effective teaching practices with young language-minority students with disabilities (hereafter referred to as language-minority students).

For young language-minority children, initial educational experiences need to be framed within familial experiences. The affective aspects of instruction should not be so dissimilar from earlier experience with families that children's ability to relate home experience to the classroom experience is affected. The authors include a discussion of the experience of Hispanic children included in the study and the family/adult interaction framework within which they function. They advise that language learning, preliteracy development, and all forms of instruction can best be implemented when the context within which a child develops is incorporated in the classroom experience.

The next sections describe dilemmas and issues and outline constructs for promoting learning and literacy in the early grades. Specific discussion focuses on (a) developing an atmosphere for success, (b) fostering mutual understanding and accommodation, (c) building language, (d) providing a challenging environment and high expectations, (e) involving parents and making a home-school connection, (f) developing a literacy-rich environment, and (g) providing instructional mediation and feedback. Finally, recommendations are provided for bilingual and monolingual teachers.

DILEMMAS AND ISSUES

Herlinda
I don't have any classes in bilingual education. I feel like I am always going back and forth between Spanish and English. Children with Spanish don't have to try as hard because they know Spanish is coming. I don't mind them using Spanish, I just don't know what is best. . . . I am always assessing myself. Is this the right way to deal with this situation?

Deborah
I believe children should be taught in their native language and taught in English when they are ready for it. I believe that we should give children the opportunities to learn in both languages. I want my monolingual English-speaking students to learn Spanish.

Connie
I don't have any training in bilingual education or in teaching ESOL. Schools should provide training. They [the school district] give us bilingual assistants, but that's not fair to the bilingual assistant. I feel my educational assistants are stressed and stretched in Spanish. . . . In my classroom, bilingual education is translation.

These statements reflect a variety of perspectives demonstrating dilemmas that special education teachers face in the education of young culturally and linguistically diverse children with disabilities. All three teachers articulate a lack of understanding of how to incorporate language effectively in the classroom. They voice the view that learning in the native language is important; however, they are unsure of how to instruct in the native language. At the same time, they realize that instruction must also be understandable in the second language. Lack of training appears to be at the root of their dilemmas.

Herlinda, a teacher with bilingual skills but no bilingual education training, is torn between when and how to use Spanish in the classroom. Her lack of training and what that entails infiltrates not only into academic domains but also into affective domains of language and learning. From her excerpt, it is evident that Herlinda does not know how to allocate language for instructional purposes in a thoughtful and effective manner. In essence, her dual-language instructional practices are a hit-and-miss venture. In the affective domain, non-English-speaking children are viewed as passive learners who wait for the translation of language. Both academic and affective domains are compromised as Herlinda struggles with her own self-doubt regarding effective instructional practices.

Although Deborah demonstrates a sensitivity to language and second language acquisition, her comments raise the issue that the determination of when a child is ready for English instruction is ambiguous and arbitrary. Sometimes the initiation of English language instruction is driven by programmatic factors concerning resource availability rather than the actual needs of the child. In the five classrooms studied, most had a 78% or higher Hispanic student population. The majority of children came from homes in which predominantly Spanish was spoken. The exceptional and developmental needs of the children were a clear program focus, because teachers involved in their instruction had backgrounds in early childhood and special education; however, the linguistic and culture-related instructional needs were not held at the same level of importance. No special education teacher indicated a strong background in bilingual or multicultural education. Primary language considerations were largely left up to the teacher to figure out and deal with.

While Deborah espouses a view that appears to be sensitive to the linguistic needs of her non-English speakers, her perspective on using both languages is not based on sound theory or research, but rather on what she perceives to be popular. She indicates that teaching two languages is a good thing because it allows monolingual English-speaking students the opportunity to learn Spanish. Her comments do not focus on the most important reason to use both languages, which is to ensure that non-English speakers have an opportunity not only to gain in their acquisition of knowledge and skills but also to develop a strong language base. Native language instruction and English language instruction for children learning English as a second language need to be carefully thought out, provided in calculated doses, and aligned with instructional goals and objectives.

Connie raises the issue of training and the often established practice for dealing with second language learners in the classroom by involving educational assistants to be the direct service providers or to bridge the gap between the use of the two languages. Without appropriate training of the educational assistants, they cannot be expected to deliver instruction more effectively than certified staff. In our classroom observations, educational assistants provided translation of communication in the classroom, but they were not equipped to provide language intervention that built and expanded existing language skills. Translation was used so that the student would not be lost in the classroom, but whether the child was actually learning and developing skills that would further literacy development is questionable.

The authors realize that due to the limited number of bilingual certified staff, monolingual teachers are often expected to rely on bilingual educational assistants. The most effective use of those bilingual educational assistants, however, can result only from well-thought-out training and planning in instructional delivery. School administrators need to be aware of and involved in the training and support efforts of both the certified staff and educational assistants.

Thus, in the three brief excerpts provided, the following concerns are apparent:

- How do early childhood special education teachers develop an atmosphere of success?
- How do early childhood special education teachers develop an atmosphere of mutual understanding and accommodation?
- How do early childhood special education teachers build on native language while teaching second language?
- How can early childhood special education teachers make instructional time challenging for second language learners?
- How do early childhood special education teachers involve the parents in making a home-school connection?
- How do early childhood special education teachers establish a literacy-rich environment?
- How can early childhood special education teachers effectively provide mediation and feedback?

CONSTRUCTS FOR PROMOTING LEARNING AND LITERACY IN THE EARLY GRADES

There are a number of constructs that when evidenced in the classroom appear to enable learning and literacy development in young children. The level of effectiveness with language-minority children is dependent on the inclusion of most, if not all, of these constructs.

Developing the Affective Dimensions of an Atmosphere of Success

Literacy in the classroom is a shared experience in which meaning and understanding emerge and expand. Educators must have a firm philosophy that engenders a genuine respect for and an affirmation of a pluralistic society. Students' sense of belonging impacts their receptiveness within the learning environment and can ultimately affect academic achievement (Nieto, 1992). Establishing that sense of belonging begins in the early grades and hopefully continues throughout the school experience. During students' early school experiences, a sense of familiarity with their environment is critical. It is during this period that students begin to develop an understanding of whether they belong in the school environment and whether they are accepted by teachers and peers. They determine whether going to school and learning is a positive or a negative venture. Early school experiences fundamentally establish the blueprint of language-minority children's attitudes about what is to come in later grades. Certainly, works by Krashen (1982) and Cummins (1984) indicate that affective concerns are important in the second language acquisition process.

During the acquisition of the first language, parents establish a warm and rewarding atmosphere in which they encourage any attempts at language by the child. The parents respect the unique attempts at verbalization without expecting the child to fit into a preestablished standard. Any mispronunciation of words and incorrect use of language are often thought of as cute and amusing. Sometimes they are woven into stories about the child's formative years (Strickland & Taylor, 1989). For the language-minority student acquiring English as a second language, the same atmosphere may not exist. Language use may be evaluated on a constant basis and may even be corrected. This often gives language-minority students the feeling that they are not living up to the expectations of the teacher, and it develops in students a feeling of incompetence. Language-minority children need to feel safe enough to use language in its current form of development. The most important consideration is whether or not children are using language to communicate and broaden their linguistic experience.

In our observations of two classroom teachers who demonstrated a genuine acceptance of the language-minority student, students appeared to be more involved in classroom activities and demonstrated more task engagement. Teachers demonstrated their acceptance through the following behaviors:

- They used terms of endearment in Spanish with the children. This matched the cultural experience that these students were exposed to at home by adults in their families.
- All children's work was displayed in the classroom.
- The teacher, educational assistant, and other adults entering the classroom were actively involved with all the children and constantly communicated with them at their level.
- The classroom reflected an understanding of the language and culture of the language-minority children in the classroom.
- The teacher was observant and watched for cues indicating that a student was not involved because he or she did not understand.

There has been much mention of the use of terms of endearment by teachers with the Spanish-speaking children in the classrooms observed. While this was important for the Hispanic students studied, it may not be as important for other culturally and linguistically diverse groups. What is important, however, is that teachers of culturally and linguistically diverse groups find cultural elements that enable students to feel more comfortable in the school environment and to sense that the teachers and others involved in their education understand their culture. From observations and interviews with parents of children in the study, we learned that the use of terms of endearment in

Spanish matched the children's cultural experience and the types of interactions used by adults in the families. It ensured that the classroom became a friendly environment that students could relate to more readily.

The display of all student work rather than that of a select few demonstrated an attitude to students that all their work was valuable and important. Classrooms in which none of the student work was displayed demonstrated less learner-friendly interactions.

In some classrooms, interactions with the children by adults in the classroom frequently demonstrated a level of recognition, validation, and acceptance. In some classrooms in which children were nonverbal due to their disability, adults interacted with them just as actively as they did with the verbal children. Constant interaction with all students enabled language building and language development, verbally or receptively.

The use of language cards for items in the classroom and pictures and books that reflected the students' culture and language was another important element that contributed significantly to students' positive feelings about school. Students were not strangers in their classroom. They could find their experiences reflected in their classroom environment. Teachers sometimes adapted a particular story or activity so that it would fit the students' language and culture.

Effective teachers observed in two of the classrooms were particularly aware of the language needs of their non–English-proficient students. These teachers ensured that children did not get left out of the instructional loop. They monitored the understanding of these students. Sometimes one teacher who was monolingual would have someone else translate for the child, or she would attempt to bridge the language gap by demonstrating what she was trying to get across or by using her limited knowledge of the child's language to make instruction understandable.

Mutual Understanding and Accommodation

In less effective classroom environments, students were expected to figure out the hidden curriculum and to fit into the preordained structure of the classroom. Student experiences were not evaluated to determine whether the student brought experiences that allowed him or her to adjust easily to the classroom environment. Often, language-minority children were left to evaluate the setting and adjust to their surroundings. While this may have been somewhat easier for students who had had some previous school experiences and were older, it was not easy for young children with disabilities involved in their initial educational experience. Language-minority children had the difficult task of figuring out the language and the additional task of interpreting the culture of the classroom, which often was very different from their own. Majority children had the advantage of entering the classroom already understanding the language as well as the culture of the school. For language-minority children, extra care must be taken to ensure that understanding and accommodation take place within the environment. Effective teachers take time to understand how differences of experience impact the ability to become actively involved in learning situations. These teachers also include aspects of the children's culture and experience in their instruction, so that students are not simply left to adjust. These teachers make it a point to understand students and the community from which they come, and the experiences that are different for those students due to both linguistic and cultural differences.

Accommodations within classroom instruction for language-minority students include incorporating instructional activities that reflect cultural understanding by the teacher. In our observations of classrooms, effective teachers had taken the time to learn enough about the Hispanic culture and the child to be able to respond sensitively. An example of accommodation is reflected in the following interaction observed in Joan's classroom:

Miguel: It's Robert's turn to chicken, chicken Robert. [Students "chicken" (check in) by standing next to the bulletin board.]

Joan: Don't call Robert chicken, Miguel. Oh, you meant "check in." I'm sorry. I didn't hear right.

Miguel: That's okay. [Smiles and motions Robert toward the bulletin board.]

Joan believed that teachers must provide a status-free environment where mutual learning and respect can occur. For example, when there was a linguistic misunderstanding between her and her student, Joan took responsibility for the misunderstanding and at the same time empowered the student by focusing on accommodation rather than correction.

Mutual Understanding and Multicultural Education

Although the teachers stated that they had an awareness of what multicultural education entailed and how it should be integrated into the classroom, one monolingual English-speaking teacher (a preschool regular education teacher) appeared to understand the limitations of the present curricular models employed in her school district. She stated, "Multicultural education is a myth. . . . Any [traditional] curriculum is heavily biased by the dominant culture because members of that culture created it." The majority of special education teachers interviewed stated that they gave a tourist version of multicultural education by introducing food, clothing, language, and so forth into the curriculum.

LANGUAGE BUILDING

Differences in linguistic and cultural characteristics can be misinterpreted as deficits in need of remediation. Children who come from linguistically diverse backgrounds and have different styles of communication and/or appear to be less verbal by mainstream standards may be seen as needing special assistance with language development. Even when language patterns appear to be culturally appropriate (but not appropriate according to assessment data), children may receive language remediation focused on the development of specific skills, beginning with vocabulary and moving toward the stringing together of short commands and sentences. Language building needs to take a completely different direction. Activities focusing on language building should not include the splintered skills of language but should revolve around things the children would be interested in communicating about. This type of language building ensures that children become competent in the language rather than merely possessing surface language skills.

In Herlinda's and Marlene's classroom, all ancillary personnel as well as the teachers took advantage of language-building opportunities. During one observation, the counselor discussed feelings (e.g., anger, sadness, happiness) with the students. She acted out the feelings and the action words discussed, and she had the children share their perspectives about the topic of feelings. All students could relate to the topic and discuss what they did when they felt angry, sad, or happy. Children were learning about the language of emotions within a meaningful context. She used the native language to modulate understanding for the potentially English-proficient students. All children were involved and actively engaged in the discussion and activities.

Such activities, while appearing to be simple, are powerful in enabling students to build language skills through active communication. Oral language development is the first step in the building of literacy skills. Oral language and reading and writing go hand in hand. Oral language enhances the opportunities for students to engage in discussion about a story that has been read or a picture in a book. For second language learners, the development of oral language in natural ways in and out of school builds the understanding and knowledge necessary to actively interact with text.

The special education teachers who were most effective in building language skills in the classrooms we observed developed language naturally by doing the following:

- They used language constantly with the students, particularly one-on-one for better understanding.

- They provided opportunities for students to constantly interact among themselves as well as with others in the classroom.

- They invited other adults (volunteers from the community and parents) to participate in instruction with the children, thereby developing multiple resources for the classroom.

- They used social as well as academic language in balanced doses. The focus was not entirely on academic skills nor on social language skills.

- They used less questioning and directives and did not adhere to teacher-initiated talk, necessitating student responses on which student knowledge was evaluated (student-response evaluation [IRE] models of instruction). Teachers acted as facilitators of classroom interaction, in which students were encouraged to dialogue through expanded language responses.

- Teachers also checked for comprehension of those students dominant in a language other than English, and they used methods to ensure comprehension.

- Teachers used language during show-and-tell, stories, rhymes, and chants. From an adult point of view, the chants sometimes appeared to be silly; however, the children enjoyed the choral chanting and predictability of the activity. Even those children with limited English-speaking skills were able to participate.

Literacy must be reflective and active, holistic and democratic. Students, in essence, must be able to reflect, discuss, and interact with the larger social network of the classroom and school community (Freire & Macedo, 1987). Language development and language learning must occur through children's own cultural framework and their own interpretations of their world. The teacher, therefore, must commit to determining how literacy development interacts with the child's exceptionality, cognitive level, native language ability, and culture and community.

Children who come from homes in which they have been exposed to reading and writing opportunities have little difficulty entering conventional literacy experiences with confidence and as risk takers. Children who have not had these opportunities are often placed in programs that ignore their previous experiences. Teacher expectations of language-minority children must be addressed within the context of a student's home experiences. If not, literacy instruction may be irrelevant and therefore ineffective.

Lack of Training and Its Impact on Language Building

Lack of training in bilingual education or English for speakers of other languages (ESOL) techniques impacted on teacher effectiveness in providing dual-language instruction. For a high percentage of the questioning used in the classroom, a wait time of at least 3 seconds was lacking, thereby not providing Spanish-dominant children enough time to understand the questions, much less respond. Attempts to check for understanding were done more frequently for the group rather than for individual children who were Spanish dominant. In addition, when we examined the type of language being used by the teachers, we found that they did not expand existing language skills or build understanding at the next level. Language expansion was not evident to the degree that would be expected for children who needed to develop their English language skills. Language expansions have the effect of reinforcing the language used by the child, while modeling more "adult-like forms" (Rice & Wilcox, 1995).

Social language in Spanish was observed often, whereas academic language in Spanish was nonexistent. Despite the fact that this classroom was an early childhood special education classroom, some academic language would have been expected, because the children were learning concepts and establishing preacademic skills. The use of academic language in the children's primary language would be critical in building oral language that will foster literacy skills. For example, including terminology that is more school related can provide exposure to terms that the children will later be expected to read. Such exposure aids in the decoding process. Open questioning that allows children to process in their own language also develops the linguistic skills necessary in an academic environment. This includes questions like, "What do you think will happen if . . .?" or "Why do you think the water overflowed in this container?" Questioning in three of the five classrooms took on the form of test questions: "What is this?" "Is this the big one or the little one?" and so forth.

In using Spanish for maintenance or existing language skills and for social purposes, a strong foundation in the primary language was not being built. Children were not being taught to think and process new information in their native language.

Challenge and High Expectations

Children should be moved through their language and literacy development at a rate at which they are constantly reviewing and building on previously acquired skills. Children should be nudged to move beyond the level they are functioning at, but care should be taken that they are not pushed too hard. Often, children will give teachers cues indicating that they are ready to move forward. They demonstrate confidence with the skills previously learned, and they use those skills in different settings. Children will also quickly make teachers aware of when they are being pushed too far, by withdrawing or refusing to participate in an activity that requires skills they do not have or do not feel comfortable performing. They may even cry or have a tantrum when asked to engage in such an activity. Effective teachers capture teachable moments and move the child to the next level in a painless and uneventful manner by nudging ever so gently and at the child's pace. Especially at an early age, challenging activities that are fun and meaningful create the most possibility for learning and the least likelihood of refusal to participate.

INVOLVING PARENTS AND MAKING A HOME-SCHOOL CONNECTION

I use a lot of Spanish. I think everyone ought to speak more than one language. The children respond to it. I like to use endearments in Spanish [e.g., m'ija, mi vida] with all the kids. The educational assistant interprets a lot in the classroom. A lot of the snacks that we serve, we tell the kids what they are in Spanish. It adds to their self-esteem. We speak in Spanish and bring things from their culture to the classroom. . . . Every child comes in with a dominant language, and basic concepts are formulated in that language. They [children] learn through modeling and interaction with their language. A child who has a solid first language will acquire the second language more so than the child who doesn't have a good basis in his/her mother tongue. . . . I want to treat the kid's spirit.

As this statement shows, Joan recognized the importance of bringing the language of the child's home and community into the classroom, but she also had an awareness of the importance of bilingual education. A major focus of the early childhood curriculum should be to ensure that all children in the classroom become active participants in the literate environments of school, home, and community (Teale & Sulzby, 1989). The school is not the only literate place. It is important to include signs, words, and other written elements that are part of the child's home and community and that the child sees every day. Slowly, those written elements can begin to have some meaning for the child and relay the idea that the written elements and symbols the child encounters regularly have a meaning.

Sometimes, teachers assume that parents of language-minority students do not have any interest in becoming involved. In our interviews with parents of young Hispanic children with disabilities, however, we discovered that a high percentage of those parents read to their children and were involved with their children in school-related activities. They may not have been reading material that was age appropriate—some of the parents complained that they did not have storybooks and other materials to read to their children—but they were reading nonetheless. Teachers can encourage reading efforts by establishing a classroom library from which parents can check out materials to read to their children. An assortment of picture books in the languages of children in the classroom, and in English, can be made available. An activity that can add books in languages other than English is to have parent sessions in which parents of certain language groups create books with their children. A series of workshops can be given by teachers to assist parents in developing book ideas and ultimately in developing the books. Once the process is started, parents can continue to develop books with their children on their own. The activity can bring the home and school together. It is a marvelous way to involve parents and make them feel that they are taking part in their child's education.

Developing a Literacy-Rich Classroom Environment

Reading aloud to children is especially important during the early grades. While the children are consumed by the story being read, they are learning vocabulary and the language of print. This translates into an ability to manipulate print when they interact with books. A book corner or a comfortable place where children can interact with books on their own or be read to by others is integral in a literacy-rich classroom environment. In some classrooms, young children were read to on the laps of adults, thereby making the experience even more enjoyable.

Meaningful print that is incorporated by the teacher into a discussion also adds to the development of literacy skills. Some teachers used print simultaneously with oral language long before the children were able to read. The association that resulted from this practice had subtle but far-reaching effects.

Chants, rhymes, and poetry can be used as a way of getting children interested in playing with language. Young children enjoy the nonsensical language that makes up some of the chants and rhymes. Activities that allow them to make up their own chants further develop their ability to use language. Children with varying English language skills can participate in the development of their own chants, because a chant can include one phrase or a series of phrases. Chants can be created from any phrase. Their repetitive nature makes them especially effective. The teacher can provide part of the chant and have the children add their own words. For example:

My favorite day is _____.

My favorite day is _____.

It's the day I like to _____.

Each child can in turn create his or her own version of the chant.

Children enjoy poetry and rhymes that speak to their actual experiences or fantasies. Shel Silverstein's *Where the Sidewalk Ends* and *A Light in the Attic* are excellent for children and can be made comprehensible when used with language-minority children. Role playing and acting out some of the poetry bring the words to life and make them meaningful to children.

MEDIATION AND FEEDBACK

Language-minority students may be best served when interventions are embedded in language and educational experiences that are meaningful and authentic and that promote social interaction, not when interventions are decontextualized, acultural, and asocial. Transmission-oriented models of teaching, in which the teacher is the primary interactor in the classroom, present difficulties for children who are potentially English proficient (PEP). Because activities often need to be simplified, they are often stripped of context, and, therefore, meaning and purpose are lost (Ortiz & Wilkinson, 1991).

Interactive teaching approaches are more effective because they are characterized by genuine dialogue between the teacher and the students, and because they focus on higher-order thinking skills as opposed to basic skills. Teachers using this approach consciously integrate language use and development into all curricular content, rather than teaching language in an isolated manner (Cummings, 1989). During these activities, teachers mediate instruction to produce meaning and provide feedback, which further aids in understanding and in the development of concepts and ideas.

Three 6-minute videotaped observations of the two monolingual teachers indicated that they used questioning as their primary instructional strategy. One teacher asked as many as 51 questions during 18 minutes of teaching time. Obviously, meditation and feedback were nonexistent. Videotaped analysis also indicated that these teachers often asked questions that required a one-word response. Unfortunately, the amount of wait time after questions asked by the teachers demonstrated that they did not allow a sufficient amount of time (at least 3 seconds) for student response. This inadequate amount of wait time may be extremely frustrating for the Spanish-speaking or PEP child who is struggling to interpret his or her environment. The two teachers frequently used directives with their students (27% and 25% of their instructional time respectively). Videotaped analyses also revealed that the teachers often determined student understanding by asking them to demonstrate their knowledge. For example, one teacher asked class members to "show me where the closet is." Multiple attempts at group understanding were moderately used (17% and 11% of instructional time, respectively), both teachers repeating or rephrasing questions to secure or maintain student involvement.

Literacy development is most effective when children are encouraged to speak and interact in a natural manner. Fradd (1987) stated:

> Often communication consists of brief utterances such as "What is this?" or "What color is that?" Students learn to reply in like form, in one- or two-word utterances. Little curriculum content or social expectation is communicated with this type of verbal exchange. Sometimes, instead of promoting the intellectual and social aspects important in learning English, the students' progress is impaired by the repetitive practice and meaningless drill.

Classroom discourse should be based on authentic language needs, not on traditional curricular models that use the students' oral language as a context for curriculum development. More precisely, literacy development needs to be based on children's real-life experiences, regardless of the language of instruction.

CONCLUSIONS

The literacy development of language-minority children cannot be left to chance. A significant body of research has led to the development and identification of effective instructional strategies that can be applied by both bilingual and monolingual teachers (Hoover & Collier, 1989; Kottler, 1994; Ortiz & Yates, 1989). While advocates of bilingual instruction view the use of native language as the best and most direct way to develop literacy, it may not always be possible to provide such instruction. Monolingual English-speaking teachers can nevertheless play an important and effective role in ensuring that language-minority students not only become proficient orally but also become literate in English. Teachers can support one another in meeting the needs of language-minority students, much like Herlinda and Marlene did in our study. When the teacher is monolingual and has a bilingual assistant, the assistant can sometimes play an important role in making instruction understandable for the student. English monolingual teachers without such support can still be effective if they remember that language learning occurs when it is meaningful, is tied to the student's experience, and is presented in a warm and accepting environment. Language skills are the basis for literacy development, and teachers need to be constantly aware that their primary role during the early grades is to ensure that language building and language expansion occurs. A strong language foundation leads to literacy development in young children. The authors have provided readers numerous examples of how to foster the development of a strong language foundation as well as develop early literacy skills. A synthesis of those recommendations is provided in the next section. Ultimately, these suggestions attempt to ensure that language-minority students are actively involved in the classroom and never get left out of the instructional loop.

SUGGESTIONS FOR MONOLINGUAL AND BILINGUAL CLASSROOM TEACHERS

Monolingual Teacher with Bilingual Educational Assistants

- Observe and respond to cues (e.g., disengagement) that may indicate a student is not understanding what is being said.
- Use ESOL techniques to teach English terms. (Ellen Kottler's book *Children with Limited English: Teaching Strategies for the Regular Classroom* is an excellent primer for those without training.)
- Involve Spanish-speaking educational assistants effectively in using primary language with children (i.e., to translate stories during group story time, to converse with children during free-play time, to read stories to Hispanic children individually, etc.).
- Use more hands-on activities, demonstrations, and guided instruction, rather than relying on large-group instruction.
- Use nonverbal and tactile as well as verbal forms of reinforcement.
- Incorporate culturally relevant instruction that reflects the home and community of the children you teach.
- Use extended wait time when using questioning during instruction.
- Learn terms of endearment in Spanish and use them effectively with children, and/or use culturally sensitive interactions that make the children feel accepted.
- Ask Spanish-speaking educational assistants and Spanish-speaking parents to work with monolingual and Spanish-dominant children.
- Access more training in ESOL and multicultural instruction if you continue to work with language-minority populations.

Bilingual Teachers

- Use your knowledge of Spanish to convey meaning, to teach new concepts, and to generally converse socially with children.
- Use both social and academic Spanish in balanced doses.
- Use culturally appropriate language and terms of endearment when speaking with Hispanic students.
- Use knowledge of the culture and language to further culturally sensitive and culturally appropriate instruction for Hispanic students.
- Allow for other individuals working with children to also work with them in the children's native language (i.e., in some cases everyone involved with a Spanish monolingual or Spanish-dominant child should work with that child in Spanish).
- Use hands-on activities, demonstrations, and guided instruction more frequently than whole-group activities involving traditional teacher-initiated and IRE models of instruction.
- Be careful not to use Spanish exclusively for reprimands and disciplinary actions.
- Have educational assistants use rich-language modeling in Spanish and work with Spanish monolingual or Spanish-dominant children.

Literacy-Development Activities

- Develop an environment that is reassuring and accepting of what students bring to the classroom.
- Develop an environment in which students use language freely and without concern for their limited competence in English.
- Use constant interaction with all children in the classroom to develop language skills.
- Incorporate language-building activities that are meaningful and relevant to the student.
- Learn about children's homes and communities and make accommodations for those differences in all literacy instruction.
- Use activities that are challenging but not frustrating so that children can move forward at a consistent and appropriate pace.
- Include the student's real-life experience in literacy activities.
- Involve parents and community volunteers in literacy activities.
- Develop a literacy-rich classroom environment.
- Provide mediation and feedback to students to ensure understanding and to build concepts and extend knowledge.

REFERENCES

Cummings, J. (1989). A theoretical framework for bilingual special education. *Exceptional Children, 56*(2), 111–119.

Fradd, S. H. (1987). Accommodating the need of limited English proficient students in regular classrooms. In S. H. Fradd & W. J. Tikunoff (Eds.), *Bilingual education and special education: A guide for administrators*. San Diego: College Hill Press.

Freire, P., & Macedo, D. (1987). *Literacy: Reading the word and the world*. Connecticut: Bergin & Garvey.

Hoover, J. J., & Collier, C. (1989). Methods and materials for bilingual special education. In L. M. Baca & H. T. Cervantes (Eds.), *The bilingual special education interface*. Columbus, OH: Merrill.

Kottler, E. (1994). *Children with limited English: Teaching strategies for the regular classroom*. Thousand Oaks, CA: Corwin Press.

Krashen, S. (1982). *Principles and practice in second language acquisition*. Oxford: Pergamon.

Nieto, S. (1992). *Affirming diversity: The sociopolitical context of multicultural education*. New York: Longman.

Ortiz, A. A., & Wilkinson, C. Y. (1991). Assessment and intervention model for the bilingual exceptional student (AIM for the BEST). *Teacher Education and Special Education, 14*(1), 35–42.

Strickland, D. S., & Taylor, D. (1989). Family storybook reading: Implications for children, families, and curriculum. In D. S.

Strickland and L. M. Morrow (Eds.), *Emerging literacy: young children learn to read and write*. Newark, DE: International Reading Association.

Sulzby, E., Teale, W. H., & Kamberelis, G. (1989). Emergent writing in the classroom: Home school connections. In D. S. Strickland and L. M. Morrow (Eds.), *Emerging literacy: Young children learn to read and write*. Newark, DE: International Reading Association.

Teale, W. H., & Sulzby, E. (1989). *Emergent literacy: Young children learn to read and write*. Newark, DE: International Reading Association.

3

Reading as a Gateway to Language Proficiency for Language-Minority Students in the Elementary Grades

Valerie Anderson
Centre for Applied Cognitive Studies
University of Toronto

Marsha Roit
SRA/McGraw-Hill

Many educators maintain that language-minority students must be fluent in oral English before they engage in learning to read in English (e.g., Wong, Fillmore, & Valadez, 1986). The practical result is that reading instruction is frequently delayed in favor of instructional efforts toward oral language proficiency. The long-range results among students are inequities that persist across the school years. In view of the increasing numbers of culturally diverse students in nonspecialized classrooms and the decreasing educational resources, even the possibility of such inequities necessitates pedagogical approaches that ensure some basic consistencies in instruction across students and grade levels.

The authors are grateful for the support of the Spencer Foundation in completing this work. Further thanks go to Elizabeth Lee for her helpful editorial assistance with the manuscript.

In the past many bilingual classrooms consisted of students from one or two language groups—often primarily Hispanic. Now due to changing immigration patterns, there are an increasing number of classrooms in which most of the students do not share a common first language. In fact, in many schools the diversity is so great that neither bilingual programs or language assistants in the classroom are a feasible solution to the problem. This chapter is specifically intended to address reading instruction in English for the language-minority students in these multiethnic classrooms.

Delaying reading for language-minority students has been recognized as a problem for some time (Goodman, Goodman, & Flores, 1979), yet there is little in the literature on how to effectively teach such students to understand what they read (Grabe, 1991), particularly when compared with the wealth of research on how to teach them to understand and speak oral English (Weber, 1991). Goodman et al. (1979) argue that reading in English should start when students begin to show receptive understanding. Like many people learning a new language, students may be reticent to speak in a new language even though they have some understanding. Because students may be equally receptive to written English, it seems reasonable that instruction in reading English should start earlier than is currently found in practice.

The potential reciprocity between learning to read and reading to learn has strong implications for developing oral language in language-minority students. Barrera (1983) noted that children learn to read in their second language before oral fluency develops. She substantiated the relationship between reading and language by pointing out that students are not limited by their oral language and that it is likely they learn English by reading in context. Despite these observations, practitioners to date have not generally taken advantage of this important reciprocity (Weber, 1991).

For nearly 10 years, we have worked extensively in the United States and Canada in grade 1–8 classrooms with high percentages of language-minority students from more than 40 countries. Our efforts have focused on helping teachers provide students with reading comprehension strategies (Anderson, 1992; Anderson & Roit, 1990, December, 1993). A natural outcome has been the informal gathering of information concerning instructional issues related to teaching the students to read. From conversations with teachers and administrators, observations of literacy teaching, and videotaped teaching sessions, we have identified six issues related to reading comprehension and language development. We state these issues as competencies that, when developed, increase both understanding of text and oral language proficiency. The competencies are English language flexibility, use of basic vocabulary that is difficult to visualize (e.g., *of, not, to*), consideration of larger contexts, determination of importance and unimportance, elaborated responses, and engagement in natural conversations.

Teaching these competencies through text has advantages over dealing with them simply on an oral basis. Spoken language is fleeting and inconsistent over time. Text, by contrast, is stable and does not pass the learner by.

When text is used, the learner can reread, reflect on, and reconsider the material to be learned, in its original form.

We focus on reading comprehension as a gateway to language development, rather than on proficient language as a prerequisite to reading. Each competency is described in one of the sections that follow. They are discussed separately for purposes of clarity; we realize that they are interrelated. We have not dealt with decoding, because there is much information on how to teach it (Adams, 1991). As with any learners, some language-minority students have decoding difficulties, but comprehension difficulties have a more direct bearing on language development and are more widespread, severe, and difficult to deal with instructionally.

The issues are followed by 10 suggestions for teaching the competencies. No attempt has been made to precisely fit suggestions to individual competencies in the way one might treat isolated skills. To do so would be out of step with current conceptions of teaching and learning (Bereiter & Scardamalia, 1989; Brown & Campione, 1990; Foresee, 1991). We offer a variety of interrelated activities, each of which could help to meet the literacy needs of language-minority students.

INSTRUCTIONAL ISSUES

English Language Flexibility

Anyone learning a new language feels good when they figure out *one* way to say something. To say something in more than one way may be initially beyond the learner. Consequently, language-minority students may respond to questions with answers in English and verbatim from the text. They find text words that correspond to a question, because they can read some of the words, but they may not know what their answers mean. They also may have difficulty putting text in their own words, because they do not understand the material or are not yet able to generate alternative ways to express it. Language inflexibility may actually be fostered by teaching in which students are expected to respond only in English. Numerous researchers (e.g., Cummins, 1989; Moll, 1994) contend that allowing children to use their first, or heritage, language to respond enhances second language learning.

Use of Basic Vocabulary That Is Difficult to Visualize

Vocabulary problems contribute substantially to language-minority students' problems in learning to understand text (e.g., Garcia, 1991). Cummins (1994) makes an interesting distinction between knowledge of surface vocabulary and knowledge of the cognitive vocabulary required for school achievement. Many teachers stress surface aspects of language, such as high-frequency nouns, verbs, and adjectives, rather than the more basic, abstract, and conceptual type of vocabulary that carries the logic of the language (e.g., negatives, conjunctions, prepositions, and other abstract words). Often, students learn these as part of their sight vocabularies, but confusions about usage and meaning persist.

Consideration of Larger Contexts

Despite frequent calls for teaching word meanings in context, typical instruction often focuses on accumulating the meanings of isolated words. While students clearly need to know more words, a concentration primarily on individual words may have unfortunate consequences. In a typical reading session, the teacher stops students at a word, asks for meaning, tells the meaning if necessary, has students repeat the word, and goes on like this every few words throughout the text. Students soon learn to grind down mercilessly on words and lose all sense of the context (Lee, 1984), further application, and ownership of the words on which they have worked so hard. When an emphasis on ungeneralizable words is coupled with a neglect of the contexts in which they occur, students begin to concentrate on minutia and ignore text meaning as a whole.

Determination of Importance and Unimportance

Unless students consider the context of words, they are unlikely to recognize important aspects of text, a crucial reading strategy (Dole, Duffy, Roehler, & Pearson, 1991). Language-minority students are surrounded by a mass of information waiting to be learned, and all readers tend to focus on highly noticeable but trivial aspects of text (Hidi & Anderson, 1987). To motivate students to speak, teachers may inadvertently underemphasize importance. For example, in classes where we observed the reading of a passage on mummies, teachers encouraged discussions on Egyptian embalmers pulling a dead person's brains out through the nose, but initiated no discussions on the cultural significance of the mummification process featured in the text. With so much input and no model of what is more or less important, what students learn from reading is often scattered and of limited applicability.

Elaborated Responses

The problems described make it understandable that language-minority students tend to respond in very few words. When prompted to say more, they commonly add as little as possible, with resulting piecemeal responses. Students rarely put together all of what they have said, and they end up with mere fragments of ideas.

Engagement in Natural Conversations

There is little chance for language-minority students to converse in English in the classroom. Gunderson (1985) found that most teachers taught reading in conventional ways and did not restructure their usual instruction to meet the special needs of students. Reading instruction is usually controlled by the teacher through teacher-generated questions, which do not encourage real conversation. Allington (1994, May) pointed out that only in schools are people constantly required to answer questions to which the asker already knows the answers—an infrequent occurrence in actual conversations. Conversations in students' homes in a first and/or second language have been shown to support the learning of a new language (Delgado-Gaitan, 1990). Yet most teachers fail to capitalize on this and may even counteract the benefits of heritage languages by discouraging students from using their first language and neglecting to foster natural conversations. Although some teachers stage "typical" conversations, these attempts do not usually capture the spontaneous and unstilted nature of real talk.

INSTRUCTIONAL SUGGESTIONS

The issues just listed involve *teachable* competencies. The following suggestions offer ways to teach these competencies through reading. Many language-minority students receive their instruction from regular classroom teachers who have little background in teaching English as a second language (Spangenberg-Urbschat & Pritchard, 1994). It is hoped that the suggestions will be especially helpful to these teachers.

The activities share the characteristics of productive practices defined by Gersten and Jiménez (1994)—practices that (a) lead to high levels of student involvement, (b) foster higher-order cognitive processes, and (c) enable students to engage in extended discourse. The suggestions also can be applied across grade levels and types of text. Further, the activities allow students to take part in a variety of ways and with different levels of English language experience. For each suggestion, we specify those grade levels, from 1 to 8, for which it seems most appropriate.

Shared Reading

Shared reading involves a teacher reading and sharing a book with students. Variations on this procedure have research support with many language-minority populations (e.g., Heald-Taylor, 1986), as well as widespread support from reading practitioners.

We suggest the following procedure for shared reading: Read a selection to the students a day or so in advance of when they are to read it. During this reading, with the help of teacher modeling, students should be encouraged to react freely to the text and to clarify any problems. Later, when the students read the selection, they will be able to contribute to a discussion in more sophisticated ways. The focus on meaning will be easier because problems with vocabulary and unfamiliar concepts will have already been addressed. Also, students will be able to clarify any remaining problems, read with more fluency and expression, and discuss what made the text enjoyable or interesting.

Although shared reading is most appropriate and commonly practiced in grades K–2, widespread anecdotal reports indicate that students at all levels continue to enjoy being read to, particularly when combined with their spontaneous input.

Vocabulary Networking

Often called semantic webbing or mapping, vocabulary networking is a current, popular, and effective way to develop vocabulary. In a semantic web, students graphically organize vocabulary from texts or other sources into related groups of words. Unfortunately, however, the activity is often carried out as a one-shot collective activity to which students do not return, or it is done too infrequently to provide the needed consistency. Alternatively, we suggest that a variety of networks be kept on separate sheets in a central location so that all students can return to them, add to them, and refer to them over time. It is critical to set a regular time for networking, or it may be neglected. The vocabulary base of the activity could also be designed to better meet the needs of the students. At the top of each sheet could be a word that the students agree is difficult. Students could organize meanings, examples, relationships, text references, and impressions for each word, drawing from their experiences, conversations, and readings. This not only increases students' understanding of particularly difficult words but also provides a source of vocabulary ideas for writing.

Since the vocabulary mapping suggested here calls on organization abilities as well as an understanding of superordinate and subordinate concepts, it is most appropriate for students in grades 3–8.

Expanding Context

Several procedures can help students become more aware of contexts for words. After clarifying a word, students can discuss what it has to do with the text, other texts, or their own experiences. Students can then exchange ideas on how they use new words in writing. Illustrating vocabulary can also put words into a context and, at the same time, encourage imagery. The important learning goal is to move from learning words in isolation to learning them in meaningful contexts. Even very young children can participate in these sorts of activities with easy texts.

Expanding context, however, applies to more than words and is appropriate at all levels. For students beyond first grade, difficult sentences and paragraphs, once understood, need to be thought of in terms of the whole text. This might be accomplished by simply asking, "What does this have to do with the rest of the text?"

Predicting

This strategy requires a sense of expanded context and is particularly important when reading narrative texts, such as stories, biographies, histories, and factual narrative episodes. It is futile to simply hope that students will predict when reading something they do not understand, so it is important that students first talk about their understandings of the text before they try to predict. It is also important for students to revisit predictions to see if text bears them out. Predictions can be written down and/or paraphrased so that all students can understand them. Gersten and Jiménez (1994) document effective teaching that includes the use of such written cues. Making predictions can be begun with very young children, as is done by most teachers. Teachers should push toward having students decide when to predict and why they wish to predict, so that students become independent in this strategy.

Imagery

Imagery (i.e., creating a mental image of text) aids comprehension in students from grade 3 on (Tierney & Cunningham, 1984). One way to encourage imagery is to talk more about illustrations. Since these do not always accurately depict important text aspects, it is critical to select texts in which the illustrations are supportive of understanding (Allen, 1994). Students could be asked to produce pictures of what they read and then to compare them with the text. Later, students might compare a text with its author's illustrations and tell whether the text and pictures match. A more sophisticated application of imagery might be judging whether the illustrations convey a text's most important, interesting, or difficult ideas. Students can begin talking about texts with supportive illustrations as early as grade 1, with the more advanced approaches carried out in grades 3–8.

Text Structures

Text structures are organizational options that authors choose when producing texts. These structures govern content to the extent that it relates to the structure chosen, such as cause and effect, compare and contrast, or problem and solution. Some studies have shown that teaching text structures to language-minority students increases their comprehension (Hague, 1990). An interesting instructional procedure, shown to be effective with students starting in grade 4 (Anderson, Chan, & Henne, 1995; McLaren & Anderson, 1992), involves teaching a text structure, such as problem and solution, by having students ask a series of questions that correspond to the characteristics of the text's structure (e.g., "What is the problem?" "What is the cause of the problem?" "What will happen if the problem continues?" "How can the problem be solved?"). Students then generate writing topics to answer the questions on the basis of their prior knowledge and use their answers to write problem-and-solution texts. The questions are scaffolds (instructional supports) for writing (Bereiter & Scardamalia, 1987). Text structures can be introduced with simple text types (e.g., narratives) in grade 1. Later, more difficult text structures (e.g., opinion texts, explanations) can be introduced. Examining text structures teaches students to ask important questions, improves reading comprehension, enhances language, encourages discussion, and integrates reading and writing.

Questioning, Identifying Problems, and Sharing Strategies

A number of recent studies show that language-minority students benefit from learning cognitive strategies for solving reading problems (e.g., Coterall, 1990). All students need to feel free to ask questions, explain their problems, and exchange and evaluate ideas for solving them. Fluent English is not necessary for such discussions. With the help of teacher modeling, think-aloud procedures have been implemented even with first graders (Pressley et al., 1992). Jiménez, Garcia, and Pearson (1996) show that language-minority students are able to think aloud about the strategies used in reading. Anderson (1992) has capitalized on this ability with culturally diverse adolescents in an instructional approach called collaborative strategy instruction, in which students and teacher work in a small group to identify aspects that make a text difficult, then work on strategies for resolving those difficulties (Anderson & Roit, 1990, December, 1993).

One strategy language-minority readers use to comprehend text is to draw on related background knowledge (Jiménez et al., 1996). Language-minority students may lack the background knowledge needed to understand some English texts. With so much to know, providing enough of this background in enough time is impossible, and it is not surprising that educators cannot accomplish the task. A more efficient way to solve the problem may be to teach students to handle a crucial lack of knowledge like the rest of us do, by questioning, identifying the problems, and finding ways to fill gaps as we read.

The use of strategies can be introduced in grade 1. At higher levels, more complex uses and variations may be introduced. From grade 5 on, students should more and more be expected to generate their own strategies and problem-solving ideas.

Text Explaining

Teachers often attempt to check understanding by allowing students to simply retell a text verbatim. This may be helpful for English speakers who know what they are retelling, but it may simply be poor practice for others. While language-minority students are often good at retelling, they may have little understanding of what they have retold. Instead of asking students to retell, teachers can encourage students to try to explain what the text means and to compare explanations with other students. This can be accomplished in collaborative groups, with simple, consistent directives that facilitate text explaining, such as, "What does this mean?" and "Can you explain it in your own words?"

Text explaining not only improves comprehension but also increases verbal elaboration and language flexibility as students exchange ideas. Text explaining also provides the teacher with a powerful way to assess whether students have really understood what they have read and to discover the sources of confusion. For language-minority students in particular, for whom so many forms of assessment are considered culturally unfair, such informal assessment is needed (Garcia, 1991).

The activity can be made less difficult with the support of teacher modeling and smaller text segments, moving to independent text explaining and larger segments as students become more proficient in English. Simple explanations of difficult words and phrases may begin in grade 1, with a gradual extension of the amount of text to be explained. From grade 4 on, more abstract ideas within text, such as seasonal change, photosynthesis, or molecules, might be explained by the students. Although a teacher may at first specify what children explain, it is more powerful to teach *them* to recognize what they think needs explaining (Anderson & Roit, 1990, December).

Conversational Opportunities

When learning a new language, most people look forward to opportunities to practice conversationally with a native speaker. These are usually lively exchanges about social or other matters, in which the conversationalists feel no discomfort from interrupting the flow of talk with language-learning questions, such as, "How do you say . . . ?" or, "Do you mean . . . ?" The purpose is to exchange information and find out about language in a friendly, enjoyable, and unintimidating way. Unfortunately, schools do not provide these opportunities. Gallimore, Boggs, and Jordon (1974) found that language-minority children were competent at home, where learning took place through group conversation, but not competent in school, where the rules were clearly different. Many researchers (e.g., Moll, 1988) have described the nonconversational recitation approach used in most schools for all children. We have pointed out that the home culture and the use of heritage languages in school can enrich school learning. It is undoubtedly true that proficiency in a heritage language is largely built from natural home conversations (Goldenberg & Gallimore, 1991).

The kind of teacher-student collaborative reading sessions reported by Anderson and Roit (1993) encourage conversational opportunities. They move away from teacher-questioning sessions to sessions in which students read and ask each other general but critical questions that stimulate real conversation: "Why is this important?" "What did I like best about it, and why?" "What is most interesting?" In other words, students are engaging in the kinds of conversations that adults engage in about their reading experiences. An added advantage of these kinds of questions is that they can be applied consistently and effectively across any number of texts. As these questions move into the hands of the students, they lead to lively and realistic conversational practice about reading and language. The intention here is not to tell students what to say to each other, but to encourage natural conversations and allow them to happen.

Many conversations occur between two people, so there should be opportunities for pairs of students to converse. These conversations need not always be between a good and a poor English speaker. Two students with poorer English can benefit from English conversational practice in which they share problems and information, and they clearly teach each other because they know different aspects of English. The challenge of such conversational opportunities is to implement them without their degenerating into stilted, teacher-controlled, and preplanned conversations. In short, ideal conversational practice should be natural, open, and freewheeling.

Conversational opportunities must be supported at all levels. The students themselves will guide the teacher in the type and level of conversation.

Culturally Fair Informational Material

Researchers have shown the importance of integrating students' cultures into teaching at all levels (Au & Jordon, 1981; Goldenberg & Gallimore, 1991; Moll & Greenberg, 1990), and educators have begun to realize the need to consider it. Perhaps the most popular and well-researched approach to including culture is through the use of culturally familiar reading materials (e.g., Rigg, 1986; Steffenson, Joag-dev, & Anderson, 1979).

Care must be taken, however, in the selection of multicultural materials. School reading materials chosen specifically for ethnic representation often illustrate sophisticated aspects of a culture, with which students actually have had little experience. In other words, while these selections could inspire pride, they may not inspire understanding. We are not suggesting that such selections be excluded, but rather that students also be provided with a relatively large set of short, simple expository passages that provide some interesting and enlightening information about very common ethnic experiences (e.g., holidays, animals, and foods). Such texts can be drawn from children's encyclopedias, trade books, and magazines. Barrera's (1992) analysis of multicultural literature and Allen's (1994) suggestions for selecting materials for ESOL students offer ideas for further sources. The students choose from these texts, read them independently, and tell the class about what they found out and how it related to their own experiences. Later, students' experience-based writing on expository topics might be added to the set of materials. In this way, students become authors, and their works become part of the class collection of relevant informational materials.

This activity has several advantages. First, it provides some culturally familiar material that students choose based on their prior knowledge and interests. Second, it gives students a chance to demonstrate their intelligence by sharing their own experiences and providing new knowledge to their peers. Third, and most importantly, it allows students to provide models for other students of at least three important reading strategies—identifying with text, reacting to text, and connecting text with prior knowledge.

In sum, the purpose of this chapter has been a practical one. We urge practitioners to avoid withholding reading from some students, while promoting it with others. The chapter describes a number of issues regarding language-minority students, some of which you may have observed. It also attempts to provide some easy-to-implement suggestions for helping students to learn English. The emphases on using strategies and collaborating allow teachers to help students use their natural social and cognitive abilities for learning to use their new language as they learn to read. Our suggestions provide equitably for student differences, because they are approaches that place value on differentiated contributions from students and that can be readily implemented on a schoolwide basis. Surely, equity is more easily accomplished in an environment where educators and students share similar learning goals and work together to achieve them.

REFERENCES

Adams, M. J. (1991). *Beginning to read: Thinking and learning about print.* Cambridge, MA: MIT Press.

Allen, V. G. (1994). Selecting materials for the instruction of ESL children. In K. Spangenberg-Urbschat & R. Pritchard (Eds.), *Kids come in all languages: Reading instruction for ESL students* (pp. 108–131). Newark, DE: International Reading Association.

Allington, R. (1994, May). *Balancing "Once upon a time" and "Scientists say."* Paper presented at the meeting of the International Reading Association, Toronto, Ontario, Canada.

Anderson, V. (1992). A teacher development project in transactional strategy instruction for teachers of severely reading-disabled adolescents. *Teaching and Teacher Education, 8*(4), 391–403.

Anderson, V., Chan, C. K. K., & Henne, R. (1995). The effects of strategy instruction on the literacy models and performance of reading and writing delayed middle school students. In *Perspectives on literacy research and practice: Forty-fourth yearbook of the National Reading Conference* (pp. 180–189). Chicago: National Reading Conference.

Anderson, V., & Roit, M. L. (1990, December). *Developing active reading behaviors with disabled adolescent learners.* Paper presented at the National Reading Conference, Miami Beach, FL.

Anderson, V., & Roit, M. L. (1993). Planning and implementing collaborative strategy instruction with delayed readers in grades 6–10. *Elementary School Journal, 94*(2), 121–137.

Anyon, J. (1981). Social class and school knowledge. *Curriculum Inquiry, 11,* 3–42.

Au, K. H., & Jordon, C. (1981). Teaching reading to Hawaiian children: Finding a culturally appropriate solution. In H. Trueba, G. P. Guthrie, & K. H. Au (Eds.), *Culture and the bilingual classroom: Studies in ethnography.* Rowley, MA: Newbury House.

Barrera, R. (1983). Bilingual reading in the primary grades: Some questions about questionable views and practices. In T. H. Escobedo (Ed.), *Early childhood bilingual education: A Hispanic perspective* (pp. 164–183). New York: Teachers College Press.

Barrera, R. (1992). The literacy gap in literature-based literacy instruction. *Education and Urban Society, 24*(2), 227–243.

Bereiter, C., & Scardamalia, M. (1987). *The psychology of written composition.* New York: Erlbaum.

Bereiter, C., & Scardamalia, M. (1989). Intentional learning as a goal of instruction. In L. B. Resnick (Ed.), *Knowing, learning, and instruction: Essays in honor of Robert Glaser* (pp. 361–392). Hillsdale, NJ: Erlbaum.

Brown, A. L., & Campione, J. C. (1990). Communities of learning and thinking, or a context by any other name. In D. Kuhn (Ed.), *Contributions to human development: Vol.*

21, Developmental perspectives on teaching and learning thinking skills (pp. 108–126). Farmington, CT: Karger.

Coterall, S. (1990). Developing reading strategies through small-group interaction. *RELC Journal, 21,* 55–69.

Cummins, J. (1989). *Empowering minority students.* Sacramento, CA: California Association for Bilingual Education.

Cummins, J. (1994). The acquisition of English as a second language. In K. Spangenberg-Urbschat & R. Pritchard (Eds.), *Kids come in all languages: Reading instruction for ESL students* (pp. 32–62). Newark, DE: International Reading Association.

Delgado-Gaitan, C. (1990). *Literacy for empowerment: The role of parents in children's education.* New York: Falmer Press.

Dole, J. A., Duffy, G. G., Roehler, L. R., & Pearson, P. D. (1991). Moving from the old to the new: Research on reading comprehension instruction. *Review of Educational Research, 61,* 239–264.

Foresee, V. (1991). Whole language practice and theory. Boston: Allyn and Bacon.

Gallimore, R., Boggs, J. W., & Jordon, C. (1974). *Culture, behavior, and education: A study of Hawaiian-Americans.* Newbury Park, CA: Sage.

Garcia, G. E. (1991). Factors influencing the English reading test performance of Spanish-speaking Hispanic children. *Reading Research Quarterly, 26*(4), 371–392.

Gersten, R. M., & Jiménez, R. T. (1994). A delicate balance: Enhancing literacy instruction for students of English as a second language. *The Reading Teacher, 47*(6), 438–449.

Goldenberg, C., & Gallimore, R. (1991). Local knowledge, research knowledge, and educational change: A case study of early Spanish reading improvement. *Educational Researcher, 20*(8), 2–14.

Goodman, K., Goodman, Y., & Flores, B. (1979). *Reading in the bilingual classroom: Literacy and biliteracy.* Rosslyn, VA: National Clearinghouse for Bilingual Education.

Grabe, W. (1991). Current development in second language reading research. *TESOL Quarterly, 25,* 375–406.

Gunderson, L. (1985). A survey of L2 reading instruction in British Columbia. *Canadian Modern Language Review, 42,* 44–55.

Hague, S. (1990). Awareness of test construction: The question of transfer from L1 to L2. In *Cognitive and social perspectives for literacy research and instruction: Thirty-eighth yearbook of the National Reading Conference* (pp. 55–64). Chicago: National Reading Conference.

Heald-Taylor, G. (1986). *Whole language strategies for ESL students.* Toronto, Ontario, Canada: OISE Press.

Hidi, S., & Anderson, V. (1987). Producing written summaries: Task demands, cognitive operations, and implications for instruction. *Review of Educational Research, 56,* 473–493.

Jiménez, R. T., Garcia, G. E., & Pearson, P. D. (1996). The reading strategies of bilingual Latina/o students who are successful English readers: Opportunities and obstacles. *Reading Research Quarterly, 31*(1), 90–112.

Lee, Y. J. (1984). Contextual reading. In B. W. Kim (Ed.), *The first yearbook of literacy and language* (pp. 93–103). Seoul, Korea: Literacy and Language Arts in Asia.

McLaren, J., & Anderson, V. (1992, December). *Instruction in two text structures: Effects on understanding and written production of expository text by elementary school students.* Paper presented at the National Reading Conference, San Antonio, TX.

Moll, L. C. (1988). Some key issues in teaching Latino students. *Language Arts, 65*(5), 465–472.

Moll, L. C. (1994). Literacy research in community and classrooms: A sociocultural approach. In R. B. Ruddell, M. R. Ruddell, & H. Singer (Eds.), *Theoretical models and processes of reading* (pp. 179–207). Newark, DE: International Reading Association.

Moll, L. C., & Greenberg, J. K. (1990). Creating zones of possibilities: Combining social contexts for instruction. In L. C. Moll (Ed.), *Vygotsky and education* (pp. 319–438). New York: Cambridge University Press.

Pressley, M., El-Dinary, P. B., Gaskins, I., Schuder, T. L., Bergman, J., Almasi, J., & Brown, R. (1992). Beyond direct explanation: Transactional instruction of reading comprehension strategies. *Elementary School Journal, 92,* 513–556.

Rigg, P. (1986). Reading in ESL: Learning from kids. In P. Rigg & D. S. Enright (Eds.), *Children and ESL: Integrating perspectives* (pp. 57–91). Alexandria, VA: Teachers of English to Speakers of Other Languages.

Spangenberg-Urbschat, K., & Pritchard, R. (1994). Meeting the challenge of diversity. In K. Spangenberg-Urbschat & R. Pritchard (Eds.), *Kids come in all languages: Reading instruction for ESL students* (pp. 1–5). Newark, DE: International Reading Association.

Steffenson, M. S., Joag-dev, C., & Anderson, R. C. (1979). A cross-cultural perspective on reading comprehension. *Reading Research Quarterly, 15,* 10–29.

Tierney, R. J., & Cunningham, J. W. (1984). Research on teaching reading comprehension. In P. D. Pearson (Ed.), *Handbook of reading research* (pp. 609–656). New York: Longman.

Weber, R. M. (1991). Linguistic diversity and reading in American society. In R. Barr, M. L. Kamil, P. Mosenthal, P. D. Pearson (Eds.), *Handbook of reading research* (Vol. 2, pp. 97–119). New York: Longman.

Wong Fillmore, L., & Valadez, C. (1986). Teaching bilingual learners. In M. C. Wittrock (Ed.), *Handbook of research on teaching* (pp. 648–685). New York: Macmillan.

PART II

The Transition Years: Intermediate School Grades

4

Recent Research on Effective Instructional Practices for Content Area ESOL

Russell Gersten
Susan Unok Marks
Thomas Keating
Scott Baker
Eugene Research Institute
University of Oregon

For many years, the specific educational needs of language-minority students have received considerable exposure, both inside and outside the field of education. The breadth of that exposure, however, has been remarkably restricted. Two issues, in particular, have dominated: whether instruction should be primarily in the student's native language or in English, especially in the early years of schooling (Crawford, 1989; Moll, 1992), and precisely when is the best time to make the inevitable transition into primarily English language classrooms. Educators familiar with bilingual education can attest to the rancorous nature in which these two issues have been debated, and also, unfortunately, to the inconclusive and occasionally insufficient data used in helping to resolve these issues.

Until recently the major topic of both debate and research in the area of bilingual education has been the language of instruction. As Moll (1992) noted, the near obsession with the topic does a disservice to language-minority students, in that little of the research and discussion has focused on the components of quality instruction and quality learning environments. C. Goldenberg (personal communication, October 8, 1994) made a similar point:

> [The] language-of-instruction debate has so dominated discussion of how best to serve the needs of language-minority children that other issues which are *at least equally important* have not been adequately addressed. For example, what are optimal instructional strategies for language-minority students who are at risk? . . . How do we promote English language development? . . . Is there an optimal balance between direct teaching strategies on the one hand and "authentic" communicatively based classroom interaction on the other?

Educators have begun to expand their conceptions of crucial issues in the development of educational programs for language-minority students to include identifying high-quality instructional practices independent of the language of instruction. In fact, researchers such as Barrera (1984) and Saville-Troike (1982) have consistently stressed that the key problem and issue is not the determination of the exact age or grade level at which to introduce English language academic instruction, but how to merge English language acquisition with academic learning in a fashion that is both stimulating and not overly frustrating to students.

This expanded focus is especially critical for language-minority students making the transition from native language instruction to English language instruction. The naturalistic research of Ramirez (1992) found that often the transition from virtually all–native-language instruction to virtually all-English-language instruction was rarely smooth for either students or teachers. In cases where the transition was especially abrupt, students often experienced major difficulties.

The purpose of this chapter is to provide an overview of an emerging knowledge base on effective instructional practices for merging academic instruction with English for speakers of other languages (ESOL). Our goal is to present this emerging knowledge base through an analysis of a research study by Tikunoff et al. (1991), supplemented by vignettes from our own observational research.

Our earlier research has resulted in the development of a set of constructs that we believe is a useful way of conceptualizing effective instruction for language-minority students. Tikunoff et al. (1991) arrived at similar conclusions and findings through presenting a range of instructional practices used by exemplary programs for English language learners. We present the emerging knowledge base as Constructs for Effective Instruction of Language-Minority Students (adapted from Gersten & Jiménez, 1994). These constructs are also elaborated on and exemplified in other chapters (Chapter 5 by Arreaga-Mayer; Chapter 6 by Gersten; Chapter 7 by Saunders, O'Brien, Lennon, and McLean; Chapter 10 by Graves; and Chapter 12 by Echevarria).

This knowledge base is primarily derived from the increasing number of programs that stress the development of English language abilities through the use of academic instruction for second language learners (Anderson & Roit, 1996; Barrera, 1984; Chamot & O'Malley, 1989, 1996; Gersten & Woodward, 1995; Northcutt & Watson, 1986). When researchers have integrated English language instruction with content area instruction in subjects such as language arts, mathematics, science, and social studies, results have been promising (Anderson & Roit, 1996; Chamot & O'Malley, 1989; Goldenberg, 1992–93). These programs are typically called content-based ESOL, or specially designed alternative instruction. (In years past, they were called sheltered instruction.) In each case, students are taught in English for the majority of the academic day. In some cases, part of the day is spent in native language instruction provided by either a teacher or a paraprofessional proficient in the students' native language. In other cases, the entire school day is in English.

Examination of Exemplary Programs for Promoting English Language Learning[1]

More than 10 years ago, Gersten and Woodward (1985) noted that the education of language-minority students is "relatively easy to write about, yet difficult to implement sensitively on a day-to-day basis" (p. 78). Part of the problem is that few studies have attempted to articulate the components of effective classroom practice for language-minority students. One of the few studies that has examined effective instructional practices for promoting English language learning for language-minority students was conducted for the U.S. Department of Education by Tikunoff et al. (1991). These researchers, in essence, attempted to explain the day-to-day realities of effective instructional practice for language-minority students.

The report by Tikunoff et al. (1991) presents the findings of a three-year study to identify and describe effective practices of nine exemplary special alternative instructional programs (SAIPs) for teaching language-minority students. The purpose of the study was to describe features of the SAIPs that appeared to contribute to positive outcomes for students from diverse linguistic and cultural backgrounds. One of the primary goals of the study was also to develop a deeper understanding of those techniques and strategies that effective teachers use while merging content area instruction with English language instruction.

Nine SAIPs were chosen from 70 programs identified as exemplary by a group of 147 educators involved in various aspects of education for language-minority students (Lucas & Katz, 1994). Qualitative and quantitative data were collected at these nine exemplary SAIP sites over a period of three years. A range of information for these programs was collected. In addition, three observational systems to describe and analyze instructional practices were used: the Description of Instructional Practice Profile, the Instructional Environment Profile, and the Student Functional Proficiency measure.

Description of Instructional Practice Profile

Observers used the Description of Instructional Practice Profile to assess teachers' use of 33 instructional practices that prior research has shown to be characteristic of effective instruction generally (Brophy & Good, 1986), as well as practices advocated specifically for the instruction of language-minority students (Chamot & O'Malley, 1989; Tikunoff, 1985). Items for the Description of Instructional Practice Profile are presented as part of the results contained in Table 4.1.

Instructional Environment Profile and
Student Functional Proficiency Measure

Additional information about the instructional environment (how instruction was organized and delivered) and about how students responded to inherent task and activity demands was obtained concurrently by two observers. The Instructional Environment Profile observations focused on class size, class composition, lesson content, number and size of groups, criteria for assignment to groups, academic task requirements, and nature of student evaluation. The Student Functional Proficiency observational measure focused on how well language-minority students performed academic tasks while acquiring English proficiency (Tikunoff, 1987). Observations focused on three areas of student performance: engagement in academic tasks, use of skills required for successful task completion, and types of instructional tasks assigned. The overall goal was to look at student engagement, the language or languages used by students, and peer interactions.

Patterns of Effective Instructional Practice

Tikunoff performed a factor analysis on the Description of Instructional Practice Profile in an effort to identify underlying patterns of effective instruction based on the 33 individual teaching practices that constituted the Description of Instructional Practice Profile. The factor analysis resulted in the extraction of nine factors that met a common standard for determining the utility and statistical soundness of factors. Four of these nine factors met an additional criterion set by Tikunoff et al (1991). Our discussion will be limited to three of the four factors, because the items in Factor 4 did not exhibit any particular conceptual coherence among them. The factors we will discuss are as follows:

- *Factor 1.* Facilitating students' comprehension of and participation in academic learning
- *Factor 2.* Structuring activities that promote students' active use of language
- *Factor 3.* Allowing use of students' native language for English language and concept development

These three key factors used 23 of the 33 observational items and are listed in Table 4.1. Table 4.1 also lists the percentages of teachers in the exemplary programs who were observed using each practice.

Table 4.1. Three Major Instructional Practice Factors and Percentage of Teachers Who Used Them

Instructional Practice	Percentage of Teachers
Factor 1. Facilitating students' comprehension of and participation in academic learning	
1 Teacher monitors students' progress toward completing instructional tasks	98
2 Teacher adjusts instruction to maximize students accuracy rates	98
3 Teacher allows students appropriate wait time for responding to questions in English	98
4 Teacher perceives that students are capable of learning	98
5 Teacher structures opportunities for students to use English	98
6 Teacher spends most of the instructional period on subject matter instruction	98
7 Teacher adjusts own use of English to make content comprehensible	96
8 Teacher provides immediate academic feedback individually to students	96
9 Teacher places a clear focus on academic goals	96
10 Teacher uses materials that maximize students' accuracy rates	96
11 Teacher checks students' comprehension during instruction	93
12 Teacher paces instruction briskly	93
13 Teacher expresses high expectations for student achievement	93
14 Teacher manages classroom well	93
Factor 2. Structuring activities that promote students' active use of language	
1 Teacher does not correct the ungrammatical utterances of students	89
2 Teacher allows students to interact with others to work on assigned tasks	83
3 Teacher assigns students to collaborate/cooperate on instructional tasks	48
4 Student talk dominates lesson	30
Factor 3. Allowing use of students' native language for English language and concept development	
1 Teacher allows students to use their native language to respond to questions asked in English	54
2 Teacher uses the students' native language for concept development/ clarification	26
3 Teacher uses students' native language to develop competence in English	24

Note. Adapted from W. J. Tikunoff et al., 1991, *Final Report: A Descriptive Study of Significant Features of Exemplary Special Alternative Instructional Programs*, Southwest Regional Educational Laboratory: Los Alamitos, CA.

Factor 1: Facilitating Students' Comprehension of and Participation in Academic Learning

Most of the instructional practices that clustered for this factor have been identified in the research literature on effective teaching (e.g., monitoring student progress, adjusting instruction to increase students' success rates, providing immediate feedback, focusing on academic goals, having reasonably high cognitive expectations, etc.). However, four teaching practices were related specifically to modifications of instruction for second language students:

- adjusting and modifying teachers' use of English to make content more comprehensible
- allowing for sufficient wait time to respond in English
- checking for comprehension during instruction
- structuring opportunities for students to use English

In the following example from our own research (Gersten & Jiménez, 1994), the reader will see how one exemplary teacher named Donna merged or adapted these principles of effective teaching to ensure comprehension with her language-minority students. Donna taught a third grade class with students who spoke at least seven different languages (including Spanish, Vietnamese, and Cambodian). Donna spoke only English.

Donna began by reading the story *Bringing the Rain to Kapiti Plain,* by Verna Aardema, to the class, in the form of a big book. She spoke to the students in a clearer, less hurried pace than she would use in normal conversation. She also used a consistent vocabulary. Both of these strategies seemed to really increase students' levels of involvement in the lesson (as judged by eye contact maintained), and, most importantly, their comprehension.

After reading two or three pages of the story, she paused to check on their understanding:

Donna: What does the bow do?
Student: Shoots arrow . . .

[Note that the question is intentionally literal, so that she could assess whether students understood a crucial vocabulary word, *bow.* Since the protagonist of the story is portrayed as a hero who causes rain to fall by shooting a feather from his bow into a cloud, it made sense that some children might benefit from hearing an explanation of this key word.]

A second question called for a moderate inference. It elicited a correct but truncated answer from a student:

Donna: What does he hope will happen when he shoots the arrow?
Student: The rain. (He motions rain falling.)
Donna: Right, the rain will fall down.

This student understood both the intent of the story and the question posed by his teacher but was unable (or was afraid) to fully express his thoughts in English. Donna extended and elaborated on the child's utterance. Her action had the dual effect of affirming the student's response and modeling a more complete English sentence structure for the others.

As Donna read the story, she seized opportunities to teach vocabulary or to engage the children in relevant ways.

Donna: How many of you girls have earrings with holes in your ears? What are they called? Pierced, pierced means you have a hole in it. If I take a piece of paper and cut it with scissors, it's pierced.

Donna cut a little hole in a piece of paper. She asked, "What's that word? *Pierce.*" She came back to this word later during this activity and repeated it. She also helped students relate what they knew to new situations and concepts. For example, she stressed the new word, *drought,* by drawing students' attention to the then current weather pattern afflicting the Southwest, because this low frequency word was crucial for understanding the plot and it was certain to be a word these students would hear and read about.

Factor 2: Structuring Activities that Promote Students' Active Use of Language

Generally, teachers used structural arrangements that facilitated student interactions (e.g., placing students in proximity to each other and setting up activities that required them to interact linguistically to complete tasks). Observations using the Instructional Environment Profile indicated that these teachers structured learning environments that promoted students' active use of English.

Tikunoff et al. (1991) note: "Structural arrangements that place students in proximity to each other and demand that they interact linguistically to complete tasks promote language use" (p. 18). One structural arrangement that has often been described in the literature as especially effective for fostering interaction among limited-English-proficient students is the use of cooperative learning groups. The following is an example from our collaborative research (Jiménez, Gersten, & Rivera, 1996). It shows how a fourth grade teacher structures effective learning groups with a class of Latino students.

> We often observed students working together in Sonia's classroom. Sonia's views concerning collaborative efforts parallel those common in many Latino homes. Children are frequently given much responsibility for their younger siblings. Her use of cooperative learning as an instructional tool was consistent with her own cultural background and that of her students. Sonia told us what cooperative learning meant to her: "I establish . . . cooperative groups, but I switch the students around each quarter. Before they can share with the rest of the class they need to bounce their ideas [in English] off of one another. They need someone they can trust [as they take risks in a new language]."

Another way that expert teachers of limited-English-proficient students continually create opportunities for students to express their own ideas in English is by providing engaging content to create a desire to communicate ideas. Students clearly benefit from opportunities for frequent, meaningful interactions among themselves as well as with the teacher. Tikunoff et al.'s (1991) results suggest that collaborative/cooperative learning and more structured teacher-directed learning seem to supply an ideal basis for promoting meaningful use of the second language, encouraging risk taking and providing many models of proficient performance.

Table 4.2. Percentage of Time Teachers and Students in Exemplary Programs Used English and Non-English Languages

Use of Language	TEACHERS				STUDENTS			
	All Grade Levels	Middle			All Grade Levels	Middle		
		Elem.	JH	HS		Elem.	JH	HS
All to most talk is in English	95	92	95	98	75	86	85	66
Talk is in both English and a non-English language	2	6	1	<1	11	8	7	22
Most talk is in a non-English language	<1	0	<1	0	7	<1	9	9

Note. Adapted from W. J. Tikunoff et al., 1991, *Final Report: A Descriptive Study of Significant Features of Exemplary Special Alternative Instructional Programs,* Southwest Regional Educational Laboratory: Los Alamitos, CA.

Factor 3: Allowing Use of Students' Native Language for English Language and Concept Development

Teachers in exemplary programs allowed students to respond to questions or class discussions in their native languages if they understood what was being asked in English but couldn't yet respond in English. This did not necessarily mean, however, that teachers were fluent in the students' languages. Instead, teachers turned to others (e.g., aides, other children) who understood the native language being used, and from these interactions they began to develop the English behind the concept. Teachers were observed to use English during 90% of the observations, and students used native languages to some degree during 36% of the observations. Table 4.2 presents the actual observed data on language use by both teachers and students.

The following example (Jiménez, Gersten, & Rivera, 1996) illustrates how a fourth grade teacher allowed students to verbalize their thoughts in Spanish before attempting to express them in English (when necessary):

> Christina considered it her responsibility to teach her students English, and she believed it necessary to provide students with opportunities to practice and use English. In other words, she did not simply insist that students speak English but instead showed students how to go about doing so. When a student answered a question in English with the Spanish word *estufa*, Christina translated it to "stove" and added it to a list she was writing on the board. If a child seemed flustered in answering a complex question in English, she asked the child to answer in Spanish and then to try to say it in English.

In our observations of expert teachers, native language responses were always accepted, but students were encouraged to try to express their thoughts in English; however, they were never forced to do so.

Tikunoff et al. and, recently, Lucas and Katz (1994) report on a variety of strategies that teachers in the observed special alternative instructional programs used to facilitate and accommodate students' use of their primary language. One example was pairing students from the same language backgrounds during instruction and activities, so that the more fluent English-speaking students could assist the less fluent students with understanding the teacher instructions and classroom assignments. Another useful strategy was to encourage students to use bilingual dictionaries, or to get help at home in their primary language from family members who were more fluent in English.

Additional Effective Teaching Practices

An additional item on the Description of Instructional Practice Profile indicated that 87% of the teachers in the exemplary programs consciously focused on English language development as an integral part of the lesson. In other words, they dedicated a portion of each lesson to language-related objectives as opposed to content-related objectives. Teachers also used multiple modalities to present material. In addition, 96% of the sample of teachers presented information both verbally and in writing. The importance of doing this for enhancing learning and language development is slowly receiving greater emphasis in the literature (Chamot & O'Malley, 1996; Scanlon, Duran, Reyes, & Gallego, 1992).

One aspect of instruction that we believe demonstrates the importance of respect for cultural differences is the finding that teachers in this study felt that "evaluation of students' academic or non-academic performance that is public (i.e., heard by others) and negative may dissuade students from participating in classroom instruction" (p. 23). These types of negative evaluations were virtually never observed in the exemplary programs. The researchers found that teachers would typically tend to support or help clarify, rather than provide negative, critical feedback. (See Gersten [1996] and McElroy-Johnson [1993] for further discussion of this critical issue.)

Observations of Student Engagement and Success

As might be expected with a group of programs that were selected based in part on their demonstration of improvements in student performance, high rates of student engagement in instructional activities (see Table 4.3) were observed. Student engagement and involvement were notably higher than those found in Tikunoff's (1985) earlier observational study of bilingual classrooms, where the mean was 82%.

The researchers also found that academic success rates were reasonably high when one considers that students were responding in a second language. The rates for responses to material in printed text were approximately 76%. This is a bit lower than the optimal rate of 80 to 85% (Fisher & Guthrie, 1983), but it is nevertheless a high rate for second language learners. In addition, the completion rate on academic assignments and activities was 97%. It appears that teachers were able to minimize frustration most of the time for many of the students.

Table 4.3. Percentage of Student Engagement in Exemplary SAIP Classrooms, by Grade Level and for Total Sample

Level	Percentage Engagement
Elementary	97
Middle/junior high school	90
High school	94
Total	92

Note. Adapted from W. J. Tikunoff et al., 1991, *Final Report: A Descriptive Study of Significant Features of Exemplary Special Alternative Instructional Programs,* Southwest Regional Educational Laboratory: Los Alamitos, CA.

FINDINGS FROM AN OBSERVATIONAL RESEARCH STUDY OF EFFECTIVE INSTRUCTIONAL PRACTICES[2]

To elaborate on the findings just described, we present findings from our own observational research. The goal of this research was to begin to describe facets of effective reading instruction for language-minority students, particularly students identified by teachers as experiencing difficulties. To do so, we followed the path of Lortie and reading researchers such as Durkin (1978–79), Duffy and Roehler (1982, April), and Richardson (1990) and began with in-depth descriptions and analyses of the realities of current practice. By doing this, we attempted to describe how the theories and concepts play out in classroom practice and delineate what teachers can actually do to refine their reading lessons to enhance students' comprehension, involvement, and language acquisition.

Our research findings are based on observations conducted in a large southwestern school district. What all the classrooms had in common was the presence of large numbers of language-minority students, some of whom had been identified by their teachers as experiencing learning difficulties. The intermediate grades were targeted for observation because they have been identified as crucial transitional periods for all students (Applebee, Langer, & Mullis, 1987), but especially for those from language-minority backgrounds (de la Rosa, Maw, & Yzaguirre, 1990; Espinosa & Ochoa, 1986; García, Pearson, & Jiménez, 1992; Ramirez, Yuen, Ramey, & Pasta, 1990).

We used a qualitative classroom observational method as the primary means of describing and analyzing the realities of teaching language-minority students. All the participating teachers were observed by at least three of the researchers over a period of two years. We also interviewed teachers to begin to understand their concerns and their beliefs concerning literacy instruction for language-minority students.

Our goal was not only to describe instructional problems—as Durkin (1978–79) and Moll and Díaz (1987) had—but also to delineate potential solutions. We defined productive instructional practices as those practices that

- led to high levels of student involvement
- fostered higher-order cognitive processes
- enabled students to engage in extended discourse

Ramirez et al. (1990) noted that these practices are rare in classrooms serving language-minority students.

A unified framework of concepts derived from the knowledge bases that influenced and served as a framework for our research is provided in Table 4.4. We have found the constructs useful when considering practices and approaches for promoting literacy and academic achievement of language-minority students. For example, as we observed, we constantly asked ourselves a set of questions based on the constructs. These included, Are the strategies increasing or decreasing student involvement? How many students are successful during this phase of the lesson—and is the teacher doing anything to ensure future success? Do students seem to be learning strategies that will be useful for them in reading other novels or stories?

THEMES FROM THE
OBSERVATIONAL RESEARCH

Perhaps the most striking finding that emerged from our observational research was the following: Many of the instructional practices typical for teaching reading to students considered at risk also seem to be effective for teaching language-minority students to read, if these practices are properly modified. Thus, we believe that with some refinement and restructuring, experienced reading teachers can enter classrooms of diverse students with a core of relevant professional knowledge.

Our research has illustrated that certain effective instructional practices loom even larger in importance for language-minority students. These practices satisfy many of the demands imposed as the students learn a new language and consolidate their grasp of English. The most useful practices from our data include the following:

- *In the area of vocabulary development*—checking students' comprehension of new vocabulary introduced in a story, and providing students opportunities for meaningful use of new vocabulary
- *In the area of mediation and feedback*—paraphrasing student remarks and gently encouraging them to expand on their responses, and including questions and activities that require elaborated responses in English so that students can practice expressing their ideas

Table 4.4. Constructs for Content Area ESOL Instructional Practices

1. *Provision of explicit structures, frameworks, scaffolds, and strategies*
a. Support provided to students by thinking aloud, building on and clarifying input of students
b. Visual organizers/story maps or other aids used to help students organize and relate information
c. Adequate background knowledge provided to students, and/or students informally assessed as to whether they have background knowledge

2. *Techniques to increase comprehension and transfer*
a. Explicit attempts to remind students to access knowledge and skills they have in their native language when performing English language activities
b. Use of consistent language—avoidance of synonyms to explain a concept or process
c. Meaningful incorporation of students' primary language

3. *Mediation/feedback*
a. Feedback that focuses on meaning, not grammar, syntax, or pronunciation during early stages of English language learning (syntactic feedback provided for more advanced English language learners)
b. Extent to which extended discourse is fostered
c. Extent to which teacher provides students with prompts or strategies
d. Prompts that press students to clarify or expand on initial statements
e. Indicating to students when they are successful
f. Assigning activities that are reasonable and challenging, while avoiding undue frustration
g. Allowing use of native language responses (when context is appropriate)
h. Sensitivity to common problems in second language acquisition

4. *Responsiveness to cultural and personal diversity*
a. Extent to which teachers show respect for students as individuals, respond to things students say, show respect for culture and family, and possess knowledge of cultural diversity
b. Incorporation of students' experiences into writing and language arts activities
c. Involvement of parents in a meaningful way in their child's education
d. Importance of teachers having the availability of multiple strategies so that instruction fits the learning style of the student rather than forcing students to fit rigid instructional approaches

Note. Adapted from W. J. Tikunoff et al., 1991, *Final Report: A Descriptive Study of Significant Features of Exemplary Special Alternative Instructional Programs,* Southwest Regional Educational Laboratory: Los Alamitos, CA.

■ *For all areas of literacy instruction*—presenting ideas both verbally and in written form, using reasonably consistent language, and minimizing use of synonyms and idioms

Another key element is the need for increased use of scaffolded instruction or cognitive strategy training. The idea behind these approaches is to make public the "secrets of reading." Often, language-minority students have been excluded from access to these "secrets" (Delpit, 1988; Reyes, 1992). These approaches are widely advocated in the reading field and, if properly implemented, seem to have great potential for language-minority students.

It is also important to note that our observations indicate that to be effective, these practices must occur as part of a consistent and comprehensive approach to instruction involving high levels of student interaction and teachers' modeling of the comprehension strategies. Spiro, Vispoel, Schmitz, Samarapungavan, & Boerger (1987) observed that only when students are allowed to "crisscross the (instructional) landscape" via a wide range of oral and written activities, do they tend to really understand the concepts presented.

CONCLUSIONS

Teaching students for whom English is a second language is a complex endeavor. In many respects, the art of instruction is a balancing act: challenging students, but not frustrating them; helping those who need help the most, but including all. For teachers of language-minority students, this delicate balance is complicated by the fact that English is a second language. Teachers can never quite be certain whether student difficulties are due to a lack of comprehension or to limited facility with English. The work of Moll and Díaz (1987) has delineated in great detail the pain and frustration that language-minority students sometimes feel when taught in all-English settings. Students may fail to understand what the teacher is talking about, and they become frustrated when they have an idea but cannot adequately express their thoughts in the new language.

We believe the study by Tikunoff et al. (1991) and our own observational research provide the beginnings of an empirical base for defining effective practice and delineate numerous specific strategies. In discussing the findings, we have attempted to elucidate key points by occasionally providing brief illustrations from our own work in the area.

Our focus in this chapter has emphasized and highlighted the effective instructional practices identified by Tikunoff et al. and our own observational research. The analysis of quantitative and qualitative data from various sources in Tikunoff et al.'s extensive study of effective practice points to two overarching findings for particular instructional practices in exemplary special alternative instructional programs for limited-English-proficient students:

- Teachers integrated principles of effective instruction with English language development in subject areas.
- Aspects of the learning environment promoted active use of English.

Our observational research arrived at similar instructional practices, as delineated in our development of the Constructs for Effective Instruction of Language-Minority Students.

At the heart of the findings of these two studies on effective instructional practices is a clear recognition that language-minority students face unique learning challenges that demand innovative practices. An all too common problem has been to view language-minority children as simply low-performing native English-speaking children (Baca & Almanza, 1991; Yates & Ortiz, 1991). This tendency has led many to merely adopt a watered-down curriculum, a simply indefensible solution. Such a posture denies language-minority children access to quality instruction and, ultimately, real academic opportunity.

Language-minority children, like all children, deserve the best possible instruction, and this demands a delicate balancing of many factors. We view the instructional strategies discussed in this chapter as a bridge linking the best present understanding to a potentially more complete set of solutions to the problems facing limited-English-speaking children and the teachers who work with them. We believe that language-minority students face unique learning challenges that demand innovative practices, but that these practices are well within the grasp of committed teachers—whether monolingual or bilingual—who are provided with relevant knowledge and support and professional development.

REFERENCES

Anderson, V., & Roit, M. (1996). Linking reading comprehension instruction to language development for language minority students. *Elementary School Journal, 96*(3), 295–310.

Applebee, A. N., Langer, J. A., & Mullis, I. V. S. (1987). *The nation's report card: Learning to be literate in America: Reading.* Princeton: Educational Testing Service.

Baca, L. C., & Almanza, E. (1991). *Language minority students with disabilities.* Reston, VA: Council for Exceptional Children.

Barrera, R. (1984). Bilingual reading in the primary grades: Some questions about questionable views and practices. In T. H. Escobar (Ed.), *Early childhood bilingual education* (pp. 164–183). New York: Teachers College Press.

Brophy, J., & Good, T. L. (1986). Teacher behavior and student achievement. In M. Wittrock (Ed.), *The third handbook of research on teaching* (pp. 328–375). New York: MacMillan.

Chamot, A. U., & O'Malley, J. M. (1989). The cognitive academic language learning approach. In P. Rigg & V. Allen (Eds.), *When they don't all speak English* (pp. 108–125). Urbana, IL: National Council of Teachers of English.

Chamot, A. U., & O'Malley, J. M. (1996). The Cognitive Academic Language Learning Approach (CALLA): A model for linguistically diverse classrooms. *Elementary School Journal, 96*(3), 259–274.

Crawford, J. (1989). *Bilingual education: History, politics, theory and practice.* Trenton, NJ: Crane.

de la Rosa, D., Maw, C. E., & Yzaguirre, R. (1990). *Hispanic education: A statistical portrait, 1990.* Washington, DC: Policy Analysis Center, Office of Research, Advocacy, and Legislation, National Council of La Raza.

Delpit, L. D. (1988). The silenced dialogue: Power and pedagogy in educating other people's children. *Harvard Educational Review, 58*(3), 280–298.

Duffy, G., & Roehler, L. (1982, April). *A study of teacher explanation behavior.* Paper presented at the annual meeting of the International Reading Association, Chicago, IL.

Durkin, D. (1978–79). What classroom observations reveal about reading comprehension instruction. *Reading Research Quarterly, 14*(4), 481–533.

Espinosa, R., & Ochoa, A. (1986). Concentration of California Hispanic students in schools with low achievement: A research note. *American Journal of Education, 95*(1), 77–95.

Fisher, C. W., & Guthrie, L. F. (1983). *The significant bilingual instructional features study. Executive summary.* (San Francisco, CA: Far West Educational Laboratory No. ED 297 562).

García, G. E., Pearson, P. D., & Jiménez, R. T. (1992). *The at-risk dilemma: A synthesis of reading research.* Champaign/Urbana, IL: University of Illinois, Reading Research and Education Center.

Gersten, R. (1996). The double demands of teaching English language learners. *Educational Leadership, 53*(5), 18–22.

Gersten, R., & Jiménez, R. (1994). A delicate balance: Enhancing literacy instruction for language minority students. *The Reading Teacher, 47*(6), 438–449.

Gersten, R., & Woodward, J. (1985). A case for structured immersion. *Educational Leadership, 43*(1), 75–84.

Gersten, R., & Woodward, J. (1995). A longitudinal study of transitional and immersion bilingual education programs in one district. *Elementary School Journal, 95*(3).

Gersten, R., Keating, T. J., & Brengelman, S. U. (1995). Toward an understanding of effective instructional practices for language-minority students: Findings from a naturalistic research study. *READ Perspectives, 2*(1), 55–83.

Goldenberg, C. (1992–93). Instructional conversations: Promoting comprehension through discussion. *The Reading Teacher, 46*(4), 316–326.

Jiménez, R., Gersten, R., & Rivera, A. (1996). Conversations with a Chicana teacher: Supporting students' transition from native-to-English-language instruction. *Elementary School Journal, 96*(3), 333–342.

Lucas, T., & Katz, A. (1994). Reframing the debate: The roles of native languages in English-only programs for language minority students. *TESOL Quarterly, 28*(3), 537–561.

McElroy-Johnson, B. (1993). Giving voice to the voiceless. *Harvard Educational Review, 63*(1), 85–104.

Moll, L. C. (1992). Bilingual classroom studies and community analysis: Some recent trends. *Educational Researcher, 21*(2), 20–24.

Moll, L. C., & Díaz, S. (1987). Change as the goal of educational research. *Anthropology and Education Quarterly, 18*(4), 300–311.

Northcutt, L., & Watson, D. (1986). *Sheltered English teaching handbook.* Carlsbad, CA: Northcutt, Watson, Gonzalez.

Ramirez, J. D. (1992). Executive summary: Longitudinal study of structured English immersion strategy, early-exit and late-exit transitional bilingual education programs for language-minority children. *Bilingual Research Journal, 16*(1), 1–62.

Ramirez, J. D., Yuen, S. D., Ramey, D. R., & Pasta, D. J. (1990). *Final report: Longitudinal study of immersion strategy, early-exit and late-exit transitional bilingual education programs for language-minority children.* San Mateo, CA: Aguirre International.

Reyes, M. de la luz (1992). Challenging venerable assumptions: Literacy instruction for linguistically different students. *Harvard Educational Review, 62*(4), 427–446.

Richardson, V. (1990). Significant and worthwhile change in teaching practice. *Educational Researcher, 19* (7), 10–18.

Saville-Troike, M. (1984). What really matters in second language learning for academic achievement. *TESOL Quarterly, 18*(2), 199–219.

Saville-Troike, M. (1982). The development of bilingual and bicultural competence in young children. *Current topics in early childhood education*. Norwood, NJ: Alex.

Scanlon, D. J., Duran, G. Z., Reyes, E. I., & Gallego, M. A. (1992). Interactive semantic mapping: An interactive approach to enhancing LD students' content area comprehension. *Learning Disabilities Research and Practice*, 7(3), 142–146.

Spiro, R. J., Vispoel, W. L., Schmitz, J. G., Samarapungavan, A., & Boerger, A. E. (1987). Knowledge acquisition for application: Cognitive flexibility and transfer in complex content domains. In B. K. Britton & S. Glymer (Eds.), *Executive control processes* (pp. 177–199). Hillsdale, NJ: Erlbaum.

Tikunoff, W. J. (1985). *Applying significant bilingual instructional features in the classroom*. Rosslyn, VA: National Clearinghouse for Bilingual Education.

Tikunoff, W. J. (1987). Mediation of instruction to obtain equality of effectiveness. In S. H. Fradd & W. J. Tikunoff (Eds.), *Bilingual education and bilingual special education: A guide for administrators* (pp. 99–132). Boston: Little, Brown.

Tikunoff, W. J. (1988). Mediation of instruction to obtain equality of effectiveness. In S. Fradd & W. J. Tikunoff (Eds.), *Bilingual education and special education: A guide of instruction* (pp. 99–132). Boston: Little, Brown.

Tikunoff, W. J., Ward, B. A., van Broekhuizen, L. D., Romero, M., Castaneda, L. V., Lucas, T., & Katz, A. (1991). *Final report: A descriptive study of significant features of exemplary special alternative instructional programs*. Southwest Regional Educational Laboratory: Los Alamitos, CA.

Yates, J. R., & Ortiz, A. A. (1991). Professional development needs of teachers who serve exceptional language minorities in today's schools. *Teacher Education and Special Education*, *14*(1), 11–18.

CHAPTER NOTES

1. Portions of this section adapted from Gersten, Keating, and Brengelman (1995). Toward an understanding of effective instructional practices for language-minority students: findings from a naturalistic research study. *READ Perspectives*, *2*(1), 55–83. Adapted by permission.

2. Portions of this section adapted from Gersten and Jiménez (1994).

5

Language-Sensitive Peer-Mediated Instruction for Culturally and Linguistically Diverse Learners in the Intermediate Elementary Grades

Carmen Arreaga-Mayer, Ph.D.
Juniper Gardens Children's Project
University of Kansas

How does one promote the second language acquisition and the academic and social integration of culturally and linguistically diverse learners (CLDLs), with or without disabilities, into inclusive environments? An effective framework is the development and/or identification of powerful instructional strategies that actively engage students instead of allowing them to be passive participants or observers. Research has documented that most students can profit from instruction in learning strategies (Cantoni-Harvey, 1987; Chamot & O'Malley, 1994; Harper, Maheady, & Mallette, 1994; O'Malley, Chamot, Stewner-Manzanares, Russo, and Küpper, 1985a, 1985b; O'Malley & Chamot, 1990). Culturally and linguistically diverse learners, for whom English is a second language, need learning strategies to assist them in managing the demands of learning a new language and academic content. These students shoulder an exceptionally heavy cognitive and linguistic load, requiring special instructional techniques and activities.

Typically, CLDLs who are limited-English proficient (LEP) spend most of their instructional time in classrooms where English is the only language of instruction used. Consequently, English-medium-classroom teachers need ways to structure the learning environment so that CLDLs at all levels of English language proficiency are included in learning activities with their monolingual English-speaking peers. The needs of CLDLs with limited English skills, with or without disabilities, are rarely qualitatively different from those of their monolingual peers, with or without disabilities. For all students to succeed, they must have high rates of active student engagement, high levels of success, clear and explicit goal and reward structures, and ample opportunity to respond to critical and meaningful academic content (Arreaga-Mayer & Perdomo-Rivera, 1996; Garcia, 1988; Greenwood, 1991). Students who speak a wide range of languages and who come from diverse cultural backgrounds can be served effectively by schools that incorporate the attributes of effective instruction relevant to language-minority students *and* emphasize student-to-student instructional tasks. Such instruction promotes the active engagement of students in instructional interactions that in turn promote higher levels of academic, social and linguistic performance (Garcia, 1988; Greenwood, Delquadri, & Carta, 1988; Maheady, Mallette, Harper, & Sacca, 1991; Slavin, 1991).

This chapter offers effective strategies to address CLDLs' instructional needs at the intermediate elementary level. Although the strategies selected are geared to students in grades 4–6, they are also appropriate for lower and higher grade levels. The present discussion will focus on the importance of language-sensitive teaching strategies and classroom organization based on effective instructional techniques through which academic, as well as linguistic and social success can be maximized. The first section discusses general constructs for effective instruction for CLDLs. In particular, it enumerates eight constructs that can be embedded in effective teaching strategies for CLDLs with limited English skills as well as English-speaking students (Gersten & Jiménez, 1994). The second section discusses three different peer-mediated learning procedures that have been used with CLDLs and that have proven to result in enhanced academic, social, and linguistic achievement: ClassWide Peer Tutoring, or CWPT (Greenwood, Delquadri, & Carta, 1988); Student Teams and Achievement Divisions, or STAD (Slavin, 1978, 1988, 1991); and Numbered Heads Together, or NHT (Kagan, 1985, 1989–90).

CONSTRUCTS FOR
EFFECTIVE INSTRUCTION

It is imperative for teachers and practitioners to understand *why* certain instructional strategies work as well as *how* they work. Simply exposing CLDLs to ample amounts of English language and conveying academic information through direct instruction have proven insufficient to the development of

Table 5.1. Constructs for Effective Instruction for CLDLs

1. Challenge
   - Implicit (cognitive challenge, use of higher-order questions)
   - Explicit (high but reasonable expectations)
2. Involvement
   - Active involvement of all students
3. Success
   - Reasonable activities that students can complete successfully
4. Scaffolding/cognitive strategies
   - Visual organizers, adequate background information, and support provided by teacher to students by thinking aloud, building on and clarifying their input
5. Mediation/feedback
   - Strategies provided to students
   - Frequency and comprehensibility stressed
6. Collaborative/cooperative learning
7. Techniques for second language acquisition/sheltered English
   - Extended discourse fostered
   - Use of consistent language
   - Incorporation of student's language
8. Respect for cultural diversity
   - Respect and knowledge of cultural diversity

Note. From "A Delicate Balance: Enhancing Literature Instruction for Students of English as a Second Language" by R. M. Gersten and R. T. Jiménez (1994). *The Reading Teacher, 47*(6), p. 440.

language and content learning. Chamot and O'Malley (1994) stated that teachers need to be aware of their students' approaches to learning and of how to expand the students' repertoires of learning strategies. The classroom is more than just one more environment in which language acquisition occurs. It can be a place that is especially conducive to language acquisition. Richard-Amato (1988) reported that for beginners up to the intermediate level, the classroom can potentially be more effective than the outside world for acquiring a second language. Language-sensitive content instruction based on effective and efficient learning strategies must (a) be effective for culturally and linguistically heterogeneous learning groups; (b) lead to high levels of student and student-student active engagement in learning; (c) foster higher-order cognitive processes; (d) enable students to engage in extended discourse in English; (e) be feasible to implement on a small-group or classwide basis; (f) be socially acceptable to the teachers, students, and parents; and (g) be responsive to cultural and personal diversity (Arreaga-Mayer, Carta, & Tapia, 1994; Garcia, 1988; Gersten & Jiménez, 1994; Maheady et al., 1991).

Gersten and Jiménez (1994) described eight basic principles for the selection and evaluation of effective instruction for CLDLs (see Table 5.1). These constructs emerged from the authors' extensive research in the areas of second language learning, effective instruction, and cognitive strategies. Their aim is at directing the selection of classroom learning activities based on (a) the level of explicit and implicit cognitive challenge; (b) the amount of active involvement of all students with the task; (c) the selection of activities that students can complete successfully; (d) the teacher's provision of scaffolding and/or cognitive strategies; (e) the frequency and comprehensibility of instructional mediation and feedback; (f) the use of collaborative and cooperative learning strategies; (g) the inclusion of techniques for second language acquisition and sheltered English; and (h) a respect for and responsiveness to cultural and personal diversity.

These principles were used as a framework for the selection of the strategies to be discussed in this chapter. The author hopes that they will serve as a basis for teachers' evaluation of learning activities and procedures to be used in their teaching. For a more detailed discussion of the framework and constructs, refer to Chapter 1 of this book.

PEER-MEDIATED INSTRUCTION

There exists an extensive research base in favor of altering the traditional teacher-to-students instruction (i.e., whole-class, lecture format) and in support of cooperative peer-mediated strategies, which have proven effective in promoting higher levels of language and academic learning and social interactions (August, 1987; Bejarano, 1987; Flanigan, 1991; Greenwood, Terry, Delquadri, & Elliott, 1992; Johnson, 1983; Slavin, 1980). Research has demonstrated that peer-mediated instruction contributes more to content mastery than do whole-class instruction, workbook exercises, and being asked to read a few sentences and answer questions during small-group instruction. The opportunity to actively practice a concept or repeatedly read a word contextually, the amount of discourse produced, the degree of negotiation of meaning that takes place, the amount of comprehensible linguistic input for new learners, and the interrelatedness of linguistic and social interactions are the keys to higher levels of academic, linguistic, and social performance through peer-mediated strategies. Peer-mediated instructional methods were designed to provide teachers with one-on-one and small-group techniques for daily instruction in the classroom. To achieve academic, linguistic, and social goals in the typical classroom, all peer-mediated learning strategies share essential components: (a) cooperative incentives, (b) group rewards, (c) individual accountability, and (d) task structures.

In peer-mediated learning strategies, students of varied academic abilities and language-proficiency levels work together in pairs or small groups toward a common goal. In these groups the success of one student depends on the help of the others. In peer-mediated instruction the class is organized in groups of two to six students to fulfill the requirements of a learning task cooperatively. The learning task to be learned varies, but the format of learning always includes interaction and interdependence among the students. In this format of learning, students and teachers participate in dynamic cooperation of learning and social interaction. The roles of the teacher and the students are somewhat different from those in the traditional whole-class, teacher-lecture format. The teacher is a facilitator of learning and a monitor of outcome performance and progress, encouraging and rewarding cooperation among the students. The students are teachers, co-teachers, and active learners. The CLDLs are no longer passive participants. They are motivated to communicate in the English language, at their own level of language proficiency, and are encouraged to access knowledge and skills they have in their native language. The CLDLs are guided and assisted by peers to engage in collaborative and cooperative learning that is challenging but provides reasonable expectations, as orchestrated by the teacher's selection of materials and heterogenous grouping. In such situations, motivation to learn a second language appears to be enhanced by decreasing the social distance between the CLDLs and/or disabled students and their English-speaking peers, through the provision of a collective learning goal.

Peer-mediated instruction is a flexible teaching approach that can be used to serve the instructional needs of CLDLs and their native English-speaking peers (Arreaga-Mayer & Greenwood, 1986; August, 1987; Flanigan, 1991). Different peer-mediated procedures emphasize the development of specific skills and content areas; consequently, it is important for the teacher to select the specific peer-mediated procedure that best fits students' instructional needs. At times the teacher might be using a number of peer-mediated instructional procedures to facilitate learning and mastery. For the purpose of this chapter, three different procedures were selected, based on their applicability to CLDLs' instructional inclusion and their proven outcomes in enhanced academic, social, and linguistic achievement: ClassWide Peer Tutoring, or CWPT (Greenwood, Delquadri, & Carta, 1988); Student Teams and Achievement Divisions, or STAD (Slavin, 1978, 1988, 1991); and Numbered Heads Together, or NHT (Kagan, 1985, 1989–90). The type of peer-mediated learning strategy selected by the teacher should be one that reflects the appropriate goal and task structure for curricular focus.

ClassWide Peer Tutoring: CWPT

ClassWide Peer Tutoring (CWPT) is a form of same-age, intraclass peer tutoring developed by researchers at the Juniper Gardens Children's Project, University of Kansas, to improve the acquisition and retention of basic academic skills (Greenwood, Delquadri, & Carta, 1988). It has been successfully applied to passage reading, reading comprehension, mathematics, vocabulary development, spelling, social studies, and science instruction with CLDLs and with regular, special education, and low-achieving students. CWPT involves the entire class in tutoring. Students are either paired randomly or matched by ability or language proficiency to partners each week. In the case of the CLDLs who have limited English skills, it is recommended that initially they be paired with students who speak their native language but have a higher level of English proficiency. Once CLDLs have a working knowledge of the English language, they can be paired at random with bilingual or native English-speaking peers. Pairs are assigned to one of two teams that compete for the highest point total resulting from daily scheduled tutoring sessions. The dyad consists of a tutor and a tutee (a teacher and a student). Students' roles are switched during the daily tutoring session, allowing each child to be both the tutor/teacher and the tutee/student. New content to be learned, teams, and tutoring pairs are changed on a weekly basis. Students are trained in the procedures necessary to act as tutors and tutees. In a given session, the students know who they are to pair with for tutoring, the material to be covered, how to correct errors, how to award points for correct responding, and how to provide positive feedback. Teachers organize the academic content to be tutored into daily and weekly units and prepare materials to be used within the CWPT format. Unit mastery is checked weekly using teacher-prepared tests in a pretest-posttest sequence, providing feedback to the students on their level of mastery. Tutoring occurs simultaneously for all tutor-tutee pairs, involving the entire class at the same time. This leaves the teacher free to supervise and monitor students' tutoring sessions.

The CWPT procedure features the characteristics of effective instruction and conforms to the eight constructs delineated by Gersten and Jiménez (1994) for effective instruction for CLDLs (see Table 5.1). It consists of four basic components:

- Weekly competing teams (culturally, linguistically, and ability-wise heterogenous grouping)
- Highly structured teaching procedure (content material, teams, pairing, error correction, system of rewards)
- Daily, contingent, individual tutee point earning and public posting of individual and team scores
- Direct practice of functional academic and language skills to mastery

A major advantage of CWPT is that it trains tutors and tutees to implement tutoring procedures. It empowers the students with a learning strategy to approach new learning tasks, independent of the CWPT classroom sessions (Delquadri, Greenwood, Stretton, & Hall, 1983). Students serving as tutors are trained to effectively create learning opportunities and increase engagement time in academics for their partners, correct errors, and give feedback and reinforcement. Students serving as tutees are trained to use auditory, visual, and writing modalities to practice and learn the new concepts.

Variation in the training of CLDLs as tutors requires the teacher or a bilingual student to simply and clearly explain the procedure to them individually and, if possible, bilingually. This will ensure that they have learned the appropriate steps to conduct CWPT. At the beginning of each week, the new content should be introduced to the CLDLs by the teacher or a bilingual student, individually or as a group, prior to the CWPT session. The CLDLs should be encouraged to access knowledge and skills they have in their native language to assist them with the new academic content (see Case 5.1). In addition, the teacher should provide support to the CLDLs by thinking aloud, using visual organizers or other aids to help students organize and relate information, and building on and clarifying the input of the students. The effort of pretutoring training with CLDLs will be rewarded many times over as CLDLs feel comfortable in approaching new material and consequently increase their academic content learning and English language skills.

Classroom Procedures. At the beginning of each week, all students in a class are paired for tutoring, and these tutor-tutee pairs are assigned to one of two competing teams. Tutoring pairs are preferably composed of a student with no or limited English skills and a student who speaks the same native language but is more proficient in the English language. Pairing of students randomly is not recommended for CLDLs with no or limited English skills, but it is advisable for English-speaking peers and bilingual English–proficient students. One student in each pair serves as the tutor or teacher for 10 minutes, while the other student is the tutee (see Figure 5.1). After the first 10 minutes have expired (signaled by a timer), the tutoring pairs reverse roles for an equivalent amount of time. The CWPT procedure focuses on students tutoring each other on prepared information in a reciprocal fashion, but the correct answers are provided for the tutor (see Table 5.2). Materials are prepared by the teacher. Tutoring content lists or study guides consist of material briefly introduced or not previously covered by the teacher (e.g., a new list of spelling words). CWPT allows for the teacher to introduce a lesson (e.g., phonics) to the whole class or small groups and then to reinforce the concept during the peer tutoring sessions (e.g., a selection of words following the specific phonetic rule, for spelling tutoring).

While the students are working in dyads, they must follow the precise teaching procedure delineated by CWPT: The tutor presents an instructional item orally and/or visually (e.g., a vocabulary word, spelling word, math fact, or social studies question from a study guide), and the tutee must respond orally and in writing. If the answer is correct (the tutor has the answer sheet), the tutor awards two points. If the answer is incorrect, the tutor conducts the error correction procedure by (a) providing the correct response (modeling), (b) requiring the tutee to write and say the correct answer three times, and (c) awarding one point to the tutee for correcting the mistake. If the tutee fails to provide the correct answer, three times, the tutor orally and visually provides the tutee the correct response and proceeds to the next item, and no points are awarded. The use of CWPT avoids direct competition between tutoring pairs but holds competition between teams. Both members of the tutoring pair are on the same team and working toward a common goal. The object of CWPT is to correctly complete as many items as possible in the allotted tutoring time. The tutee is to proceed through the tutoring list or

---

CASE 5.1. Scenario: Pretutoring of CLDLs in a Heterogeneous Classroom

The teacher, Mrs. Mayberry, is a monolingual English speaker. She is introducing the weekly spelling and vocabulary words to her class, which consists of Hispanic, Hmong, African American, and Caucasian students. The CLDLs represent a continuum in the level of English language proficiency. The teacher used a multimodality approach to introduce the spelling-vocabulary words for the week to the whole class.

> **Mrs. Mayberry:** Today we will be studying the words that are on this chart. Please note that I have colored each syllable in a different color and that I have drawn a picture to represent each word.
> The first word is *cheetah.*

> **All students:** Repeat, "Cheetah," and spell, "c-h-e-e-t-a-h."

> **Mrs. Mayberry:** A cheetah is a wild cat that runs very fast.

Marta, could you explain in Spanish what a cheetah is to the class?" [Marta is a bilingual Spanish- and English-speaking student.]

Marta: Una cheetah es un gato salvaje que corre muy rápido. Es de la familia del leon y tigre y vive en las selvas. [A cheetah is a savage cat that runs very fast. Is from the family of the lion and tiger and lives in the jungles.]

Mrs. Mayberry: Class, say, "Cheetah, c-h-e-e-t-a-h, cheetah."

All students: Repeat, "Cheetah, c-h-e-e-t-a-h, cheetah."

Mrs. Mayberry: Class, repeat after me: "A cheetah is a wild cat that runs very fast."

All students: A cheetah is a wild cat that runs very fast. [Procedure continues.]

---

reading passage as many times as possible during the 10 minutes. The more correct items the students complete, the more points they earn for themselves and for their team, and the more learning is taking place. Teams are rewarded with recognition (e.g., clapping of hands, stickers, privileges) and point posting on a classroom chart.

While the students are tutoring, the teacher moves about the classroom and awards bonus points for appropriate tutoring behaviors: (a) clear presentation of materials, (b) appropriate awarding of points, (c) correct use of the error correction procedure, and (d) positive comments and reinforcers to the tutoring partner. Immediately after the tutoring session, students total their daily points, and these are recorded on a laminated Team Points Chart posted in the front of the classroom. This provides another opportunity for the teacher to verbally reinforce students for their daily progress by evaluating their previous day's performance. Each day, a team is announced as the daily winner. Students clap to congratulate the winner and quietly transition to the next class period.

FIGURE 5.1. ClassWide Peer Tutoring is a flexible and effective teaching approach that can be used to serve the instructional needs of culturally and linguistically diverse learners in inclusive classrooms.

Table 5.2. CWPT Tutoring List Sample

SPELLING-VOCABULARY **CWPT** LIST WEEK OF SEPTEMBER 1–5	
Spelling Words	**Vocabulary Definitions**
1. always	all the time, forever
2. bright	shining with light, full of light
3. detect	to discover, to find out
4. insult	to treat or speak to someone with disrespect
5. orphan	without mother or father (they are dead)
6. stag	full-grown male deer
7. thermos	bottle or jug that keeps liquids at original temperature
8. volant	flying or capable of flying

Tutoring sessions typically occur four to five days during the week (30 minutes each for most subject areas, 40 to 45 minutes for reading). At the end of the week, students' progress is assessed with a teacher-prepared test covering the same material tutored during that week. Some teachers choose to tutor four days and allocate Fridays as a testing day. Students take tests individually and earn 5 to 10 tutoring points for each correct answer. These points are also recorded on the Team Points Chart. At the end of the week, all points, including bonus and test points, are totaled, and the winning team of the week is announced. The team is rewarded with a clapping of hands as well as through achievement certificates or special privileges. The second-place team is rewarded with a clapping of hands for their efforts and sportsmanship.

The CWPT for reading follows basically the same procedures, with some minor variations. It uses the basal text or supplementary reading material (e.g., novels, weekly readers) for the daily tutoring content. Two points are awarded for reading complete sentences, one point is awarded for a corrected sentence, and no points are awarded when a second reading error is made during the correction procedure. At the end of the first 10 minutes (reading passage tutoring), the tutor conducts a reading comprehension check (5 minutes) by asking the tutee five or more questions based on the passage, using the who, what, where, when, and why question format. Students are trained in how to query. Two points are awarded for correctly answered questions. A variation that has been implemented with culturally and linguistically heterogeneous classrooms is the provision of written questions by the teacher, using wall charts or an overhead projector. After the first 15 minutes, the tutor-tutee pair changes roles, and CWPT begins again. Another variation of CWPT for reading is on the Friday test. The teacher either chooses three low-achieving students and two average-achieving students to monitor on a weekly basis, or he or she assesses every student by administering a 1-minute reading rate check on one of the passages read that week, followed by five comprehension questions. A words-per-minute rate as well as error and comprehension scores are calculated and charted on graphs. The graphs can be posted in the classroom or kept by the individual students.

CWPT has been shown to be highly effective across subject areas (e.g., reading, spelling, math, language arts, social studies), across age levels (K–12), across instructional settings (e.g., regular, special, English for speakers of other languages classrooms), and across heterogeneous groups (e.g., low-, average-, and high-achieving students, CLDLs, LEP students, and students with disabilities). The most comprehensive study to date included more than 400 low-achieving minority and majority students enrolled in four separate schools across four years of implementation (grades 1–4) and a follow-up of the same students in junior high and in high schools. Results of the four-year implementation demonstrated significantly greater gains in spelling, reading, and math for the CWPT students than for students in classrooms emphasizing teacher-lecture, whole-class instruction. Furthermore, the CWPT students exceeded or approached the national norms in all three academic domains, as measured by the Metropolitan Achievement Test (Greenwood, Delquadri, & Hall, 1989). Students and teachers consistently rated all CWPT components favorably. Furthermore, teachers have consistently reported higher levels of peer social interaction during the remainder of the school day and positive self-esteem outcomes as a result of CWPT (see Case 5.2).

CASE 5.2. Teachers' Experiences with CWPT

We have been totally amazed at the results we are witnessing. We are getting a large percentage of learned vocabulary with correct spelling and definitions by all our students. The reading comprehension and enjoyment have both soared. The finished written products on and about the readings are done quicker and with greater understanding of content.

Many other teachers in our building have expressed interest in the program because of what they see our students doing. I am very impressed by this program.

Sue Mayberry (grades 3–4)

My first experience with Juniper Gardens began this fall with a short in-service on ClassWide Peer Tutoring. I have had some experience and training in the area of peer tutoring; however, this program had a number of components that had been absent in other models. I tried it with my class and immediately realized its potential.

We have seen much improvement from the program in the areas of not only spelling, oral reading, and the comprehension of our students, but also in the areas of positive self-esteem and a motivation to read. The program has proven to be beneficial to children of all reading levels. In today's classrooms, this is very important.

Cheryl Sparks (grade 5)

Student Teams and Achievement Divisions: STAD

Student Teams and Achievement Divisions, or STAD (Slavin, 1991), is a peer tutoring technique based on raising students' motivation for learning by focusing on the cooperation of members within each team. Each team is made up of four to five members, including high-, average-, and low-performing students and students of different ethnic and language backgrounds. The STAD procedure is used to review teacher-presented material on worksheets through peer tutoring. Following team practice with the material, students are individually assessed on the content. Individual scores are determined by the amount of improvement shown (gain score) over a previous test/quiz score average (base score). Individual scores are the basis for the team points; that is, individual improvement scores are added to form a team score. Teachers are encouraged to use rewards at both the individual and team levels by recognizing improved team and individual scores in a weekly, one-page class newsletter. In addition, special privileges and/or small prizes can be used as optional rewards.

By providing each individual with the opportunity to contribute to the team score, the STAD procedure raises the students' motivation to succeed, even for low-achieving students, CLDLs with limited English skills, and students with disabilities who are at risk for academic failure under regular teaching procedures (Slavin, 1991). Dramatic classroom changes have been reported as the teacher and students become more familiar with and consistently use the STAD procedure (Slavin, 1983, 1988, 1991). Students begin helping each other learn the assigned material, rather than taking exception to those who always know the correct answers or making fun of those who have difficulties. Students see learning activities as cooperative instead of isolated, exciting instead of boring, promising instead of threatening. They begin to see the teacher as a guide and manager during the activities. As a result, CLDLs feel a camaraderie with their classmates in a climate of cooperation and acceptance. This procedure equips CLDLs with the opportunity to compete at the same level as peers and to contribute to a team effort.

The STAD procedure has been used to teach factual information in grades 2–12, with low-achieving, regular, special education, and LEP students. It has been used effectively to improve students' performance in mathematics, reading comprehension, language arts, spelling, geography, science, and English for speakers of other languages. In specific, STAD procedures are recommended for teaching well-defined objectives with single answers, such as math computations and applications, language usage and mechanics, geography and map skills, and scientific facts and concepts. In addition to having a positive effect on student achievement, peer relations, and self-esteem, the STAD procedure increases students' liking of school, feelings of control over what happens at school, desire to do well in school, and cooperativeness (Slavin, 1983, 1986, 1991).

The STAD procedure adheres to the constructs for effective instruction for CLDLs (see Table 5.1) by (a) using higher-order questions, (b) actively engaging all students in the academic task, (c) assigning activities that pertain to the learning content of the class, (d) providing scaffolding strategies for building on and clarifying concepts and questions, and (e) scheduling collaborative and cooperative learning activities.

The STAD procedure follows six basic steps: (a) organization of small heterogeneous groups (e.g., by ethnicity, ability, exceptionality), (b) presentation of the teaching unit by the teacher, (c) assignment of cooperative peer group work on a worksheet, (d) administration of individual quizzes, (e) computation of students' improvement scores, and (f) team recognition.

Classroom Procedures. The teacher makes a list of the students in the class, ranking them from highest to lowest achievement. The ranking can be based on curriculum-based assessments or criterion reference test scores developed by the teacher or textbook publishers. These scores serve as the students' base scores. These rankings are for teacher use only and to direct her or his curriculum activities. The ranking list is then divided into four equal groups (e.g., high, high-average, low-average, and low). The teacher assigns students to STAD teams of four, selecting a student from each of the four performance-based groups. This selection procedure for peer-team members results in balanced groups of four each, with no single team having an advantage. Given the number of students in the class, some groups might have more than four members. It is recommended that every two months the divisions be re-evaluated, allowing students to move to a different division, based on their performance.

Table 5.3. Sample Answer Key and Worksheet for STAD

Answer Key Unit: Spanish Colonies (pp. 34–40)	Worksheet Unit: Spanish Colonies (pp. 34–40)
1. New Spain covered much of <u>South America</u>, and all of <u>Central America</u> and <u>Mexico</u>.	1. New Spain covered much of _____ _____, and all of _____ _____ and _____.
2. What did the Spanish find in Mexico and Peru? <u>Gold</u> and <u>silver</u>.	2. What did the Spanish find in Mexico and Peru? _____ and _____.
3. San Juan, Puerto Rico, was founded by the <u>Spanish</u> in the year <u>1521</u>.	3. San Juan, Puerto Rico, was founded by the _____ in the year _____.
4. Name the first three Spanish colonies in the United States: <u>San Juan, Puerto Rico</u>; <u>St. Augustine, Florida</u>; and <u>Santa Fe, New Mexico</u>.	4. Name the first three Spanish colonies in the United States: _____; _____; and _____.

The teacher introduces the teaching unit/material in any format (e.g., lecture, discussion, audiovisual). Worksheets developed based on the teaching unit are distributed to the different teams. The group members proceed to study together, first in pairs and then as a whole group. Each pair is provided with a worksheet and an answer sheet. All the worksheet items ask about factual or objective information with only one right answer (see Table 5.3). The students study together in preparation for the daily individual quiz, which follows the study period. Most often, the students quiz one another to discover any content or work problems together. The team is the most important feature of the STAD procedure (Slavin, 1991). It is the responsibility of each team member to learn and to help her or his peers learn the material.

After one or two sessions of teacher presentation and team practice, students take individual quizzes based on the material previously studied. After the individual quiz, scores are calculated. Each student's contribution to the team score is based on his or her individual gains. For example, if the quiz score is higher than the base score by four points (base score = 78%; quiz score = 82%), four points are added to the team score. If students score at or below their base score, no points are added to the team score. The team score is computed and posted on the bulletin board, and the winning team is recognized.

The STAD procedure promotes language use and acquisition and academic content learning through the active participation and the opportunity for communication exchanges among individuals on the team. Furthermore, peers on the teams are likely to engage in talk that is more comprehensible to each other and to ask for clarifications and definitions of meanings (Slavin, 1991). Overall, for CLDLs, heterogeneous small groups provide a more meaningful social environment for promoting language use and comprehension than does the traditional whole-class instruction format.

Numbered Heads Together: NHT

Numbered Heads Together (NHT) is a teacher questioning strategy designed to actively engage *all* students during teacher-led instruction and discussion (Kagan, 1985, 1989–90). Its primary goal is to improve student cooperation and to promote informal sharing of ideas. There are five basic steps to the successful implementation of NHT: (a) creating heterogeneous (culturally, linguistically, and ability-wise) learning teams; (b) training the students in the steps of the procedure and coaching them in the use of collaborative studying or tutoring; (c) asking higher-order questions as well as factual questions; (d) providing equal opportunity to all teams; and (e) providing positive reinforcements and recognition.

NHT makes use of a question format that engages *all* students simultaneously in the activity. The CLDL research supports the use of questioning in the classroom to (a) facilitate the use of students' previous knowledge and cultural backgrounds, (b) increase motivation and interest in lessons, (c) challenge students with higher-order inquiry, and (d) improve students' comprehension of the material (Anderson, Everson, & Brophy, 1979; Gersten, Carnine, & Williams, 1981; Gersten and Jiménez, 1994; Maheady et al., 1991). Unfortunately, in traditional classrooms, questioning is mostly characterized by the use of direct questions to the whole class, with one student responding to the inquiry. For CLDLs with limited English skills, this whole-class form of query is most often frustrating and demeaning, because they have to negotiate not only new academic content but also the English language (Chamot & O'Malley, 1994). The NHT procedure offers an alternative that actively engages both the low- and the high-achieving students in questioning and answering, and at the same time affords low-achieving students or CLDLs with limited English skills an opportunity to collaboratively negotiate new learning in a small-group situation. Furthermore, NHT gives students the opportunity to negotiate an answer by allowing time between the question and the answer for the team members to work and learn together (see Figure 5.2).

Classroom Procedures. In NHT, students are placed into four-member heterogeneous learning teams. Each team consists of one high-achieving student, two average-achieving students, and one low-achieving student. The teams should be composed of a mixture of students that is consistent across groups, so that no one team has an advantage over another. The purpose of this composition is to provide collaboration and stimulation among all team members. Within each team, the students are then numbered from 1 to 4. Each team sits together during the NHT lessons. The teacher makes the instructional presentation to the whole class (e.g., a lecture on mammals or a short video on volcanoes). Then she or he directs questions to the whole class. Students are instructed to "put their heads together" (i.e., work together to come up with the right answer). Each member of the team can contribute to the answer, but each member needs to know the correct response, because only one will be asked to reply. It is important for the teacher to decide

FIGURE 5.2. Numbered Heads Together is a teacher questioning procedure designed to actively engage all students during teacher-led instruction.

beforehand the amount of time that will be allocated for collaborative discussion (e.g., one to two minutes). The end of the collaborative discussion time is signaled by a timer. The teacher then asks, "Which student number 3s [or 1s, 2s, or 4s] know the answer?" After a randomly selected student number 3 [or 1, 2, 4] responds, the teacher asks, "Which other student number 3s [or 1s, 2s, or 4s] agree or disagree with that answer?" or "Which other number 3s [or 1s, 2s, or 4s] can expand on the answer?" The teacher gives the opportunity for other students to respond and contribute to the answer. The teacher then recognizes and rewards students who provide the correct response, and those who expand on or agree with the correct answer. The rewards can be tokens or poker chips with different value points (e.g., red = 1, blue = 5, white = 10). These tokens can be counted at the end of each session, and the team with the most points for the day is the winner. The points can also be accumulated for a weekly team winner or exchanged for small prizes or privileges.

An element added to the procedure by Maheady and colleagues (1991) was the use of daily quizzes at the end of each NHT session. These quizzes were based on the same material discussed in the lesson. The daily team quiz scores were then recorded on a posted chart. A daily and/or weekly winner could then be selected. Variations such as this can be provided by the teacher not only to maintain a record of the students' progress but also to motivate students in their collaborative participation and learning.

In NHT, it is important that the teams be changed regularly (once a month or every two weeks), to allow the students to interact as a team with a variety of classmates. As in all previously discussed procedures, training of students in the procedure is a very important contributor to its success. The use of this procedure provides the students with the opportunity to succeed by offering the means to become successfully involved in their own learning and achievement.

SUMMARY

The purpose of this chapter was to introduce teachers in inclusive settings and serving CLDLs in the intermediate elementary grades to three research-based and highly effective peer-mediated instructional procedures. The three procedures are time- and cost-efficient as well as quite feasible to implement. In addition, teachers and students have consistently chosen these procedures over whole-class instruction (Greenwood, 1991; Harper, Maheady, & Mallette, 1994; Slavin, 1991).

Unlike traditional teacher-mediated instruction (i.e., whole-class, lecture format), peer-mediated procedures create a more favorable climate for the individualization of instruction, provide opportunities for all students to be actively engaged with the learning task, and facilitate socialization among classmates. Peer-mediated instruction supports higher levels of student engagement, academic learning time, challenge, success, collaboration, integration, and positive feedback—processes that have been demonstrated to optimize students' academic, linguistic, and social gains. The challenge is to empower teachers to better assist *all* students in their classrooms, by adopting procedures that have been demonstrated to be fun, effective approaches to accelerating and maintaining learning.

REFERENCES

Anderson, L. M., Everson, C. M., & Brophy, J. E. (1979). An experimental study of effective teaching in first-grade reading groups. *Elementary School Journal, 79,* 193–222.

Arreaga-Mayer, C., Carta, J. J., & Tapia, Y. (1994). Ecobehavioral assessment of bilingual special education settings: The opportunity to respond revisited. In R. Garner III, D. Sainato, J. Cooper, T. Heron, W. Heward, J. Eskleman, & T. Grossi (Eds.), *Behavior analysis in education: Focus on measurably superior instruction* (pp. 225–240). Pacific Grove, CA: Brooks/Cole.

Arreaga-Mayer, C., & Greenwood, C. R. (1986). Environmental variables affecting the school achievement of culturally and linguistically different learners: An instructional perspective. *Journal of the National Association for Bilingual Education, 10*(2), 113–135.

Arreaga-Mayer, C., & Perdomo-Rivera, C. (1996). Ecobehavioral analysis of instruction for at-risk language minority students. *Elementary School Journal, 96*(3), 245–258.

August, D. L. (1987). Effects of peer tutoring on the second language acquisition of Mexican American children in elementary schools. *TESOL Quarterly, 21*(4), 717–736.

Bejarano, Y. (1987). A cooperative small-group methodology in the language classroom. *TESOL Quarterly, 21*(3), 483–504.

Cantoni-Harvey, G. (1987). *Content-area language instruction: Approaches and strategies.* Reading, MA: Addison-Wesley.

Chamot, A. U., & O'Malley, J. M. (1994). *The CALLA handbook: Implementing the cognitive academic language approach.* Reading, MA: Addison-Wesley.

Delquadri, J. C., Greenwood, C. R., Stretton, K., & Hall, R. V. (1983). The peer tutoring spelling game: A classroom procedure for increasing opportunity to respond and spelling performance. *Education and Treatment of Children, 6,* 225–239.

Flanigan, B. O. (1991). Peer tutoring and second language acquisition in the elementary school. *Applied Linguistics, 12*(2), 141–158.

Garcia, E. E. (1988). Instructional discourse in an effective kindergarten classroom: A case study. In L. M. Malave (Ed.), *Theory, research and applications: Selected papers* (pp. 48–71). Buffalo, NY: State University of New York at Buffalo.

Gersten, R. M., Carnine, D. W., & Williams, P. B. (1981). Measuring implementation of a structured educational model in urban school districts. *Educational Evaluation and Policy Analysis, 4,* 56–63.

Gersten, R. M., & Jiménez, R. T. (1994). A delicate balance: Enhancing literature instruction for students of English as a second language. *The Reading Teacher, 47*(6), 438–449.

Greenwood, C. R. (1991). Longitudinal analysis of time, engagement and achievement in at-risk versus non-risk students. *Exceptional Children, 57,* 521–535.

Greenwood, C. R., Delquadri, J. C., & Carta, J. J. (1988). *Classwide peer tutoring (CWPT).* Seattle, WA: Educational Achievement Systems.

Greenwood, C. R., Delquadri, J. C., & Hall, R. V. (1989). Longitudinal effects of classwide peer tutoring. *Journal of Educational Psychology, 81,* 371–383.

Greenwood, C. R., Terry, B. J., Delquadri, J. C., & Elliott, M. (1992). *Classwide peer tutoring (CWPT) as measurably superior instruction: Practices, issues, evidence and implications.* Kansas City, KS: Juniper Gardens Children's Project.

Harper, G. F., Maheady, L., & Mallette, B. (1994). The power of peer-mediated instruction. In J. S. Thousand, R. A. Villa, & A. I. Nevin (Eds.), *Creativity and collaborative learning* (pp. 229–240). Baltimore, MD: Paul H. Brooks Publishing.

Johnson, D. M. (1983). Natural language learning by design: A classroom experiment in social interaction and second language acquisition. *TESOL Quarterly, 17*(1), 55–68.

Kagan, S. (1985). *Cooperative learning.* Riverside, CA: University of California–Riverside.

Kagan, S. (1989–90). The structural approach to cooperative learning. *Educational Leadership, 47*(4), 12–15.

Maheady, L., Mallette, B., Harper, G. F., & Sacca, K. (1991). Heads together: A peer mediated option for improving the academic achievement of heterogeneous learning groups. *Remedial and Special Education, 12*(2), 25–33.

O'Malley, J. M., & Chamot, A. U. (1990). *Learning strategies in second language acquisition.* New York: Cambridge University Press.

O'Malley, J. M., Chamot, A. U., Stewner-Manzanares, G., Russo, R. P., & Küpper, L. (1985a). Learning strategies used by beginning and intermediate ESL students. *Language and Learning, 35,* 21–46.

O'Malley, J. M., Chamot, A. U., Stewner-Manzanares, G., Russo, R. P., & Küpper, L. (1985b). Learning strategy applications with students of English as a second language. *TESOL Quarterly, 19,* 285–296.

Richard-Amato, P. A. (1988). *Making it happen: Interaction in the second language classroom— from theory to practice* (pp. 20–30). New York: Longman.

Slavin, R. E. (1978). Student teams and achievement divisions. *Journal of Research and Development in Education, 12,* 39–49.

Slavin, R. E. (1980). Effects of individual learning expectations on student achievement. *Journal of Educational Psychology, 72,* 520–524.

Slavin, R. E. (1983). *Cooperative learning.* New York: Longman.

Slavin, R. E. (1986). *Using student team learning.* Baltimore, MD: Center for Research on Elementary and Middle Schools, Johns Hopkins University.

Slavin, R. E. (1988). Cooperative learning and student achievement. *Educational Leadership, 45*(2), 31–33.

Slavin, R. E. (1991). *Student team learning: A practical guide to cooperative learning.* Washington, DC: National Education Association.

RESOURCES FOR
PEER-MEDIATED INSTRUCTION

ClassWide Peer Tutoring Manual: Together We Can, Sopris West, P.O. Box 1809, Longmont, CO 80502-1802. Phone (800) 547-6747; fax (303) 776-5934.

ClassWide Peer Tutoring training and information, Carmen Arreaga-Mayer and Barbara Terry, Juniper Gardens Children's Project, 650 Minnesota Avenue, 2nd floor, Kansas City, KS 66101. Phone (913) 321-3143; fax (913) 371-8522.

Student Teams and Achievement Divisions manual and information, The Johns Hopkins Team Learning Project, Center for Social Organization of Schools, Johns Hopkins University, 3505 North Charles Street, Baltimore, MD 21218. Phone (301) 338-8249.

Numbered Heads Together Manual, Video and Cooperative Learning, Resources for Teachers, 27128 Paseo Espada, Suite 622, San Juan Capistrano, CA 92675.

6

The Double Demands of Teaching Language-Minority Students

Russell Gersten
Eugene Research Institute
University of Oregon

D uring the past 15 years, the United States has experienced the greatest surge of immigration in its history. The fact that one out of every seven children grows up speaking a language other than English has profoundly reshaped the nature of education (Barringer, April 28, 1993).

Increasing numbers of teachers have become, by default, teachers of second language learning. They face the daunting task of simultaneously building literacy, developing writing ability, and enhancing English language growth. The complexity of this challenge can cause even seasoned and accomplished teachers anxiety. The large number of students involved and the great diversity of languages spoken, ranging from Hmong to Russian to Haitian Creole, have led many to conclude that all teachers need more training in this area.

Teaching students for whom English is a second language requires helping them with the double demands of acquiring a new language while mastering academic content. A quote from a recently arrived student from Sierra Leone illustrates the frustrations of these double demands: "All the English-speaking kids should learn a foreign language. Then they'd know how hard it is for us sometimes" (Leslie, Glick, & Gordon, 1991, p. 57).

From "The Double Demands of Teaching English Language Learners" by R. Gersten, 1996, *Educational Leadership*, 53(5). Reprinted with permission of the Association for Supervision and Curriculum Development.

LITERATURE AND
CONTENT AREA INSTRUCTION

Over the past decade, teaching English for speakers of other languages through content area instruction, particularly through the use of literature, has increased significantly. This approach is sometimes called *sheltered content area English* (Echevarria, in press) or bilingual immersion (Gersten & Woodward, 1995). Proponents argue for moving away from the rather sterile emphasis on grammar and syntax or a contrived conversational approach and toward building knowledge of the new language by integrating language acquisition with understanding and enjoying and talking about quality literature.

In an articulate plea for the integrating of reading with English language development, Anderson and Roit (1996) note, "Spoken language is fleeting and inconsistent over time. Text is stable and does not pass the learner by. It allows one to reread and reconsider that which is to be learned in its original form" (p. 2).

Another current of educational thought evokes the power of using literature from many cultures (Au, 1993; Banks & Banks, 1993; Greene, 1993). Here, the emphasis is not only cognitive and linguistic but also personal and sociocultural. The authors note the potential of multicultural literature for breaking down some of the boundaries that often exist between non-European immigrant students, who are predominantly working class, and their teachers, who are, by and large, middle class and white.

Greene (1993) demonstrates this with a quote from the novel *Lucy* by Jamaica Kincaid, a recent immigrant: "Outside I seemed one way, inside I was another; outside false, inside true" (1990, p. 18). The vocabulary is relatively simple, yet its power to resonate with students' lives is fierce. Greene (1993) passionately urges teachers to make "imaginative efforts [that] cross the distances and [allow the teacher to] look through diverse others' eyes" (p. 13).

In this approach, process writing is as crucial as literature-based instruction. An emphasis on process writing has the potential to push students, regardless of their current English language capabilities, to begin to "pursue the meanings of their lives—to find out *how* things are happening, to keep posing questions about the 'why.'" The ultimate goal, in Greene's words, is "to reach out for the proficiencies and capacities, the craft required to be fully participant in this society, and to do so without losing the consciousness of who they are" (p. 17).

More than 10 years ago, Woodward and I (1985) noted that "education of language minority students [is] relatively easy to write about, yet difficult to implement sensitively on a day to day basis" (p. 78). Our recent observations and interviews revealed that the majority of the 26 teachers we studied understood the benefits of integrating English language learning with academic content instruction but were overwhelmed with the intricacies of putting it into practice.

Many aspired to use literature and writing to stimulate interaction between themselves and their students, but they didn't possess the tools and techniques to do so. For example, Reyes (1992) notes that the high regard that Hispanics hold for teachers as authority figures indicates that they rely on and expect direct instruction. Yet many teachers routinely made only indirect requests of their students.

The issue of how to balance literature-based, personal instruction with explicit instruction is a dilemma that consistently emerged in our interviews with teachers. Only the creative synthesis of many techniques seemed to enable expert teachers to consistently engage their students and actively promote language learning. It is, I believe, the type of dynamic synthesis that researchers such as Reyes (1992), Delpit (1988), and McElroy-Johnson (1993) have constantly advocated as optimal for working-class children from immigrant families.

LOOKING FOR PICTURES
OF EFFECTIVE INSTRUCTION

Experts in professional development, like Judith Little (1993), argue that training in intricate topics, such as combining ESOL instruction with content area instruction, requires very different methodologies: "There is no well developed picture of what these principles look like in practice" (p. 131).

My goal here is to create pictures of productive teaching strategies as well as an understanding of principles that underlie effective practice. Whereas prior research on second language students has often focused heavily on the philosophical, policy, and program-planning levels (Cziko, 1992), our project focused squarely on the observed learning environment of the child.

For three years a team of seven researchers observed 26 classrooms in five schools in two large metropolitan areas: San Diego, California, and El Paso, Texas. We observed more than 200 hours of reading/language arts instruction provided to language-minority students in grades 3–6. Although most of the students were not fluent English speakers, most had graduated from their bilingual or sheltered English programs. By district standards, they were no longer considered limited in English proficiency. Our goal was to look at the quantity and quality of instruction offered to these students, and the coherence or fragmentation of the instructional program.

Like Moll (1992), we observed that typical instruction in many of the 26 classrooms was "intellectually limited, with an emphasis on low-level literacy . . . skills" (p. 20), even though most teachers were using literature rather than basal texts as the basis of their reading and language arts curriculum (Gersten & Woodward, 1995). However, 5 of the 26 teachers appeared to provide instruction that met the criteria set by researchers of being intellectually stimulating, clear, and explicit (Delpit; 1988; McElroy-Johnson, 1993; Reyes, 1992). These teachers seemed exceptionally artful in translating contemporary research on literacy and language learning into realistic instructional strategies. Gently but consistently, they encouraged students to reason, to use English to express their ideas, and to justify their conclusions. To analyze these seemingly productive situations, we interviewed these 5 teachers several times.

These expert teachers seemed not only to embody principles of the whole-language movement (such as use of literature as opposed to basal texts, and the integration of reading and writing) but also to sensitively incorporate many of the instructional strategies and techniques from the effective-teaching research of the 1980s (Brophy & Good, 1986). Following is one example of a particularly effective fourth grade teacher.

A LOOK AT MARIA TAPIA'S CLASSROOM

Although Maria Tapia[1] is bilingual, her classroom instruction is in English, except for a 30-minute Spanish language arts block. In fact, when a student asks a question in Spanish, Maria answers in English, because "this is the English part of the day." The students are in their second year in a primarily English language instruction classroom.

Students sit on the floor as Tapia reads *Wilfred Gordon McDonald Partridge,* an Australian story about a woman losing her memory. The readability of the book is well below the fourth grade level, but the emotional and thematic content is complex and subtle. Children listen with rapt attention.

Tapia asks students to predict what the story will be about. Even the more reticent students volunteer their predictions, which Tapia records on the flip chart. She provides prompts to students who seem to be floundering, such as, "With a title like this and this picture on the cover, Fernando, what do you think this story will be about?"

At the conclusion of this brief story, a discussion of mood ensues. Tapia asks, "What did you think about it?" One student answers, "It was kind of sad." Tapia responds, "How do you know?"

Miguel, one of the students she has earlier described as a student with learning difficulties, says, "Because old people." Since the idea is on the right track, even though the English grammar is incomplete, the response is evaluated for content rather than for the extent that it conformed to correct language use.

Tapia never labels responses as right or wrong, but sometimes students are asked to explain the rationale for their answers or opinions. Jorge, for example, explains that he "liked it because it was sad and it was happy," and he proceeds to provide several examples.

Tapia chooses words for the class to analyze in depth, words that represent more-complex ideas—adjectives like *anxious, generous,* and *suspicious,* and nouns like *memory*—and that second language students are likely to need help with.

Later, she tells students they can use three sources of data to explain why they think a character is anxious. She lists the sources on a chart: actions, speech (or dialogue), and appearance. The class uses this list for discussing subsequent stories as well, and as a guide while writing in their journals. Tapia consistently challenges students to incorporate more-complex structures in

---

[1] This is a pseudonym.

their analyses by referring to the list. For example, in response to student essays, she says, "None of you provided dialogue." Students then search for dialogue to support their inferences about a particular character.

Throughout our three years of observations, "You have to prove it to me" was Tapia's consistent message. Teacher and peers evaluated, but never directly criticized, all attempts to develop or support an inference. Tapia continually prompted students to provide evidence for predictions, hypotheses, or inferences. In our observations, this sense of intellectual accountability was rare (Gersten, 1996).

EFFECTIVE LITERACY INSTRUCTION

Our analyses of observational and interview data revealed four productive teaching practices for teaching language-minority students. These practices are discussed in the following sections.

Use Evocative Words as an Explicit Focus of Lessons

Teachers we observed chose words that relate to human motivation and are critical for literary analysis (such as *anxious* and *memory*). On the surface, some of these words seem too easy for fourth or fifth graders. Yet, the words are critical for second language learners, and discussion of their meanings can go well beyond standard dictionary definitions. The teachers also chose words, especially idioms, that were likely to be difficult for second language students, because these words have the power to sharply increase comprehension.

The expert teachers did not drill students on lengthy word lists, even though districts or publishers usually provided such lists. Rather, they focused on two or three critical words and emphasized these for several days. When possible, teachers used short stories or below-grade-level books and personal writing projects to amplify understanding of the concepts. These types of activities helped establish the semantic networks critical to deep vocabulary learning, a subject that has been the cornerstone of pioneering research on vocabulary instruction (Beck, McKeown, & McCaslin, 1983).

We saw a dramatic difference in the mood of students in a typical fifth grade class, where they had to incorporate in a story as many of the day's 12 new words as possible, and the mood of students working in cooperative groups, pooling together their evidence on why a given character was "generous" or "vile" or "brave, but also frightened."

Use Explicit Strategies to Help
Students Become Better Readers

Expert teachers frequently used scaffolds to help second language students. Tapia's request that students cite data sources for evidence is an excellent example; she encouraged students in their search for examples of dialogue and warmly rewarded them for their efforts.

While discussing another story, the class concluded that the leading character had transformed himself from a "bad man" (a thief) to a "good man" (one who helps people). When Tapia asked for examples, even the most reticent students volunteered to provide evidence as to how they knew the thief had become a good man.

Tapia made it clear that she would take all predictions seriously. On the other hand, though she never called a response incorrect or illogical, when a student predicted that the people in the story "will have a ranch," a statement that seemed to make no sense, she asked him to provide some evidence. When he was unable to answer, she neither praised nor criticized him, but merely moved on.

Effective teachers of second language students seem to be aware of the negative impact of telling students they're wrong. During an interview with Tapia, I asked her whether this was intentional. She replied, "Absolutely. It's intentional. . . . When I was a child, I was taught that way . . . this is right . . . that is wrong. I'd never do that to a child."

In one case, Tapia's class was unable to provide an adequate explanation for calling a character "disobedient." The students provided partial responses, such as, "She was dying for gum." Finally, Tapia provided the full response: "She is disobedient because she eats gum despite what her mother tells her." This technique, however, was a last resort. Typically, she elicited increasingly sophisticated responses from the students.

Teach Children How to Transfer into English
What They Know in Their Native Language

Not long ago, bilingual education theorists believed that once students were academically proficient in their native language and could understand abstract concepts, they would easily transfer these abilities into English, provided they'd had adequate exposure to English and were motivated to learn English (Cummins, 1980). More recent research has shown that this type of transfer is, in fact, much more difficult and complicated for children than was previously believed. Even proficient readers need to put a good deal of energy into transferring knowledge from one language to another. For less proficient readers, this problem is immense (Jiménez, García, & Pearson, 1995).

The research has also found that proficient bilingual readers use specific strategies to help them transfer what they know from Spanish to English. Chamot and O'Malley (1996) suggest that we may need to explicitly teach students how to access knowledge in their native language to successfully perform in English language activities. Yet few concrete guidelines exist for facilitating this process.

Tapia and other teachers consistently provided feedback to Spanish responses during the English language arts part of the day. In our observations, expert teachers always accepted Spanish responses but also encouraged students to try to answer again in English. They did this with the same gentleness, the same attentiveness, that they displayed when asking students to explain how they reached their conclusions. Allowing students to organize their thoughts in their native language before risking an English response seemed to be an effective technique.

Encourage Students to Speak
and Write about Their Lives

Although some topics were difficult and delicate to discuss, the expert teachers did not sidestep the issue of poverty when it came up in students' stories. They allowed students, for example, to write about broken-down television sets or the time wasted sitting by a highway waiting for their truck to be towed.

Less proficient teachers, partly because of their discomfort, tried to guide students away from talk about poor living conditions, with the consequence that students withdrew from the teachers. Although merely allowing free expression of not-so-pleasant experiences is hardly a panacea for the complex tasks facing teachers, it does begin to break down barriers that often exist between middle-class teachers and working-class students, and it helps maintain the integrity of each student's experience.

BREAKING DOWN BARRIERS

With the increasing demands on all teachers to learn how to teach second language students, articulation of the lessons learned from teachers like Tapia becomes increasingly important. Their strategies, techniques, and tools for providing students with intellectually demanding content without unduly frustrating them, for appropriately using below-grade-level material to reinforce concepts and enhance English language growth, and for consistently supporting reticent or low-performing students are a basis for professional development efforts. These teachers' sensible, often gracious, means of breaking down class and cultural barriers can and should serve as models for practice.

REFERENCES

Anderson, V., & Roit, M. (1996). Linking reading comprehension instruction to language development for language minority students. *Elementary School Journal.*

Au, K. (1993). *Literacy instruction in multicultural settings.* New York: Harcourt Brace Jovanovich.

Banks, J. A., & Banks, C. A. M. (1993). *Multicultural Education, 2nd ed.* Boston: Allyn & Bacon.

Barringer, F. (1993, April 28). When English is foreign tongue: Census finds a sharp rise in 80's. *New York Times,* pp. 1, 10.

Beck, I. L., McKeown, M. G., & McCaslin, E. S. (1983). Vocabulary development: All contexts are not created equal. *Elementary School Journal, 83*(3), 177–181.

Brophy, J., & Good, T. L. (1986). Teacher behavior and student achievement. In M. Wittrock (Ed.), *The third handbook of research on teaching* (pp. 328–375). New York: Macmillan.

Chamot, A. U., & O'Malley, J. M. (1996). The Cognitive Academic Language Learning Approach (CALLA): A model for linguistically diverse classrooms. *Elementary School Journal, 96*(3), 259–274.

Cummins, J. (1980). The cross-lingual dimensions of language proficiency: Implications for bilingual education and the optimal age issue. *TESOL Quarterly, 14*(2), 175–187.

Cziko, G. A. (1992). The evaluation of bilingual education. *Educational Researcher, 21*(2), 10–15.

Delpit, L. D. (1988). The silenced dialogue: Power and pedagogy in educating other people's children. *Harvard Educational Review, 58*(3), 280–298.

Echevarria, J. (in press). Preparing text and classroom materials for English language learners: curriculum adaptations in secondary school settings. In R. Gersten & R. Jiménez (Eds.), *Promoting learning for culturally and linguistically diverse students: classroom applications from contemporary research.* Pacific Grove, CA: Brooks/Cole.

Gersten, R. (1996). The double demands of teaching English language learners. *Educational Leadership, 53*(5), 18–22.

Gersten, R., & Woodward, J. (1985). A case for structured immersion. *Educational Leadership, 43*(1), 75–78.

Gersten, R., & Woodward, J. (1994). The language-minority student and special education: issues, trends, and paradoxes. *Exceptional Children, 60*(4), 310–322.

Gersten, R., & Woodward, J. (1995). A longitudinal study of transitional and immersion bilingual education programs in one district. *Elementary School Journal, 5*(3), 223–240.

Greene, M. (1993). The passions of pluralism: Multiculturalism and the expanding community. *Educational Researcher, 22*(1), 13–18.

Jiménez, R. T., García, G. E., & Pearson, P. D. (1995). Three children, two languages, and strategic reading: Case studies of bilingual and monolingual readers. *American Educational Research Journal, 32*(1), 67–97.

Kincaid, J. (1990). *Lucy.* New York: Farrar, Straus & Giroux.

Leslie, C., Glick, D., and Gordon, J. (1991, February 11). Classrooms of Babel. *Newsweek.*

Little, J. W. (1993). Teachers' professional development in a climate of educational reform. *Educational Evaluation and Policy Analysis, 15*(2), 129–151.

McElroy-Johnson, B. (1993). Giving voice to the voiceless. *Harvard Educational Review, 63*(1), 85–104.

Moll, L. C. (1992). Bilingual classroom studies and community analysis: Some recent trends. *Educational Research, 21*(2), 20–24.

Northcutt, L., & Watson, D. (1986). *Sheltered English teaching handbook.* Carlsbad, CA: Northcutt, Watson, Gonzalez.

Reyes, M. de la luz (1992). Challenging venerable assumptions: Literacy instruction for linguistically different students. *Harvard Educational Review, 62*(4), 427–446.

7

Making the Transition to English Literacy Successful

Effective Strategies for Studying Literature with Transition Students

William Saunders
University of California, Los Angeles

Gisela O'Brien
Deborah Lennon
Jerry McLean
Los Angeles Unified School District

S tudents who receive instruction in their native language during the early years of schooling eventually transition into mainstream English. Transition can occur anywhere from the early elementary grades to middle school or later, depending on the school's program, when a student begins the program, and individual student characteristics and achievement.

Although many educators consider this period a positive indication that English learners are entering the mainstream, transition can be problematic for both students and teachers. Teacher expectations tend to drop, and thus students' cognitive learning opportunities decrease (Berman et al., 1992). If transition is handled too abruptly, and this is often the case, achievement can decline precipitously (Ramirez, 1992). Students are also more likely to be referred for compensatory or special education during the transition years (Gersten, 1996). In sum, transition is a crucial period during which many English learners are especially vulnerable to academic underachievement.

Unfortunately, educators have little research on which to base policy and practice (Goldenberg, 1996). Teachers tend to describe themselves as overwhelmingly uncertain about the appropriate methods to use during transition (Gersten & Woodward, 1994). Even in schools and districts recognized for their exemplary bilingual programs, transition is often a conundrum (Berman et al., 1992). Much of the existing research has focused on the timing and duration of transition (e.g., Ramirez, 1992). Far less attention has been devoted to empirical studies of effective transition instruction and curriculum (Gersten, 1996).

For the past five years we have been involved in a research and development project at five predominantly Latino elementary schools in the Los Angeles area, where, on average, 84% of the students are limited-English proficient (LEP) upon enrollment. Teachers, project advisors, and researchers are collaborating to develop, implement, and describe an instructional program that significantly improves the chances that limited-English-proficient children from Spanish-speaking backgrounds will successfully transition from Spanish bilingual instruction to all-English mainstream instruction. The fundamental goal is to substantially increase the development of both Spanish and English academic literacy.

Informed by the current and previous work of researchers collaborating with us (Goldenberg & Gallimore, 1991; Goldenberg & Sullivan, 1994; Saunders, Goldenberg, & Hamann, 1992; Tharp & Gallimore, 1988), other available research (García, 1992, 1995; Gersten, 1996; Gersten & Jiménez, 1993, April; Ramirez, 1992), and our own evaluation studies (Saunders & Lennon, 1993, 1996), the project team has developed and implemented a three-year transition program involving three phases: Pre-Transition, Transition I, and Transition II (optimally, grades 3–5). As part of this effort, we developed language arts curricula and performance assessments for each phase of the program. Four fundamental theoretical premises undergird the program; all of these premises are assumed to promote first and second language acquisition and academic achievement:

- *Challenge.* Consistently challenge students academically—challenge them to think, learn, and engage intellectually

- *Comprehensiveness.* Address both meaning and skills, both higher-level thinking and appropriate drill and practice, and provide complementary portions of student- and teacher-centeredness

- *Continuity.* Achieve continuity in curriculum and instruction as students move from primary to middle to upper grades, and from Spanish to English language arts

- *Connections.* Build on and make explicit connections between students' existing knowledge, skills, and experiences and the academic curriculum to be learned (including language, literacy, and content)

Preliminary evaluations (while the program was being developed) suggest the three-year transition program, in comparison to the transition programs students normally take part in, cultivates higher levels of Spanish and English literacy, as well as healthier attitudes toward biliteracy and more-sophisticated understandings of reading and writing.

In this chapter, we first provide an overview of and background on the three-year transition program. We then focus on the central component of our program—literature units—and four strategies that make the units successful: (a) building students' background knowledge, (b) drawing on students' personal experiences, (c) assisting students in rereading pivotal portions of the text, and (d) promoting extended discourse through writing and discussion. We explain the four strategies and the theoretical rationale behind them. Next, we describe the conduct of an actual literature unit (*Annie and the Old One*) from beginning to end and highlight the use of the four strategies. Following the unit description, we discuss the positive effects of the three-year transition program, as indicated by our evaluation studies. We close with a discussion of the major premises that undergird our transition program.

OVERVIEW AND BACKGROUND ON THE THREE-YEAR TRANSITION PROGRAM

Similar to concerns in other parts of California (Berman et al., 1992) within the administrative region of our district, there was substantial concern about low levels of student achievement as students transitioned, and tremendous uncertainty about what to do with regard to transition curriculum and instruction (Saunders & Lennon, 1993). Our project team (18 teachers, 3 project advisors, 1 researcher) was formed to first examine how transition was operating in the project schools and then research and develop a more successful program.

Three-Year Conceptualization of Transition

The three-year conceptualization of transition optimally spans grades 3–5. Grade 3 is explicitly considered a Pre-Transition year, grade 4 is Transition I, and grade 5 is Transition II (see Table 7.1). The three-year conceptualization of transition presumes two things: (a) students receive effective language arts instruction, and (b) students receive a coherent program of language arts instruction in grades 3–5, from primary language through transitional language arts.

In the district where we work, all Spanish-speaking LEP students enrolled in the bilingual program receive language arts and content area instruction in Spanish while they are acquiring oral English proficiency, addressed primarily through 20 to 30 minutes of daily ESOL instruction. This program continues until students demonstrate grade-level proficiency in Spanish reading and writing and basic oral English proficiency, as measured by district-developed assessments. When students demonstrate these proficiencies, they qualify to

Table 7.1. Three-Year Conceptualization of Transition: Goals and Outcomes

Phases	Optimal Grade	Goal	Measurable Outcome
	K–2nd	Initial reading and writing proficiency (Spanish)	Existing norm- or criterion-referenced measures
		Early production II (oral English)	
Pre-Transition	3rd	Grade-appropriate reading and writing proficiency (Spanish)	Pass CARE (district transition instrument)
		Speech emergence (oral English)	
Transition I	4th	Initial reading and writing fluency (English)	Existing norm- or criterion-referenced measures
		Academic oral language proficiency (English)	
		Grade-appropriate reading and writing proficiency (Spanish)	
Transition II	5th	Grade-appropriate reading and writing proficiency (English)	Reclassification: LEP to FEP

transition and begin English reading and writing instruction, during which time they are to continue receiving Spanish language arts as well. According to the district guidelines, transitional language arts should last approximately three to six months and concentrate on nontransferable English skills, vocabulary development, oral and reading comprehension, and written language. After this period, students enter a mainstream English program. Students are officially reclassified as fluent-English proficient (FEP) when they demonstrate grade-level or close-to-grade-level reading, writing, and oral language skills on standardized English language achievement tests (i.e., at or above the 36th national percentile).

As we began work at the project schools, two things were readily apparent: (a) students were not being effectively prepared to qualify and enter transition, and (b) the transitional program students received when they did qualify was, at best, underspecified.

The concept of a Pre-Transition component is designed to emphasize the fundamental role of the Spanish reading and writing and oral English instruction that precede transition. Large numbers of students were not qualifying to enter transition because they were not functioning at or close to grade level in Spanish literacy, and they were not acquiring oral English skills. The understanding we tried to develop at project schools was that problems with the transition program could not be addressed without devoting attention to Spanish language arts and oral English development in the early grades. As part of this effort, we explicitly included grade 3 as a Pre-Transition year in the larger transitional program. The thrust of this phase is intensive Spanish reading and writing instruction and extensive oral English development.

The problem with transition itself was that schools grossly underestimated the amount of time that might be devoted to a transitional language arts

Table 7.2. Instructional Components for the Three-Year Transition Program

Units of Study	Skill Building	Other Supporting Components
Literature units (experience-text-relationship approach)	Comprehension strategies	Pleasure reading
	Assigned independent reading	Teacher read-alouds
Literature logs	Dictation	Interactive journals
Instructional conversations	Conventions lessons	
Culminating writing projects (writing-as-a-process approach)	Oral English language development through literature	

Note: All components are used in each phase of the three-year transition program, except for English language development (oral English), which applies to the Pre-Transition year(s), and interactive journals, which are used primarily at the beginning of Transition I (and also in the primary grades).

program. The district's three- to six-month guidelines encouraged schools to think of transition as a relatively short period of time sandwiched between Spanish and mainstream English language arts, so short as to prohibit any serious attention to curriculum or training. Consequently, only one of the project schools had an articulated transition program. The concept of Transition I and II is designed to make explicit the need for a concrete transition program of serious substance and duration. The goal across the two years is reclassification: Students have transitioned and can perform successfully in a mainstream program when they have grade-level or close-to-grade-level English skills.

Instructional Components
for the Language Arts Program

As part of our work on the transition program, we identified 12 instructional components that seemed most effective in serving the needs of students throughout the three phases of the program (see Table 7.2; Appendix 7.1 includes brief descriptions of each component). Some of these instructional components were intended specifically to address the needs of transition students, but many of the components can stand on their own as effective language arts strategies for the middle and upper elementary grades. However, operationalizing these components, integrating them together in a total language arts program, developing complementary management systems, and applying them to programs for LEP students making the transition was essential to our project.

Studying literature, for example, is one of the major emphases in the California Language Arts Framework (1987). Yet, like many schools in California (Gersten, 1996), the project schools had provided only minimal training in literature-based approaches to reading instruction. Teachers were not at all sure how to use literature effectively, and they were not certain about how to balance basic skills and the new meaning-oriented approaches. This was particularly challenging for transition teachers who, following district guidelines, took as their primary responsibility teaching discrete, nontransferable skills (e.g., letter sounds, vocabulary, possessives, syntax, homonyms).

FOUR STRATEGIES THAT MAKE STUDYING LITERATURE WORK

Across all phases of the program, from Pre-Transition to Transition II—from Spanish to English language arts—literature units are the central instructional component. Discussions, writing projects, social studies content, and supplementary readings are all coordinated around the literary selection being studied. Four specific instructional strategies have proven fundamental to the success of studying literature with transition students:

- building students' background knowledge
- drawing on students' personal experiences
- assisting students in rereading pivotal portions of the text
- promoting extended discourse through writing and discussion

Literature units are the central component in our program because we hypothesized that transition students would benefit from more extensive and intensive opportunities to work with text, to study interesting stories under the tutelage of a teacher. Based on research conducted as part of the Kamehameha Elementary Education Program in Hawaii (Au, 1979, 1992; Tharp & Gallimore, 1988) and research in Spanish-speaking Latino communities in southern California (Goldenberg, 1992–93), we adapted the experience-text-relationship approach as our framework for studying literature. Through ongoing discussions, writing activities, and reading, the teacher helps students study the story in relationship to their own experiences and a central theme. The metaphor for this approach to studying literature is weaving (Tharp & Gallimore, 1988). With the assistance of the teacher, students weave together new and existing knowledge, experiences, and concepts.

Building students' *background knowledge* prior to and throughout the literature unit helps contextualize story themes, content, and vocabulary. Drawing on, sharing, and discussing students' related *personal experiences* sustains motivation and helps students make concrete and conceptual connections to the text, its content, and the themes under study.

The media for this weaving are writing and discussion—also called instructional conversations, or ICs (Goldenberg, 1992–93; Tharp & Gallimore, 1988)—both of which can promote *extended discourse,* the opportunities for students to use language to elaborate and develop ideas. Discussions set up writing assignments and writings inform subsequent discussions throughout the course of the literature unit. Writing—at least at the point of composing—is an individual opportunity for each student to think about and articulate ideas, interpretations, and related experiences. Discussions provide a social opportunity for students and teacher to collaboratively build more elaborated and sophisticated understandings.

Within this dynamic of reading, writing, and discussion, however, there are critical junctures at which students need careful *rereading assistance* from the teacher to fully comprehend the content of the text. Typically, this comes at pivotal points in the story, where the stylistic or semantic qualities of the text have to be highlighted and clarified for the students.

In terms of literacy development, students are learning to comprehend text, to make connections between the text and their own lives, and to develop more fully formed concepts through this recurrent process of individual and social discourse—of reading, writing, and discussing. Students are learning to engage in meaningful discourse by participating in it. "For literacy, meaningful discourse is both the destination and vehicle" (Tharp & Gallimore, 1988, p. 93).

In terms of second language acquisition theory (Cummins, 1989; Krashen, 1987), our working hypothesis is that these four strategies help provide substantial comprehensible input—language that includes slightly more sophisticated structures or vocabulary than the learner can produce on his or her own, but is understandable within the total context in which it is used. Starting with *background building* activities, continuing with written and oral sharing of students' *personal experiences,* supported by timely *rereading assistance,* and ultimately promoting *extended discourse* through writing and discussion, the literature unit becomes a meaningful social context in which words, phrases, language structures, and concepts are used, acquired, and learned.

USING THE FOUR STRATEGIES: AN EXAMPLE LITERATURE UNIT

This section illustrates how teachers in our project conduct a literature unit and employ the four strategies. As part of our effort to document the program, project advisors and teachers have been writing detailed descriptions of what transpired as they taught particular units. This section is a condensed version of a unit write-up prepared by Gisela O'Brien and Jerry McLean (an advisor and a teacher). They have been developing this unit for *Annie and the Old One* over the last four years and conducted it with both fourth and fifth grade transition students. (Appendix 7.2 includes a one-page planner for the total unit.)

The section begins with some preliminary explanations about the story, theme, and conduct of the unit. The second part describes activities conducted at the beginning of the unit to build students' background knowledge and draw on their personal experiences prior to reading the story. The third part describes two lessons conducted during the unit when teacher and students are reading and working the text. One lesson shows the application of background knowledge and further efforts to help students connect their personal experiences to the story. The other lesson shows the teacher assisting students in carefully rereading a pivotal passage. The final section describes the culminating writing project, one way that the unit promotes extended written discourse. Although we do not include transcript excerpts, our descriptions indicate the ways that discussions promote extended oral discourse throughout the course of the unit.

About the Story, Theme, and Conduct of the Unit

Why *Annie and the Old One*? Teachers in our project typically use *Annie and the Old One* (Miles, 1971) near the end of Transition I (grade 4) or the beginning of Transition II (grade 5). *Annie and the Old One* has many benefits as a reading experience for transition students. It is a fifth grade core literature selection for our school district, so students are reading the same level material as their fluent-English-speaking peers. The language is challenging but manageable with the appropriate scaffolding (i.e., background building, discussion, assisted rereading).

In choosing this book for a literature study for transition students, not only readability but also the content and potential themes of the story are considered. *Annie* is about a young Navajo girl who learns about the natural cycle of life and death from her grandmother—the Old One. The first part of the book describes Annie's environment and daily activities, and it introduces her grandmother, who tells Annie it is time for her to learn to weave. Annie declines her mother's subsequent invitation to help with the weaving of a new rug. But shortly thereafter, the Old One announces she will "return to mother Earth" when the new rug is finished, and she asks each family member to choose a gift. Annie chooses the Old One's weaving stick, but then, thinking she can forestall her grandmother's death, Annie tries to disrupt her mother's work on the rug. The Old One discovers Annie's efforts, and in a short but dramatic exchange on the top of a mesa overlooking the desert, the Old One explains that death is a natural part of life. Annie comes to a new understanding and in the closing scene begins to weave "as her mother had done, as her grandmother had done."

The Legacy Theme. Throughout our use of the book, the most successful and motivating theme deals with the concept of *legacy*. All human beings affect those people whose lives they touch. Whether a person dies or simply moves away, there is a legacy left behind. Most upper-elementary students have dealt with the death of an older relative or separation from a friend. At the same time, they are ready to develop more complex and sophisticated views of separation and loss, particularly in relationship to the idea of a legacy. Initially, students often talk about the concrete sense of missing someone or not being able to do things with them. But they are less likely to grasp the ways in which that person has contributed to their lives and the ways in which we carry on and remind ourselves of such people through memories and artifacts. This is one of the many themes that can be studied through *Annie and the Old One*.

Integrating with Social Studies. *Annie* also lends itself to the study of Native American cultures, which is part of the fourth and fifth grade history–social studies curriculum. Background-building lessons and activities support the literature unit and provide a means to integrate language arts and social studies. Students complete supplemental reading about Native Americans through assigned independent readings, teacher read-alouds, and books available for pleasure reading.

Whole-Class and Small-Group Activity. Initial lessons and activities completed before we begin reading the book are usually conducted as a whole class. Once we begin the process of reading and working the text, however, all lessons are carried out in small groups. Small groups give each student more opportunity and responsibility to contribute to the discussion and share his or her logs. Small groups also make it easier for the teacher to gauge how each student is understanding the text and address the needs of those who are having difficulty.

Time Devoted to the Unit. The unit takes about eight weeks: two weeks for beginning activities, five weeks for working the text, and one week for the culminating project. This chronology is based on the three-group rotation system developed by this particular teacher and project advisor. Rather than rotate through all groups each day, the teacher devotes an entire 70-minute time block to one group each day.[1]

Reading and Writing That Supplements the Unit. Understandably, devoting eight weeks to a 44-page text may be difficult to imagine. How do you get students to stay with the text that long? Isn't it an insufficient amount of reading for students to do? Sustaining interest comes as a result of the many varied assignments we do as part of the literature unit. As part of the language arts program, students are also doing a large amount of assigned independent reading that supplements the literature study. For example, during the *Annie and the Old One* unit, students read and complete assignments for other selections dealing with similar content and themes—*Nanabah's Friend, Blue Wings Flying, Through Grandpa's Eyes,* and *A Gift for Alicia* (short stories from the Houghton-Mifflin Transitional Reading series, 1986); *Dancing Drum, Turquoise Boy, Little Firefly, Clamshell Boy, Quill Worker,* and *Ka-ha-si and the Loom* (from the Watermill Press Native American Legends series, 1990).

Beginning the Unit

We begin a literature study by building pertinent background knowledge and drawing on students' related personal experiences. The goal is activating and developing a schema relevant to the story and theme.

We began the *Annie* unit by asking students to make predictions based on the cover of the book, which has a number of clues about the content of the story.[2] Asking students for predictions allowed us to identify and clarify—for the whole class—that which was not readily apparent to the students. For example, many students did not grasp the term *the Old One*. Some thought it referred to an inanimate object of some sort, because they did not grasp the usage of the word *One*. Some understood it to refer to an older person, but they did not grasp the subtlety of *the*, which helps convey the singular importance of that particular older person. These language and conceptual issues had to be discussed and clarified.

We also conducted two activities to more fully develop this initial schema. To establish a concrete reference for the concept of the Old One, students wrote, shared, and discussed a literature log about an important older person in their own lives. To elaborate on their understanding of the time, place, and culture depicted in the story, the class developed short reports on the four major North American cultures from which most of the many different tribes evolved. Reports were prepared by small groups of students using material from the social studies textbook.

Log Entry: Drawing on Students' Related Personal Experiences. Students' responses to the log prompts varied. Many students described a very close and important relationship with an older person. Some had not actually experienced such a relationship but described the benefits they thought such a relationship might provide. A small number of students wrote about clearly negative experiences with an older person.

The responses were informative because they provided us with an indication of those students who might have more difficulty understanding Annie's perspective in the story—a critical part of comprehending the text and working with the legacy theme. However, the range of responses was beneficial because students who had no positive and/or direct experiences with an Old One heard the experiences of those who did. As a result, it was still possible to provide all students with concrete examples of the Old One concept—a central concept in the story.[3]

Using what students shared in their log entries, the teacher charted various things that the students mentioned: the kinds of people who were the Old One, activities children did with the Old One, and the feelings students mentioned about having such a relationship. These charts were saved and later revisited to compare Annie's relationship with her grandmother to the ideas and experiences students mentioned.

Native American Cultures Reports: Building Background. We felt the students needed background knowledge in two areas. First, they needed a working knowledge of certain philosophical views that are a part of many Native American cultures: reverence for nature; unity and harmony between humans, animals, and earth; and the cyclical process of life and death. These concepts are woven throughout the story. Second, the story includes numerous references to geographical features of the setting (e.g., mesas, hogans, bluffs, pastures, desert) and the daily activities of Annie and her family (e.g., herding, harvesting, weaving, silversmithing), and students needed to know more about these.

Each group of students was assigned a portion of the social studies text that dealt with the four main Native American ancestral cultures in North America. The textbook provides an overview of the regional differences that shaped the cultural, economic, and social life of the various peoples. Before students began to read the text, we explained the terms *ancestors* and *descendents* by using the teacher's family tree to depict a lineage—current generation, parents, grandparents, great-grandparents. We were then able to clarify that the textbook dealt with the ancestors of Native Americans, and that we were going to study early Native American ancestors to learn about the roots of Native American culture.

As part of their group assignment, students had to read the text and complete a graphic organizer that categorized information (e.g., environment, shelter, clothing, food, religion, art). Each group then synthesized all the information and created a single version of the graphic organizer that served as a guide for the group's presentation of information to the whole class. During the reports, other groups and the teacher asked questions and clarified issues that were unclear, after which groups returned to the social studies text to gather additional information, clarify ambiguities, and identify essential ideas in the reading material.

During a second round of presentations, the teacher highlighted and talked about the relationship between the characteristics of each tribe and their geographical surroundings, how each tribe adapted its means of subsistence to flourish in a particular area, and the central role nature played in the development of all the tribes. This provided the historical background necessary to introduce the philosophical views of Native Americans—specifically, their reverence for nature and their belief in a natural cycle of life and death.

Our goal with the reports was to create a backdrop of understanding about Native Americans. Specific terms and concepts (e.g., the term *going to Mother Earth* or the concepts of mesa and harvesting) could be further and better clarified as we began reading the story, but defining specific terms while reading is more efficient and effective when students have a broader knowledge base or schema for those terms.

Working the Text

Working the text means studying it carefully—reading it, rereading it, discussing it, writing about it, and listening to what others have written about it. In preparation for the unit, the teacher chunks the book into sections. The chunks set a pace at which students and teacher study the story. At least one lesson (small-group session) is devoted to each chunk. The goal of chunking is to create manageable portions of reading and meaningful junctures to engage the students in discussion and writing. Some chunks are short because the content is complex and critical to the larger understanding of the story and themes. Other chunks are longer because the content is more straightforward. In those cases, there is less of a need to intervene to work the text.

Table 7.3 provides details on the five chunks for *Annie and the Old One,* including page numbers, synopses, understandings to develop, discussion topics, and literature log prompts. By "Understandings to Develop," we mean ideas that are central to a complete understanding of the story. Discussion topics and literature log prompts focus directly on those critical understandings. Discussion is designed to solidify students' grasp of the literal details and the potential meaning and implications of the chunk in relationship to the theme and story as a whole. The literature log is intended to help students connect the events and ideas expressed in the story to their own lives, first so they can increase their understanding of the characters' motives and actions, and second so they can see the relevance of the story and themes to their own experience.

Rather than discuss each chunk in detail, we will focus on chunks 3 and 5. These two chunks provide ample opportunity to illustrate the role of the four strategies during the portion of the unit when we are actually working the text with the students.

Chunk 3: Applying Background Knowledge and Connecting Personal Experiences. The study of chunks 1 and 2 focused primarily on Annie's relationship with her grandmother and Annie's uncertain reaction to her grandmother's invitation to learn to weave. We discussed with students the role of weaving as a tradition handed down from one generation to the next in this story. We also discussed how learning to weave represented a benchmark in Annie's growth and maturation—like taking on new, more adult-oriented chores and responsibilities (the topic of literature log 2). Both of these issues are important to understanding the significant events in chunk 3, when suddenly the Old One tells her family that she will soon die, and Annie surprisingly chooses the Old One's weaving stick as her gift.

There were three critical things we wanted the students to understand in chunk 3: (a) the Old One's ability to anticipate her own death; (b) the practice of letting family members choose one of the Old One's possessions as a gift, which relates directly to the legacy theme; and (c) Annie's choice of her grandmother's weaving stick, which is noteworthy because in the previous chunk Annie told her mother she was not yet ready to weave.

The background building we had done at the beginning of the unit facilitated discussion about the Old One's announcement and her ability to anticipate death. Most students grasped what the Old One meant when she said, "When the new rug is taken from the loom, I will go to Mother Earth." Students were familiar with the Native American belief that the Earth is the source of all life. For those students who did not make the connection, we defined the phrase for them (*going to Mother Earth* means she is about to die; she will be returning to the source of all life—Earth).

The other point that needed clarification, however, was the marker of time the Old One used—the new rug being taken from the loom. We asked the students to consider whether the Old One meant that exactly as she said it (i.e., she would pass away when the rug was complete) or in some other way

Table 7.3. Chunking for the *Annie and the Old One* Literature Unit

Pages	Synopsis of Chunk	Understandings to Develop	Discussion Topics	Literature Logs
1–7	Describes Annie's environment, activities, and relationship with the Old One (grandmother), who tells Annie it's time for her to learn to weave.	The closeness between Annie and the Old One; fragility of the Old One—suggesting she may not have too long to live.	What have you learned about Annie and Old One? (Who's Annie? What's expected of her? What kind of relationship does she have with the Old One?)	Write about someone you are very close to, and describe your relationship. Or, write about a time you thought someone you loved might die.
8–13	Annie seems lost in thought as she watches her mother weaving a new rug; Annie tells her mother she is not ready to start weaving.	The role of weaving—passed on from one generation to the next; Annie's uncertainty about learning to weave.	Why do the Old One and Annie's mother think it is time for Annie to learn to weave? Why does Annie feel she is not ready to weave?	Describe an important responsibility you have at home that makes you feel grown up. Why does it make you feel more grown up?
13–17	The Old One tells family she will die when the new rug is finished, then asks each member to choose a gift; Annie chooses the Old One's weaving stick.	Old One's anticipation of death; the role of the gifts—a memory, legacy; significance of Annie's choice, because she has not yet chosen to weave.	How come the Old One knows she will die? Why does she let them each choose a gift? Why does Annie choose the weaving stick?	The Old One gave her family gifts. Write about a gift you received that is a memory of someone you loved who died or moved away.
18–37	Thinking she can forestall the Old One's death, Annie tries to disrupt her mother's work on the rug; later she begins removing portions of the rug.	Annie does not understand the rug is only symbolic—a way to mark time; her actions show how deeply she cares for the Old One.	How did Annie react to the Old One's news? Why? How would you react if someone you loved told you they were going to die? Why?	Annie can't accept that the Old One is going to die. If you could speak with Annie, what would you say to her or what advice would you give her?
38–44	The Old One discovers Annie's efforts and explains to Annie that death is natural part of life, after which Annie declares herself ready to weave.	The Old One's descriptions of the natural cycle of life; Annie's thoughts and actions as she listens to the Old One and looks out on the desert before her.	What does Old One mean when she says, "Earth, to which all creatures finally go . . ."? What does Annie see, do, and think as she listens to her grandmother? What does she come to understand?	Why do you think Annie is now ready to weave?

(i.e., as a more general way to mark time). Some students grasped the idea—and explained in the discussion—that the Old One and her family probably all knew about how long it takes to weave a rug and that her words were a way of saying, "In a few weeks or so." We wanted to emphasize this issue because in the next chunk, it becomes clear that Annie makes a literal connection between the status of the rug and her grandmother's imminent death.

Background knowledge also facilitated discussion of the Old One's ability to anticipate her own death. When we posed the discussion question, "How come the Old One knows she is about to die?" we asked students to locate an excerpt from the text that specifically helped to answer that question. Students noted the explanation Annie's mother gave to Annie: "Your grandmother is one of those who live in harmony with all nature—with earth, coyote, birds in the sky. They know more than many will ever learn. Those Old Ones know."

The excerpt provides an explanation, but interpreting its meaning requires the kind of background knowledge we studied as part of the Native American cultures reports. The key phrase is *living in harmony with all nature*. We had specifically introduced the words *harmony* and *unity* as part of the background-building lessons. In the discussion, students grasped the idea of living in close relationship to nature. Being sensitive to and knowledgeable and respectful of the Earth and its creatures and their natural life cycles helps people better understand how they too are part of that natural cycle. The Old One probably did not know exactly when she would die, but her knowledge of nature provided her with a feeling for such things.

The discussion then turned to the practice of choosing gifts, and the question, "Why does the Old One let each family member choose a gift?" We wanted students to understand the idea of a legacy—when people leave us, we often have something tangible (or intangible) that helps us feel we are not completely separated from them. The legacy links us to that person forever, despite the separation of distance or even death. We asked students to share experiences they'd had that were similar to Annie's. Students described gifts they had received that helped them remember a special person who had died or moved away. This oral sharing activity served as a form of prewriting for the literature log entry that we then used with chunk 3: "The Old One gave her family gifts. Write about a gift that is a memory from someone you loved who died or moved away."[4] The assignment of the literature log concluded the lesson. Students completed the log as homework or at the independent center.

The next lesson began with the sharing of the literature logs, which provided an opportunity to examine the relationship between students' experiences and those of Annie and her family (see Figure 7.1 for samples of students' writing).[5] The teacher charted how the gifts they had received helped them remember an important person and the particular things the gifts called into mind. We did the same for the gifts Annie and her family selected. Our point was that different gifts remind you of different things about that special person.

The students' logs provided a springboard for discussing why Annie would choose the weaving stick as her gift when she had not expressed any interest in learning how to weave. Some students thought Annie chose the stick because she associated it with her grandmother, who used the stick every day. Other students thought she chose the stick specifically because her grandmother had recently announced that it was time for Annie to learn to weave. These students argued that Annie would soon begin to weave but simply

FIGURE 7.1. Literature Log 3 for Sergio and Raul

Sergio	Raul
In the last two years I went to Mexico and my grandma died and she was 86 years old. She gave me a fotograf. Every time when I remember her I get the picture and I see it. That makes me feel like she is right there but she ain't. She used to play with me. I mis her so much.	One day my grandpa was going to die. I felt so sad. Before he dies he told my brothers and me to line up because he was going to give us a surprise. I got a cap and money and my brothers go money I miss him.

needed some time to get herself ready for that big step. Still other students thought that the Old One's announcement of her impending death changed Annie. It made her realize that she needed to learn to weave in order to carry on her grandmother's tradition. Our objective here was not to resolve this issue one way or the other; in fact, the text offers little with which to make a clear determination. Each of these interpretations is plausible. We told this to the students and then explained that this was the kind of situation where you have to read on in the story to confirm possible interpretations.

Chunk 5: Assisting Students in Rereading a Pivotal Passage. In chunk 5, the Old One discovers Annie's efforts to forestall the completion of the rug. The next morning, she takes Annie to the top of a small mesa overlooking the desert, where she explains how life and death are part of a natural cycle. As her grandmother speaks, Annie observes various forms of life around her. Connecting her observations with her grandmother's words, Annie comes to a heightened understanding. In the subsequent and final scene of the story, Annie begins to weave.

The climactic scene on the top of the mesa is a complex but pivotal passage that required careful rereading. First, the text itself contains multiple forms of narrative prose: description of the physical setting, the Old One's words, and description of Annie's thoughts and actions. Second, much of the language in the passage is figurative and requires students to make inferences about the meaning of the language (e.g., "Earth, to which all creatures finally go"). Yet the scene is critical to understanding the change Annie undergoes.

The focus of the lesson on chunk 5 was twofold: What actually happens? and What does it mean in relation to the whole story? Because the mesa scene is so complex, we had to devote a significant portion of time to assist the students in rereading the passage. To do this, we broke the passage down into three parts: the initial description of Annie and the Old One sitting on the mesa; the Old One's explanation; and Annie's immediate reaction and reflection.

We started by recounting what had transpired thus far in the story. Students reviewed their books and described key events, which the teacher listed in sequence on chart paper. When we arrived at the pivotal scene in chunk 5 where Annie follows the Old One to the top of the mesa, we stopped and staged the scene, with students role playing Annie and her grandmother, walking together, sitting down on the edge of a desk, and looking out across an imagined desert.

We reviewed the story and staged the critical scene as a way of reconstructing the context in which the scene takes place—what had happened previously, and the immediate circumstances of the scene. Then we told students that we had arrived at a very dramatic and important part of the story. Students voiced their agreement, saying this is where Annie changes her mind and decides she is ready to weave. With that, we were able to pose the question that would guide a close rereading of the passage: What happens here that leads Annie to change her mind?

Then we turned our attention to the paragraph containing the Old One's explanation, identifying the sentences in quotation marks, which indicate the Old One's words, and those not in quotation marks, which are part of the narrator's description:

> "My granddaughter," she said, "you have tried to hold back time. This cannot be done." *The desert stretched yellow and brown away to the edge of the morning sky.* [Italics added.] "The sun comes up from the edge of earth in the morning. It returns to the edge of the earth in the evening. Earth, from which good things come for the living creatures on it. Earth, to which all creatures finally go."

Referring back to our staging of the scene and asking students to imagine themselves as the characters, we asked the students why the author might have put that descriptive sentence ("The desert stretched . . .") right in the middle of the grandmother's words. Many students understood that the author was describing the scene, but they did not see the connection between that description and the grandmother's words. We needed to explain that the Old One was using what she saw before her (the morning sky) to explain her ideas ("The sun comes up from the edge of the earth in the morning"). It was important to draw students' attention to this because in the next paragraph, Annie begins to the do the same thing—using what she sees around her to explain to herself the cycle of life and death.

Then we considered the Old One's two concluding lines: "Earth, from which all good things come for the living creatures on it. Earth, to which all creatures finally go." Initially, students locked onto the second sentence—all creatures go back to Earth. Some interpreted that literally to mean, when one dies, one is buried in the earth. We had to explain how the two sentences work together: Earth provides good things for those creatures that live on it; when creatures die, they return to the earth; in returning to the earth, they help provide good things for those still living. In this way, there is an ongoing cycle that keeps moving as time carries on.

With that, we returned to the Old One's first remark: "You have tried to hold back time. This cannot be done." What does the Old One mean by "hold back time"? Having examined the entire paragraph, students understood that she meant the ongoing cycle—Annie could not hold back her grandmother's death. It was as inevitable as the sun rising and setting each day.

The next section of the passage is similarly complex, but it revisits the same ideas, only this time as Annie seemingly internalizes them:

> Annie picked up a handful of brown sand and pressed it against the palm of her hand. Slowly, she let it fall to earth. She understood many things.
> *The sun rose but it also set.*
> *The cactus did not bloom forever. Petals dried and fell to earth.* [Italics added.]
> She knew that she was part of the earth and the things on it. She would always be a part of the earth, just as her grandmother had always been, just as her grandmother would always be, always and forever.
> And Annie was breathless with the wonder of it.

The author describes Annie's actions and her thoughts, rather than having her articulate her thoughts, as her grandmother had done in the previous paragraph. We had to bring this switch to the students' attention because they didn't understand that the statements were not a description of the desert, but rather of what Annie was thinking. As we had done earlier in the lesson, we returned to the staging of the scene, with two students portraying Annie and her grandmother. While the students carried out Annie's actions—picking up the sand, pressing it against her palm, and letting it fall to earth—we highlighted the lines that described Annie's thinking: "The sun rose but it also set. . . ."

To help students identify with the way Annie was connecting this knowing to what she saw around her, we asked students about similar examples we could point to in our own lives. Students mentioned, for example, pets that are born, grow up, have babies, and then pass away; fruit that ripens and degrades but leaves a pit or seeds behind. On the basis of these examples, we then examined the last part of the passage. We asked the students to reread the entire passage once again and then consider what the last two paragraphs meant. What did Annie understand?

> She knew that she was part of the earth and the things on it. She would always be a part of the earth, just as her grandmother had always been, just as her grandmother would always be, always and forever.
> And Annie was breathless with the wonder of it.

Students said that Annie knew that just like the petals of the cactus flower dried and became part of the earth, so too did human beings—her grandmother, her, her family. And if people were still part of the earth when they died, then they could still be with you in your mind and in your heart. That became a way for the students to express it—that the Old One would always be there for Annie as part of the earth and in Annie's heart and mind.

In the final portion of chunk 5—the last scene in the story—Annie begins to weave. Discussion of the last scene took place in the next lesson. As a way to prepare for that discussion, we assigned the following literature log: "Why does Annie begin to weave?" The key understanding that came across in virtually every student's entry was that Annie had come to understand that she could not hold back time. Her efforts to disrupt completion of the rug could and would not forestall her grandmother's death. The students also talked about Annie's new understanding of death. Despite the fact that her grandmother would die, they said, Annie's grandmother would still be with her as a part of the earth; she would be alive in Annie's heart and mind. (See Figure 7.2 for writing samples.)

A handful of students, however, went further in their analysis to introduce the idea of Annie carrying on her grandmother's legacy. In her decision to begin weaving, Annie was carrying on the traditions passed on to her by her grandmother:

> I think Annie began to weave because now she knows that her grandmother will always be with her and that just as the sun can't be stoped from coming up and down she can't stop her grandmother from dying. *She also knows that her grandmother left her the knowledge of learning to weave.* [Marcos, literature log 5; italics added]

> Annie now is ready to weave because her grandmother is going to die and *Annie could cap [keep] the tradition of weaving so she could remember about her grandmother.* She could remember when she started to weave and always remember her grandmother is going to be with her. [Luis, literature log 5; italics added]

The array of responses in the logs provided a promising set of circumstances for the next lesson, in which we wanted to work on the legacy theme as it pertained to the final scene in the story. On one level, Annie begins to weave because she has come to terms with her grandmother's death. On another more sophisticated level, she is carrying on her grandmother's legacy: "[Annie] slipped the weaving stick in place, as her mother had done, as her grandmother had done." Based on the log entries, almost all of the students understood chunk 5 at the first level. A few understood it at the second level, and their log entries provided a starting point for discussing the legacy theme.

The final discussion focused primarily on the many things that Annie would possess to carry on her grandmother's memory. After logs were shared, the teacher summarized the prevailing idea that Annie now had a better understanding of the inevitability of death and that death meant only a physical separation. Then, using the logs of those students who mentioned something about Annie carrying on the traditions of her grandmother, we asked the students to consider what things Annie would have that could preserve her grandmother's memory when she did pass away. Students listed a number of things: the weaving stick, Annie's knowledge about how to weave, the many stories her grandmother had told her, memories of special times they'd had together, and also the wisdom her grandmother had passed on about life. Through each

FIGURE 7.2. Literature Log 5 for Sergio and Raul

Sergio	Raul
I think Annie is now ready to weave because she is interested and because she could hando the weaving stick. I think she is big inof to weave and for her grandmother won't be sad. Because when Annie finish the rug her grandmother could be part of the earth and because she understood that her grandmother was still going to die because all people are part of earth. Even thou she is a person she still going to be part of earth.	Annie began to weave because she did understand about death because she understood that no one can stop anyone from dying. I think she did not worrie anymore because she knew that her grandmother will be in her heart and she would remember the good days when they were together. Annie also knew that her grandmother will be part of mother earth and she will be around in some ways.

of these, her grandmother would live on for Annie in her heart and mind, and in the many things she would do, like weaving.

Culminating the Unit: Extending the Written Discourse

Culminating writing projects serve two goals: (a) developing a deeper understanding of some aspect of the unit (content, themes, related personal experiences); and (b) developing a high-quality piece of writing. As part of the writing project, students share their drafts, receive feedback from peers and teacher, and revise and edit their work. The process is designed to address most directly goal b—developing a high-quality piece of writing. But it also addresses goal a; through the process of writing and revising, students spend more time thinking about and articulating some aspect of the unit.

In our experiences with the *Annie* unit, the most compelling topic has been literature log 3, in which students write about a gift they received that helps them remember someone who died or moved away. Almost all students have had such an experience, but there is a consistent pattern in their initial drafts. They focus primarily on the gift itself, and they do not develop the circumstances in which it was received, their relationship with the person, or how the gift endures and continues to remind them of that person. When students shared their entries during the *Annie* unit, invariably their peers began to ask them questions about these important details.[6]

As students respond to these questions, it often seems that it is the first time they have begun to unpackage and articulate the emotional impact and the meaning of the gift, elaborating on both the experience itself and the way they describe it. Perhaps that is why students are so willing to work on this log entry for the culminating project. It is a form of discovering and making explicit the legacy of an important relationship, just like Annie does.

FIGURE 7.3. Culminating Writings for Sergio and Raul

My Grandmother's Gift

by Sergio G.

For the last two years I have been going to Mexico in the summer to visit my grandmother. After my last visit she gave me a photograph of herself. Two weeks after we returned from our visit last summer we got a call from my aunt. She told us that my grandma died because she was 86 years old and sick.

Every time when I remember her I get the picture out and I look at it. That makes me feel like she is right there beside me even though she isn't. She used to play with me every day when I was in Mexico. I miss her so much. What made my grandma special was that she used to play with me and care about me. She used to tell me stories about a little monster. The stories would scare me but I knew she was just playing with me.

A Special Gift

by Raul C.

When I lived in Mexico four years ago my grandpa was very sick and dying. One morning before he died he called my five brothers and me to come into his room because he wanted to give us a gift to remember him. We were very surprised. My brothers and I got money but I also got his cap. He wore the cap when he was a captain of the cavalry in the Mexican Army.

That day I felt very sad because I knew he was going to die. We started to cry when he told us he would always be in our hearts forever. Soon he died. I will never forget him because I love him so much.

Note: First drafts for these pieces are presented in Figure 7.1.

As with each log, students wrote down the questions posed by their peers and the teacher. These questions became the first source of consideration when students began a second draft. As part of the rotation process, the students worked independently on a second draft. As each group came to its time with the teacher, the students shared the second drafts. As each student read his or her draft, students and teacher listened for how well the suggestions had been incorporated in the piece. The next revision was accomplished through individual conferences with peers. A final revision came as a result of conferencing with the teacher, which ultimately led to a final draft (see Figure 7.3 for samples). Final drafts were shared with the whole class and at home, and then displayed in the room.

POSITIVE IMPACT OF THE TRANSITION
PROGRAM: EVALUATION RESULTS

Do transition students benefit from the kind of literacy instruction described in the previous section? Our evaluation studies suggest they do (Saunders & Lennon, 1996). Data were collected for samples of project students and students from comparable, neighboring schools in the district. All students were enrolled at their respective school since first grade and participated in a Spanish

Table 7.4. Mean National Percentile Scores from Grades 1–5 for Project and Nonproject Students on Standardized Measures of Spanish and English Reading and Language Achievement

		READING		LANGUAGE	
Grade	Language of Test	Project	Nonproject	Project	Nonproject
1st	Spanish	44	44	40	41
2nd	Spanish	55	47	49	41
3rd	Spanish	62	49	73	61
4th	Spanish	72	52	78	62
5th	English (n = 14 and 14)	36	27	55	31
	Spanish (n = 4 and 4)	48	23	40	16

Notes: Data are based on same 18 project and 18 nonproject case study students. Spanish language test is APRENDA (Psychological Corp.); English is California Test of Basic Skills, Form U (CTB/McGraw-Hill).

bilingual program following the same district guidelines. The two samples were matched based on first grade standardized measures of Spanish reading and language achievement.

The results presented here are for those project students who were part of Jerry McLean's fifth grade classroom, the same class featured in the previous section. These particular students (n =18, and 18 matched comparison students) provide the best gauge of the program's impact because we began intensive research and development at McLean's school earlier than at other project schools. As a result, across grades 3–5, students participated in our most advanced implementation of the program. In fact, as early as second grade, these students began receiving Spanish language arts instruction that included many of the components that comprise our program (including the oral English development component of our program).

These data indicate the program is providing students with a profoundly more successful transition experience. First, with regard to literacy achievement, from the end of first to the end of fourth grade, as gauged by standardized Spanish language achievement tests, project students made significantly higher gains in Spanish reading and language than nonproject students (see Table 7.4). Mean national percentile scores for project students increased from the 44th to the 72nd in reading, and from the 40th to the 78th in language. In comparison, percentile scores for nonproject students showed smaller gains: from the 44th to the 52nd in reading, and from the 41st to the 62nd in language.[7]

At the end of grade 5, whether tested in English or in Spanish,[8] project students scored significantly higher than nonproject students (see Table 7.4). Project students tested in English (14 of 18) scored, on average, at the 36th national percentile in reading and at the 55th in language; nonproject students tested in English (also 14 of 18) scored at the 27th and 31st percentiles, respectively. To be reclassified, students must score at or above the 36th national percentile in both English reading and language; 50% of the project students

Table 7.5. Results from Grade 5 for Project and Nonproject Students on Project-Developed Performance-Based Measures of English Language Arts Achievement

Assessment Task Name, Question, Description, Measure	Indicators	Project (*n* = 18)	Nonproject (*n* = 18)
Self-selected story—Are students remembering and understanding stories they have read? Students select a story, summarize it, and write a short essay about a theme of the piece. Scored for completeness of summary and explanation of theme.	Mean score	3.06	2.33
	% 4 or better	28%	0%
	% 3 or better	78%	33%
Assigned story—Can students read and understand a grade-appropriate story? Students read about two-thirds of a grade-appropriate, unfamiliar story, summarize what they read, and write an ending. Scored for comprehension.	Mean score	3.00	2.33
	% 4 or better	22%	6%
	% 3 or better	78%	28%
Assigned article—Can students read and understand a grade-appropriate informational text? Students read a grade-appropriate informational text, synthesize the most important points, and write a short essay based on an inference question. Scored for comprehension.	Mean score	3.39	2.44
	% 4 or better	44%	0%
	% 3 or better	89%	44%
Conventions—Can students use written conventions effectively in their own writing? Summary portion of self-selected story task is scored for correct usage, mechanics, and spelling.	Mean score	3.17	2.67
	% 4 or better	39%	17%
	% 3 or better	78%	50%
Dictation—Can students accurately write what is dictated to them? Students take dictation for a grade-appropriate selection; scored for correct usage, mechanics, and spelling.	Mean score	3.28	2.83
	% 4 or better	39%	33%
	% 3 or better	83%	67%
Overall: Average across all five measures.	Mean score	3.18	2.52
	% 4 or better	11%	0%
	% 3 or better	67%	17%

Notes: All tasks are scored on a 6-point scale: A score of 4 means students are meeting challenging grade-level standards; 3 means students are demonstrating at least basic competence and approaching those standards.

(9 of 18), but only 11% (2 of 18) of the nonproject students, took English tests, met the criteria, and were reclassified (LEP to FEP).

At the end of fifth grade, project students also scored significantly higher than nonproject students on project–developed performance–based measures of English reading and writing (see Table 7.5). In fact, 67% of project students, in comparison to 17% of nonproject students, demonstrated at least basic competence on all five measures.

Important qualitative differences between project and nonproject students are also apparent in the data we gathered at the end of fifth grade. For example, 61% of project students, but only 22% of nonproject students, were able to list 10 or more books they had read on their own over the previous year (the average numbers of items for each sample were 11.27 and 5.88, respectively). Moreover, 67% of project students, in comparison to 33% of nonproject students, said they had used the public library during the previous year and listed specific books they had checked out. As another indication of these differences in reading experiences, a third of the nonproject students (33%) could not think of a story they knew well enough to write about (see the self-selected story task, Table 7.5) other than a familiar fairy tale (e.g., *Goldilocks and the Three Bears*); the figure was about half that for project students (17%).

Project students also responded quite differently from nonproject students when asked to describe the characteristics of a good reader and a good writer. The vast majority of nonproject students said good readers read or practice a lot; a substantial number said good readers know how to pronounce all the words. Only 11% of nonproject students mentioned any kind of mental actions involved in reading. In contrast, 67% of project students listed specific strategies that good readers use, such as summarizing, asking yourself questions, and stopping to think. The same pattern emerged when we asked students about writing. Most nonproject students (89%) said good writers practice a lot, spell words correctly, and write neatly. Only 11% mentioned any kind of concrete strategies. In comparison, 61% of project students mentioned specific writing process strategies, such as clustering ideas before you write, thinking about what you want to say, rereading as you write, making more than one draft, and reading your paper to someone else.

Finally, while students in both groups reported positive attitudes toward English literacy, project students were significantly more likely to report positive attitudes toward Spanish literacy. For instance, 94% of nonproject students and all project students said they liked reading and writing in English. In contrast, only 44% of nonproject students, in comparison to 89% of project students, said they liked reading and writing in Spanish. Moreover, all students in both samples said they wanted to continue to learn to read and write well in English, but only 50% of nonproject students, in comparison to 89% of project students, said they wanted to continue to learn to read and write well in Spanish. In short, while the vast majority of project students reported healthy attitudes toward English and Spanish, fully half of the nonproject students said they did not like and had little interest in continuing to learn how to read and write well in their home language.

DISCUSSION

We close by returning to the four premises that undergird our program: challenge, comprehensiveness, continuity, and connections. These premises represent key understandings we have arrived at over the course of our work conceptualizing and implementing effective programs for transition students.

First, transition can and should concentrate heavily on *challenging* content: engaging stories, information, concepts, themes, ideas, and knowledge. As illustrated in the *Annie and the Old One* unit, with proper support and assistance, transition students *can* read, discuss, and write about challenging material. In fact, as indicated by our evaluation results, they appear to benefit from such opportunities. Transition students also need explicit language instruction and practice (our next point), but we view the intellectual substance of the literature units as the driving force in our program. From the perspective of project teachers, the literature units—supported by the specific strategies discussed in this chapter—foster a motivating, academic context that is often lacking during the transition years:

> It thrills me when I see my students now making connections. What was before just a book now has a purpose, a meaning in their own life. I think that is what our literature studies have given our students, which then makes everything more pleasurable. And they can bring enthusiasm into the study, and when you bring enthusiasm, well, then you are going to learn more because you want to, because it means something. I think that the greatest success of our program is bringing meaning and pleasure to what we study. [LM, project teacher, team meeting, February 1995]

Second, transition instruction should be *comprehensive*. In this chapter, we featured our approach to studying literature. There are other instructional components, however, that play significant supporting roles in our program, including those that focus directly on language and literacy skills, such as dictation, conventions lessons, comprehension strategies, and assigned independent reading, and those that foster broader literacy-related experiences and attitudes, such as pleasure reading, teacher read-alouds, and interactive journals. This array of components might appear eclectic, perhaps even contradictory. But in designing the program and adapting each of these components, we consistently tried to address the needs of the students, as we identified them.

For example, although studying literature drives the program, it does not—as we found—provide students with sufficient reading practice and experience. A year of instruction involves only three to five literature units. Our pleasure reading program helped address this need only to some extent. Students' self-selected reading is based more on interest—as it should be—rather than on increasingly sophisticated texts supporting skill development. Consequently, we developed assigned independent reading centers, at which students were required to read specific material (including basal selections) and complete fairly conventional assignments (e.g., answering comprehension questions). These centers addressed an important need and improved our total program.

Like transition teachers described elsewhere (Gersten, 1996), teachers and advisors in our project saw the need to be comprehensive, to synthesize across rather than pit in opposition various approaches to teaching and learning (directed lessons and instructional conversation, literature and basals, writing projects and dictation). The benefits of this comprehensiveness are reflected in the results of our evaluation studies, which reveal important differences between project and nonproject students on a range of standardized and performance-based measures of basic skills and higher level achievement, as well as literacy-related attitudes and understandings.

Third, there should be *continuity* across the transition and pretransition years. Helping students make successful transitions depends heavily on an effective primary- and middle-grade Spanish literacy program (as well as on solid oral English development). Our strongest evaluation results—like those presented in this chapter—come from project schools where students were exposed to the program's instructional components beginning in second grade and then at close to full implementation across Pre-Transition, Transition I, and Transition II in grades 3-5. Project teachers and advisors see this continuity in curriculum and instruction as extremely important. To begin with, the instructional components yield higher levels of Spanish literacy at grades 2 and 3, so students transition with a stronger first language foundation. But continuity yields a related and equally important benefit, which leads us to our final point.

Fourth, during transition, every effort must be made to make explicit *connections* between learning English and students' prior learning and experiences in Spanish. In our program, English literacy is initiated in Transition I through the same instructional components students experienced in Spanish during Pre-Transition in third grade (and even in second grade). This, of course, saves time, because students are familiar with the kinds of activities and assignments they will do, but more importantly, it allows teachers to make a direct connection between what students learned to do in Spanish and what they are being asked to do in English. The same students who participated in the *Annie and the Old One* unit at the beginning of grade 5 participated in similarly designed units based on Spanish literature in grades 2 and 3. Explicitly connecting Spanish and English learning and creating greater continuity between Spanish and English instruction have helped reduce the stark and often destructive disjunctures students face when they transition.

ACKNOWLEDGMENTS

Our thanks to the administrators, teachers, and children at the project schools who made this work possible, especially members of the project team: Abbey Alessi, Kris Bullivant, Dolores Beltrán, Victor Chavira, Rafael Delgado, Susan Dickson, Melissa Dodd, Teresa Franco, Mae Hom, Gerardo López, Cindy Kim, Albert Martínez, Celia Mata, Lydia Moreno, Sylvia Salazar, Liz Salcido, Susan Sandberg, Imelda Valencia, Sally Wong, and Rossana Yñiguez. Thanks also to Tina Saldivar, Russell Gersten, and Claude Goldenberg for their helpful comments on the chapter. The project described here was supported by a Title VII grant from the U.S. Department of Education, Office of Bilingual Education and Minority Languages Affairs. Additional research support was provided by the Spencer Foundation, the National Center for Research on Cultural Diversity and Second Language Learning, and the Urban Education Studies Center, UCLA Graduate School of Education. No endorsement from any source should be inferred.

APPENDIX 7.1

Critical Components
of an Effective
Language Arts Program

Literature Units
(Experience-Text-Relationship Approach)

On average, students engage in four literature units across the year. Titles are chosen to fit the students' grade level and language proficiency (in particular across Transition I and II). The literature unit is propelled by an ongoing process of reading, writing (literature logs), and discussion (instructional conversations). Discussions are conducted in small groups of 6 to 10 students and managed through a specifically designed rotation system (teacher specific). The instructional framework for the literature units is called experience-text-relationship (Mason & Au, 1986); throughout the course of unit, the teacher tries to help students understand the relationship between their own experiences, the content of the literary selection, and one or more major themes that apply to the selection (e.g., friendship, sacrifice, perseverance, commitment, justice, cultural identity). In addition to those three critical elements (experience, text, theme), the teacher enriches the unit with lessons, activities, and supplementary readings that build background knowledge necessary for developing a deeper understanding of the selection and themes. Typically, units culminate with a writing project (see "Writing Projects") through which students elaborate on some aspect of the literature unit.

Literature Logs

Teachers divide the literary selection into chunks (manageable portions of reading) and assign a literature log entry for each chunk. Students complete the log entry at an independent center, and typically small-group discussions begin with some or all students sharing their logs. Literature log prompts might ask students to (a) write about a personal experience (related to the story), (b) elaborate on something that has happened in the story (e.g., assume the role of the character), or (c) analyze/interpret some aspect of the story or theme. In preparing a literature unit, teachers develop specific log prompts for each chunk, but often, prompts emerge naturally from small-group discussions.

Small-Group Discussion (Instructional Conversation)

Throughout the course of the literature unit, teacher and students meet in small groups to discuss the story, log entries, related personal experiences, and the themes for the unit. The amount of time allotted to the discussion segment and the frequency vary from teacher to teacher, but on average students spend at least 45 minutes a week engaged in discussion. The discussion provides the teacher with the opportunity to (a) hear students articulate their understanding of the story, themes, and related personal experiences and, in the process of facilitating the discussion, (b) challenge but also help students to enrich and deepen their understandings. Facilitated by the teacher, the small-group discussions, also referred to as instructional conversations (Goldenberg, 1992–93), allow students to hear, appreciate, and build on each others' experiences, knowledge, and understandings.

Writing Projects (Writing-as-a-Process Approach)

On average, students complete four major writing projects across the year, taking the pieces through the entire process of writing: prewriting, drafting, sharing, receiving feedback, revising, editing, and preparing a final, polished piece of work (Calkins, 1986, 1991; Graves, 1983, 1991). Typically these projects are directly related to the literature units, which conclude with a culminating writing (e.g., a fully developed literature log or a writing assignment tailored to the themes and content of the literature study). The key to this process is revision. Two things seem to promote meaningful revision: (a) helping students learn to share and receive/provide feedback, and (b) discussing examples (student or published) of the kind of writing students are working on, highlighting for students things they might incorporate in their own pieces when they revise.

Conventions Lessons

Students receive directed lessons about the conventions of written language (punctuation, capitalization, grammar, word usage). Lessons include a presentation from the teacher, opportunities for guided and independent practice, and then application to writings the students are working on (e.g., literature logs, writing projects, even dictation passages). The key is connecting what is studied in the lessons to the actual writing students are doing.

Dictation

The most extensive dictation program (Seeds University Elementary School, UCLA, 1992) includes students engaged in dictation exercises weekly, taking a cold dictation of a grade-level appropriate passage (at the beginning of the week), studying the features of that particular passage and practicing the dictation (throughout the week), and then completing a final dictation (at the end of the week). But as we've found, even a less extensive dictation program (two times per week) is beneficial. Two elements are critical for successful dictation:

(a) explanations from the teacher about language and punctuation items featured in the dictation passage, and (b) opportunities for the students to proofread and check their dictation against the actual passage.

Assigned Independent Reading

Students are regularly assigned reading selections from available materials (basals, literature titles, and any other sources) to read independently. Optimally, selections are related to the themes and topics being discussed in the literature units. Students complete various accompanying assignments to promote comprehension and hold the students accountable for what they read (summaries, comprehension questions, graphic organizers, paired and group activities). Readings and assignments are completed in class as part of an independent center and/or for homework.

Comprehension Strategies

Students are taught specific strategies to use while they are reading, in order to monitor their own comprehension (McNeil, 1984; Palinscar & Brown, 1985). The two essential strategies are pausing intermittently during reading to (a) summarize what they've read and (b) formulate and answer testlike questions about the reading material. Strategies are introduced during two-week training modules provided at the beginning of and midway through the year. Students practice the strategies in pairs at the assigned independent reading center.

Teacher Read-Alouds

At least three times per week, teachers read to students for approximately 20 minutes. Read-alouds (Trelease, 1985) serve various purposes: they promote pleasure reading; expose students to the language of expert writers and the fluency of an expert reader; engage students in reading material they may not yet be able to read themselves; and allow students to become familiar with different genres of writing.

Pleasure Reading

A portion of time each day (or, at the upper grades, each week) is scheduled for students to select and read things on their own for pleasure and interest. Students keep and review with the teacher a record of their ongoing readings (reading inventory), and often complete assignments related to their readings: preparing summaries and synopses, oral presentations for book-sharing time, drawings, and so forth. Teachers can do three things to help promote pleasure reading: (a) introduce students to numerous selections (through trips to the library, a full classroom library, lending read-aloud selections, making recommendations); (b) explicitly teach students how to choose and try out books (reading the cover synopsis, reading a portion of the book, reading various books from the same author); and (c) giving students a chance to share and discuss with each other and the teacher what they are reading.

Oral English Language Development (ELD)
through Literature

Used in grades K–3, the ELD program is based on a natural language approach and children's literature (Beltran & O'Brien, 1993). Literature provides a meaningful, motivational, and enjoyable context for learning and practicing specifically targeted English oral language skills. It also exposes children to English print well in advance of formal transition to English reading. On average, students receive 30 minutes of ELD per day. Lessons are conducted in small groups organized by English language production level. Organizing groups by production level allows the teacher to focus more successfully on students' specific needs.

Interactive Journals

Used primarily in grades K–2 and perhaps at the beginning of transition, interactive journals provide students with regular, nonthreatening opportunities to write about topics of their own choice and participate in a written dialogue with the teacher (Flores et al., 1991). Teacher response occurs as often as possible and provides students with examples of conventional writing. Interactive journals help kindergarten and first grade students break the written language code; later, in grades 1 and 2, they help students develop initial writing fluency.

APPENDIX 7.2

Unit Planner for *Annie and the Old One*

Title and Story Synopsis: *Annie and the Old One.* The story is about a young Navajo girl, Annie, who finds out her beloved grandmother will soon pass away. Although at first she is unable to accept it and does a number of things she thinks will forestall it, through her grandmother's guidance Annie comes to understand that death is a natural part of the cycle of life and that her grandmother will always live on in Annie's heart and mind.

	Lesson/Activities
BB	■ Examine and discuss details in the illustration on the cover of the book and the title of the book; make and discuss predicitons: What's the story probably about? ■ Initial literature log: Write about an important older person in your life. ■ In small groups, develop, present, and discuss reports on the four ancestral Native American tribes (source material: social studies textbook).

	Pages	Synopses of Chunks	Understandings to Develop
W O R K I N G T H E T E X T	1–7	Describes Annie's environment, activities, and relationship with the Old One (grandmother), who tells Annie it's time for her to learn to weave.	The closeness between Annie and the Old One; fragility of the Old One—suggesting she may not have too long to live.
	8–13	Annie seems lost in thought as she watches her mother weaving a new rug; Annie tells her mother she is not ready to start weaving.	The role of weaving—passed on from one generation to the next; Annie's uncertainty about learning to weave.
	13–17	The Old One tells family she will die when the new rug is finished, then asks each member to choose a gift; Annie chooses the Old One's weaving stick.	The Old One's ability to anticipate death; the role of the gifts—a memory, legacy; significance of Annie's choice to not yet weave.
	18–37	Thinking she can forestall the Old One's death, Annie tries to disrupt her mother's work on the rug; later she begins removing portions of the rug.	Annie not understanding the rug is only symbolic—a way to mark time; her actions, which show how deeply she cares for the Old One.
	38–44	The Old One discovers Annie's efforts and explains to Annie that death is a natural part of life, after which Annie declares herself ready to weave.	The Old One's descriptions of the natural cycle of life; Annie's thoughts and actions as she listens to the Old One and looks out on the desert—she comes to a realization.

	The Writing Assignment	Understandings to Develop
CW	Revise and edit the literature log for chunk 3 ("Write about a gift . . .") to better explain who the person is, the circumstances under which the gift was received, and why the person is so important (how s/he touched you).	Like Annie, we have people in our lives who have touched us, whose memory we cherish, and whose legacy we carry on.

Theme(s): The major theme we work on in the unit has to do with the concept of legacy: All human beings affect those people whose lives they touch. Whether a person dies or simply moves away, there is a legacy left behind. That person remains with us through memories, artifacts, knowledge, and the traditions we carry on. By the end of the unit, students should develop a fuller understanding of the concept of a legacy so that they can better understand the changes Annie undergoes in the story and value the legacies they've been left and are carrying on in their own lives.

Understandings to Develop	
■ Physical and cultural setting of the story and main characters (desert, Navajo peoples, young girl and her grandmother).	
■ The concept and examples of an Old One (a cherished elder).	BB
■ Native American philosophies, such as a reverence for nature (harmony) and the cycle of life and death; relevant cultural and geographical terms (e.g., *hogan, mesa*).	

Discussion Topics	Literature Logs	Pages	
What have you learned about Annie and the Old One? (Who's Annie? What's expected of her? What kind of relationship does Annie have with the Old One?)	Write about someone you are very close to, and describe your relationship. Or, write about a time you thought someone you loved might die.	1–7	W O R K I N G T H E T E X T
Why do the Old One and Annie's mother think it is time for Annie to learn to weave? Why does Annie feel she is not ready to weave?	Describe an important responsibility you have at home that makes you feel grown up. Why does it make you feel more grown up?	8–13	
How come the Old One knows she will die? Why does she let them each choose a gift? Why does Annie choose the weaving stick?	The Old One gave her family gifts. Write about a gift you received that reminds you of someone you loved who died or moved away.	13–17	
How did Annie react to the Old One's news? Why? How would you react if someone you loved told you he or she was going to die? Why?	Annie can't accept that the Old One is going to die. If you could speak with Annie, what would you say to her, or what advice would you give her?	18–37	
What does the Old One mean by, "Earth, to which all creatures finally go . . ."? What does Annie see, do, and think as she listens to her grandmother? What does she come to understand?	Why do you think Annie is now ready to weave?	38–44	

Activities/Lessons	Writing Goals	
Revise (add) content based on group questions/feedback; revise, based on lesson, phrases that clarify sequence of events; edit, based on conferences, clarity, and conventions.	More description and details; sentence clarity; conventions (spelling, punctuation).	CW

Note: BB refers to background building; CW refers to culminating writing project.

REFERENCES

Au, K. H. (1979). Using the experience-text-relationship method with minority children. *Reading Teacher, 32,* 677-679.

Au, K. H. (1992). Constructing the theme of a story. *Language Arts, 69,* 106-111.

Beltran, D., & O'Brien, G. (1993). English language development through literature. Workshop and documentation presented at the annual conference of the California Association for Bilingual Education, Anaheim, CA.

Berman, P., Chambers, J., Gandara, P., McLaughlin, B., Minicucci, C., Nelson, B., Olson, L., & Parrish, T. (1992). *Meeting the challenge of language diversity: An evaluation of programs for pupils with limited English proficiency* (Executive Summary, Vol. 1). Berkeley, CA: BW Associates.

California State Department of Education (1987). *English-language arts framework for California public schools, K–12.* Sacramento, CA: California State Department of Education.

Calkins, L. M. (1986). *The art of teaching writing.* Portsmouth, NH: Heinemann.

Calkins, L. M. (1991). *Living between the lines.* Portsmouth, NH: Heinemann.

Cummins, J. (1989). *Empowering minority students.* Sacramento, CA: California Association for Bilingual Education.

Flores, B., Garcia, E., Gonzalez, S., Hidalgo, G., Kaczmarek, K., & Romero, T. (1991). *Bilingual holistic instructional strategies.* Unpublished manuscript.

García, E. (1992). Effective instruction for language minority students: The teacher. *Journal of Education, 173*(2), 130–141.

García, E. (1995). Educating Mexican American students: Past treatment and recent developments in theory, research, policy, and practice. In J. Banks & C. McGee Banks (Eds.), *Handbook of research on multicultural education* (pp. 372–387). New York: Macmillan.

Gersten, R. (1996). Literacy instruction for language minority students: The transition years. *Elementary School Journal, 96*(3), 227–244.

Gersten, R., & Jiménez, R. (1993, April). Language minority students in transition. Symposium presented at the annual conference of the American Educational Research Association, Atlanta, Georgia.

Gersten, R., & Woodward, J. (1994). The language minority student and special education: Issues, themes, and paradoxes. *Exceptional Children, 60*(4), 310–322.

Goldenberg, C. (1992–93). Instructional conversations: Promoting comprehension through discussion. *The Reading Teacher, 46,* 316–326.

Goldenberg, C. (1996). Commentary: The education of language-minority students: Where are we, and where do we need to go? *The Elementary School Journal, 96*(3), 353–361.

Goldenberg, C., & Gallimore, R. (1991). Local knowledge, research knowledge, and educational change: A case study of first-grade Spanish reading improvement. *Educational Researcher, 20*(8), 2–14.

Goldenberg, C., & Sullivan, J. (1994). *Making change happen in a language-minority school: A search for coherence* (EPR No. 13). Washington, DC: Center for Applied Linguistics.

Graves, D. H. (1983). *Writing: Teachers and children at work.* Portsmouth, NH: Heinemann.

Graves, D. H. (1991). *Build a literate classroom.* Portsmouth, NH: Heinemann.

Krashen, S. (1987). *Principles and practice in second language acquisition.* Englewood Cliffs, NJ: Prentice-Hall.

Mason, J. M., & Au, K. H. (1986). *Reading instruction for today*. Glenview, IL: Scott, Foresman.

McNeil, J. D. (1984). *Reading comprehension: New directions for classroom practice*. Glenview, IL: Scott, Foresman.

Miles, M. (1971). *Annie and the Old One*. Boston: Little, Brown.

Palinscar, A., & Brown, A. (1985). Reciprocal teaching: A means to a meaningful end. In J. Osborn, P. Wilson, & R. C. Anderson (Eds.), *Reading education: Foundations for a literate America* (pp. 299–310). Lexington, MA: D. C. Heath.

Ramirez, J. D. (1992). Longitudinal study of structured English immersion strategy, early-exit and late-exit transitional bilingual education programs for language minority children (Executive Summary). *Bilingual Research Journal, 16*(1 and 2), 1–62.

Saunders, W., Goldenberg, G., & Hamann, J. (1992). Instructional conversations beget instructional conversations. *Teaching and Teacher Education, 8*, 199–218.

Saunders, W., & Lennon, D. (1993). Developing academic literacy in English through a program of integrated language arts: Year 3 evaluation (Project TOO3AOO185). Washington, DC: Office of Bilingual Education and Minority Affairs, U.S. Department of Education.

Saunders, W., & Lennon, D. (1996). Developing academic literacy in English through a program of integrated language arts: Year 5 evaluation (Project TOO3AOO185). Washington, DC: Office of Bilingual Education and Minority Affairs, U.S. Department of Education.

Seeds University Elementary School. (1992). *Dictation program: An approach to written language development*. Los Angeles: Seeds University Elementary School, University of California, Los Angeles.

Tharp, R., & Gallimore, R. (1988). *Rousing minds to life*. Cambridge, England: Cambridge University Press.

Trelease, J. (1985). *The read-aloud handbook*. New York: Penguin.

CHAPTER NOTES

1. This organization scheme includes two other centers: one led by the aide (who works on Spanish language arts as part of Transition I, and English reading comprehension strategies or other types of language arts instruction for Transition II), the other designed for independent work—assignments for the literature unit or assigned independent reading.

2. The cover bears the title and shows a profile of Annie—with a single bead woven into a strand of hair—looking over at a loom positioned in front of her hogan. In the background, there is a mesa and an expansive horizon.

3. This is a worthwhile illustration of the role of personal experiences and the importance of log sharing. Every student in the class does not necessarily have to have accessible, concrete experience related to the text. If experiences are shared, all students will—with the assistance of the teacher—be able to see similarities between the experiences of characters in the story and their own experiences, even if these experiences come by way of their peers.

4. The oral sharing sets up the log entry. During the oral sharing, students have the opportunity to voice a potential experience that is relevant to the particular log; they also have the opportunity to hear the experiences of others. When the sharing is complete

and the log prompt is announced, most students already have identified relevant content to write about (related personal experiences). If some students recount experiences that stray from the prompt, the teacher can use examples introduced by other students to clarify the focus of the prompt. For students who do not have an experience called for by the prompt, an alternative is assigned.

5. Student samples are printed exactly as they were written, without copyediting. For consistency, all samples included in this section were authored by the same two students, whose work is generally representative of how most students responded to the various writing assignments discussed in this section. Names are pseudonyms.

6. Students ask the authors questions as a part of the log-sharing process. Our approach to sharing and response draws on the work of Graves (1983) and Calkins (1991).

7. Comparisons reported here have been subjected to appropriate statistical significance testing. The term *significant* is used in those cases where differences are statistically significant ($p < .05$). All analyses of standardized test data were conducted on normal curve equivalent (NCE) scores; mean NCEs have been converted to national percentile ranks for summary purposes only. See Saunders & Lennon (1996) for a more technical analysis.

8. Based on district guidelines, LEP students are eligible to take standardized tests in English three semesters after they formally qualify to begin transition, prior to which students continue to take Spanish language tests.

8

Interactive Semantic Mapping and Charting:

Enhancing Content Area Learning for Language-Minority Students

Elba I. Reyes
Candace S. Bos
University of Arizona

A s a growing number of language-minority children enter school, teachers are increasingly required to teach literacy and engage students in content learning as they assist students in acquiring English as a second language. They are challenged to become teachers of English language learning by default (Gersten, 1996). Students whose primary language is other than English also face challenges in reading and learning as they participate in content area classes in English. They are expected to use cognitive and metacognitive strategies for negotiating information in text while also deepening and broadening their knowledge through reading. Yet these students often have difficulty developing higher-level language skills in English and learning content at a level on par with their peers. This is because instructional practices continue to be aimed at remediating an apparent lack of basic reading and language skills and center around basal-type texts and language drills that result in lower levels of language and cognitive development (Diaz, Moll, & Mehan, 1986; Duran, Dugan, & Weffer, 1996, February; Reyes & Molner, 1991). To move students to conceptual learning that results in school success, educational environments need to provide opportunities for conceptual learning that helps students develop higher-level language and cognitive skills in English (Bos & Reyes, 1996; Chamot & O'Malley, 1996; Reyes, 1994). The critical question is, How is this done? This chapter presents an interactive instructional model that assists students in developing English language skills while learning content, and that builds on theories of second language acquisition and effective content area instruction and learning.

The first part of this chapter provides the theoretical framework that supports our guiding principles of teaching. The second part provides information on how to use interactive teaching strategies, and the third part describes how to assist students in using interactive strategies to guide their learning.

AN INTERACTIVE MODEL OF TEACHING AND LEARNING: GUIDING PRINCIPLES

Students learn most effectively when they are actively engaged with the content through discovering the meaning of the ideas and comparing new learning to previous learning (Bos & Anders, 1992a). For several reasons, this is especially important for second language learners.

First, students learning the content in a second language often have some knowledge of the concepts being taught but do not have access to the concepts in the second language. Providing cues in the first language assists students to access their knowledge. Second, teachers need to guide students through the connections of ideas to assist them in seeing the relationships between their own experiences and the key content concepts presented.

The interactive learning principles used to guide and actively engage students with the content are illustrated in Table 8.1. These principles are derived from theories of second language acquisition, concept learning and development, and cognitive development.

Second Language Acquisition and Effective Instructional Practices for Second Language Learners

Teaching and learning occur in an environment where academic success depends on the students' ability to interpret a variety of language situations. This is particularly important for second language learners who may be at various stages of acquiring a second language. The second language acquisition process closely follows the natural process of first language development (Cummins, 1994; Krashen,1982). First, the learner experiences a preproduction or silent period during which receptive language (in this case, English) is developing and during which the learner understands more than she or he produces. Next, early production of language emerges, characterized by short, one- or two-word sentences and, often, grammatical and syntactic errors. As the language learner interacts with more proficient speakers, speech emerges with improved levels of correctness.

Instruction that is sensitive to this language acquisition process, that is well organized, and that provides students with opportunities to consistently

Table 8.1. Principles of Interactive Teaching and Interactive Learning

Interactive Teaching Strategies	Interactive Learning Strategies
Teach concepts in relation to the content to be learned in a comprehensible learning environment.	—
Design cooperative knowledge sharing activities that allow students to incorporate their own experiences and use others as a resource for information and consensus building.	Utilizing cooperative knowledge sharing by sharing each other's experiences and ideas and using others in a group as a resource for information and consensus building.
Activate students' background knowledge and encourage them to access their natural language skills.	Activating and using prior knowledge and developing new knowledge base through peer interaction.
Relate new knowledge to students' old knowledge.	Tying new knowledge and information to old knowledge.
Provide opportunities for learners to discuss and predict meanings and relationships among concepts.	Discussing meanings of concepts and predicting the relationships among ideas and concepts.
Provide opportunities for students to justify meanings and relationships among concepts.	Justifying meanings and relationships among concepts.
Encourage learners to confirm their understandings.	Confirming or modifying own understanding.
Provide students with an overview and scaffold for learning and language development.	Assisting or guiding each other through the learning and language development procedures.

participate in interactive activities is effective for bilingual students (Tikunoff, 1987). Such instruction facilitates students' communication by providing opportunities for purposeful language interactions and optimizing the comprehensibility of both language learning and content learning.

Schema Theory, Concept Learning and Development Theory, and the Sociocultural Theory of Cognitive Development

Understanding a concept or knowing what a vocabulary word means implies that one knows the definition and its relationships to other concepts. Students learn concepts and new information best when (a) the new information is systematically organized and related to an organizational framework that builds on prior knowledge (Carr & Thompson, 1996); (b) when they are taught in ways that demonstrate the organization of the concepts (Farnan, Flood, & Lapp, 1994; Hudson, Legnugaris-Kraft, & Miller, 1993); and (c) when examples of a concept are presented and used during activities that ask students to identify and name defining attributes of the concepts. For example, when

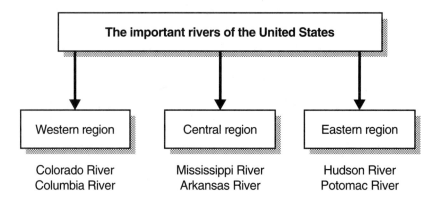

FIGURE 8.1. Content Organization for Important Rivers of the United States

studying the important rivers in the United States, students found it helpful to discuss the organization of the content, as illustrated in Figure 8.1. Other content matter may have other organizational frameworks, such as the cyclical frameworks evident in the weather cycle that causes precipitation.

In the social setting of the classroom, learning through problem solving and practical activities provides students with opportunities to confirm or modify their prior knowledge and integrate it with new learning, and to increase their participation in regulating their own learning process (Vygotsky, 1978). Dialogue can serve as the vehicle to content and strategy instruction. Dialogue between the teacher and learners and among the learners provides less skilled students with language and learning models to guide their learning process (Diaz, Neal, & Anaya-Williams, 1990; Moll & Diaz, 1987). Such instruction allows the students to use their existing language resources within an accepting classroom environment as they develop new and more complex language forms in context, and as they learn to use instructional strategies to mediate their learning (Collier, 1995, Fall; Reyes, Duran, & Bos, 1989; Richard-Amato, 1996; Voltz, 1995).

INTERACTIVE TEACHING STRATEGIES

In our work with both teaching and learning strategies, we have used two instructional, content-enhancing tools: interactive semantic charting (Anders & Bos, 1986; Johnson & Pearson, 1984) and interactive semantic mapping (Pearson & Johnson, 1978; Scanlon, Duran, Reyes, & Gallego, 1992). We have found that both tools make content more comprehensible to learners. Steps in the teaching process include (a) conducting a content analysis, (b) making a map or chart, and (c) using the strategy.

Conducting a Content Analysis

Regardless of the tool used, the first step in preparing for content instruction is for the teacher to complete a content analysis. The content analysis provides an opportunity for teachers to think about the concepts associated with the chapter or unit to be taught and the language inherent to that content domain. It also assists the teacher in determining the organizational framework for the content and how well the features used in the text, such as headings, subheadings, and key vocabulary, match the organizational framework. This process assists the teacher in determining which ideas are relevant to an overall understanding of the content, and which ideas are isolated details that provide little or no additional understanding or information. The process of doing a content analysis can be divided into three steps, followed by the mapping or charting process.

First, read the text to be used. Review the information to be presented keeping in mind the students' needs and abilities. For second language learners, analyze the content for its level of comprehensibility and design your instruction at a level that is a little beyond the students' present level of linguistic competence.

Second, make a list of the concepts that are central to understanding the content. Pay particular attention to the textual cues (e.g., titles, headings, highlighted words, pictures). Identify and include on your list any vocabulary and concepts that may present difficulties for second language learners due to students' limited background knowledge in English, such as metaphors, analogies, idioms, figurative language, and words that have multiple meanings. New vocabulary can be framed within word phrases already familiar to students learning English.

Third, determine the superordinate concept (i.e., the main idea) of the chapter by reviewing the list and asking yourself, What is the all-inclusive idea or concept? That superordinate concept becomes the name of your relationship chart or map.

For example, "Mountain Regions Today" is the title of a chapter from a social studies textbook (published in both English and Spanish) that we have used in our work and that we will use in this chapter to explain the process. Notice in Table 8.2 the list of concepts that we made as we reviewed the chapter. The chapter title in the textbook did not represent the superordinate concept. The overall concept is better represented by the statement "Mountain regions are valuable."

Making a Map or Chart

First, determine the type of content-enhancing tool you want to use for the content, such as a semantic chart or semantic map. In our work, we construct the tool that we plan to use during instruction, in this case either a chart or map. For a relationship chart (Figure 8.2), we create an open-ended matrix in which the subordinate concepts (important, supporting details) are placed along one axis, and the coordinate concepts (labels or headings for categories

Table 8.2. Key Concepts and Lanugage Difficulties for the Chapter "Mountain Regions Today"

KEY CONCEPTS		LANGUAGE DIFFICULTIES
English	**Spanish**	"little" farming
mines	minas	steep (vs. *step*)
forest	bosques	sloping
park	parques	coal (vs. *cold*)
ranches	ranchos (granjas)	fuel
jobs	ocupaciones	layers
coal	carbón	clear (has multiple definitions)
metals	metales	precipitation
trees	árboles	cattle
lumber	madera	graze (could be confused with *grass*)
recreation	recreación	splendid
cattle	ganado	
ranchers	rancheros	
wool	lana	
skiing	esquiar	
houses	casas	
hiking	caminatas	
sheep	ovejas	
silver	plata	
copper	cobre	
fishing	pescar	
paper	papel	
meat	carne	
schools	escuelas	
miners	mineros	
fuel	combustible	
gold	oro	

of concepts or ideas) are listed along the other axis. For a relationship map, the ideas are arranged by coordinate and subordinate concepts with lines drawn to demonstrate the relationships (Figure 8.3).

Second, construct the chart or map as you determine the coordinate-level concepts. To do this, group the vocabulary and concepts from your list by categories and then decide on a concept that describes each category. We have often found that some coordinate-level concepts are not labeled in the text. When this is the case, it is important to add those concepts to the concept list and to the map or chart, particularly for second language learners who may not as easily generate the implicit concepts (Jiménez, García, & Pearson, 1996) and who may not be familiar with the new meanings and relationships.

RELATIONSHIP CHART
CUADRO DE RELACIONES

MOUNTAIN REGIONS ARE VALUABLE
El Valor de las Regiones Montañosas

Key: + = related; ? = undecided
Leyenda: + = relacionado; ¿ = no puedo decidir

Important Ideas / Ideas Importantes		Important Places		Lugares Importantes	
		Mines / Minas	Forests / Bosques	Ranches / Ranchos	Parks / Parques
resources / recursos	coal / carbón				
	gold / oro				
	silver / plata				
	copper / cobre				
	trees / árboles				
	fish / peces				
	cattle / ganado				
	sheep / ovejas				
product / producto	meat / carne				
	wool / lana				
	lumber / madera				
	fuel / combustible				
recreation / recreación	hiking / caminatas				
	skiing / esquiar				
	fishing / pescar				
jobs / ocupaciones	miners / mineros				
	ranchers / rancheros				

FIGURE 8.2. Chart for the Chapter "Mountain Regions Today"

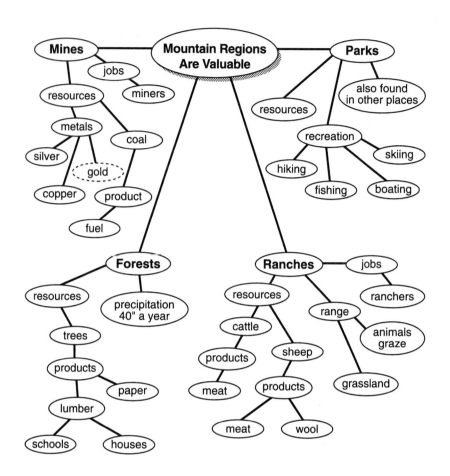

FIGURE 8.3. Map for the Chapter "Mountain Regions Today"

From our list on mountain regions, we grouped *mines, coal, metals, copper, silver, miners,* and *gold* together into one category. We identified the category (coordinate level) as mines/mining. Coordinate categories can be based on different types of relationships, depending on how the content is organized. They can be organized by steps in a process (e.g., evaporation, condensation, and precipitation in a water cycle) or by different aspects of the superordinate concept. For example, in the chapter "Mountain Regions Today," the concepts can be grouped by the major activities or places found in mountain regions—mining, forests, ranching, and parks.

Third, organize the subordinate concepts on the map or chart in relation to the coordinate concepts. In both cases, these concepts represent the important words that flesh out the coordinate-level ideas. For example, in "Mountain Regions Today," the concepts of resources, products, and jobs are important ideas, particularly in the sections on mining, forests, and ranching.

In organizing this level, you may find that concepts from the list are not needed on the map or chart because they are not important to the overall understanding of the superordinate idea. In this case they are not added. At this level it is also helpful to add related concepts that are particularly familiar to your students. For example, although gold was not explicitly mentioned in the text, we added the concept of gold to the other products from mines, because gold and gold mines were familiar to our particular Latino students in the Southwest.

Using the content analysis and the mapping or charting processes results in a map or chart that can serve as a blueprint for teaching. It determines what content and concepts are important to teach, the language inherent to the content, and the concepts and language that may be particularly difficult for second language learners. It is important to remember that the resulting map or chart is the teacher's interpretation of the relationships among the relevant concepts.

Employing the Interactive Teaching Strategies

With interactive teaching strategies, the teacher engages the students in mediated discussions, builds on the model's guiding principles, and uses the map or chart as a visual guide for assisting students in defining the key concepts and predicting relationships among the concepts.

First, present the topic through visual media when possible (e.g., films, videos, CD-ROMs), particularly if the students are not familiar with the topic. Many students who are learning a second language are familiar with television and videos, and a growing number are familiar with computers and CD-ROMs. Often, these students are interacting with these media in English. Next, introduce the superordinate concept by writing it on the board, on an overhead, or on a large sheet of butcher paper. We found it effective to introduce the idea in such a way that we could display it in the room and keep it for future reference. Next, have the students brainstorm what they already know about the concept and, as they make suggestions, list their ideas. It is important to ask the students to share what made them think of the idea as you write it on the list. In this way, the language activity is designed so that effective communication is modeled by the teacher and by more expert peers, and all students have opportunities to engage in the purposeful use of language.

Second, introduce the relationship map or chart. In our work, we have introduced the map by presenting the list of concepts generated from our content analysis and then adding the concepts the students generated from the brainstorm session. In our classes, the concepts were generated by the students and listed in both English and Spanish. In this way, students have access to both languages and can use them as a resource for understanding (Jiménez et al., 1996; Ovando, 1993; Reyes et al., 1989). This process assists students' cognitive shift into English. Using interactive discussions, we then guided the students in constructing a relationship map, encouraging them to discuss and predict the meaning of the different concepts on the list and in determining likely coordinate concepts. When introducing the chart, we have given the students copies of the chart with the superordinate concept and coordinate-level concepts, and then had the students add the concepts they generated during brainstorming. Again, initially the concepts were listed in both languages. As with the mapping procedures, we used interactive discussions to assist the students in predicting the meaning of the different concepts on the list, making predictions about the relationships among the concepts, and noting the relationships on the chart by filling in the boxes, as indicated by the key (see Figure 8.2).

Third, use the map or chart as a guide to set purposes for reading. For example, in constructing their map for "Mountain Regions Today," students were not familiar with the concept of resources. Consequently, they did not incorporate it into the map that the class generated before reading. Therefore, we set one purpose for reading as clarifying the concept of resources and determining and justifying where it might fit on the map.

Fourth, guide and encourage the students during reading to confirm or disconfirm the predictions made on the map or chart and to clarify their understanding of the key concepts.

Fifth, review the map or chart with the students and integrate what was learned from reading the text. We have found that students often make changes in the map or chart and make predictions that go beyond the text (Pressley, Brown, El-Dinary, & Afflerbach, 1995).

Sixth, demonstrate and assist the students in using the map or chart as a study tool and a guide for writing summaries of the content. Explain that students can assist each other as they review and draw conclusions from the map or chart. For example, José helped Lupita arrive at a conclusion when he asked her, "¿Porqué dice el libro que las minas, los bosques, y los ranchos nos dan recursos?" (Why does the book say that mines, forests, and ranches provide resources?).

Using interactive teaching strategies assists students in recalling the important concepts presented in a chapter. The written recall of Lupita, a fourth grade bilingual student with specific learning disabilities, demonstrates how she understood the overall structure of the chapter entitled "Mountain Regions Today" (Figure 8.4). When asking Lupita about using the relationship chart, she commented, "It helped me remember the ideas from the chapter and that mountain regions are valuable. It also helped me read the chapter because I had seen the hard words in English and Spanish. This makes it easier to learn and remember."

INTERACTIVE LEARNING STRATEGIES

Interactive learning strategies are based on the same theoretical notions and principles as interactive teaching strategies. These learning strategies are used when the goal is for students to acquire the strategies associated with learning (strategic knowledge). In this way the students learn the strategic knowledge

The things I learned was that
Mountains are valuable to us people
because they have things like,
mines, coal, fuel, forest, parks, recre
asion, and other things too. I learned
that they product lots of thing like
places to go, and they have animals
that product lots of things like
meat, wool, milk, and other thing. And
I learned that mountains are very
valueable to people. Well mountain are
made, of rocks, dirt, and water. Well
I cant think of any other thing to tell
you. Well bye.

FIGURE 8.4. Lupita's Written Recall for "Mountain Regions Today"

needed to cooperatively generate their own chart or map and use it to learn the content (Bos & Reyes, 1989, December). It is this process that assists the students in moving from guided instruction to independent learning. Teaching strategic knowledge during content learning establishes a context and purpose for learning the strategic knowledge.

The steps in the interactive learning process are similar to those in the teaching strategies, except that now the students learn to use the strategies for their learning. First, the teacher conducts a content analysis of the material for the learning strategies, and then helps the students to employ the strategies.

Conducting a Content Analysis

When using interactive learning strategies, it is important for the teacher to complete a content analysis before teaching, as explained in the previous section on interactive teaching strategies. The content analysis provides the teacher with a framework to guide the students as they explore the structure of the content, and it allows the teacher to serve as an informed mediator during students' learning.

Employing the Interactive Learning Strategies

During this phase, the students use the following steps in small groups. The relevant principles (see Table 8.1) are included for your reference.

1. *Make a brainstorm list* using what you know about the topic. (Activating prior knowledge.)

2. *Make a clue list* using what the text tells you about the topic. (Tying old knowledge to new knowledge.)

3. *Make a relationship map or relationship chart* to predict how you think the concepts are related. (Predicting meanings and relationships among concepts.)

4. *Read to confirm your understanding* and the relationships among the concepts. (Justifying meanings and relationships.)

5. *Review and revise the map or chart.* (Confirming meanings and relationships.)

6. *Use the map or chart* to study or write about what you have learned.

The students apply the principle of cooperative knowledge sharing as they carry out these steps in their groups.

Step 1: Make a Brainstorm List. First, the teacher introduces the superordinate concept using a visual medium (e.g., a film, video, or computer CD-ROM). Next, the students work in cooperative groups to develop a brainstorm list based on their prior knowledge about the topic. Students activate prior knowledge by encouraging each other to share ideas related to the superordinate concept, writing them on self-stick notes, and placing them on the brainstorm list. It is important for students to understand that all ideas are accepted for inclusion on the brainstorm list. The only criterion is that for each idea, students must talk about what made them think of the idea or how it relates to the superordinate concept.

Step 2: Make a Clue List. Next, students survey or skim the text to develop a clue list of key concepts presented in it. Students are cued to pay attention to the author's clues such as headings, subheadings, bold type, italic words, words in margins, pictures, maps, and so forth. Again, students are encouraged to write the concepts on self-stick notes, put them on the clue list, and, through discussion, justify their selections. Ideas that are found in the text and that have already been listed on the brainstorm list are simply incorporated into the clue list by moving the self-stick notes. For example, during a brainstorm discussion by a group of students on the chapter "Mountain Regions Today," one student suggested that there were mountains in China, and the concept *China* was added to the brainstorm list. As the students skimmed the text for clues while making their clue list, they found in bold type the word *Himalayas* with the ideas *China* and *Asia*. While *Himalayas* and *Asia* were added as new concepts to the clue list, the self-stick note for China was moved from the brainstorm list to the clue list. In this way the background knowledge is physically integrated with the new text information, analogous to the way in which both are used to construct meaning from text when reading. Meanings are also discussed and clarified through this selected reading.

Step 3: Make a Relationship Map or Chart. Students organize the concepts from the clue list and other ideas from the brainstorm list into a chart or map predicting the relationships among the concepts. Predictions and justifications of the relationships are encouraged through discussion. As with interactive teaching, these first three steps serve as prereading activities.

Step 4: Read to Confirm Understanding. The students read the text in small groups to confirm their understanding of the concepts and the relationships among the concepts as they check their map or chart. During these reading sessions, one student may volunteer to read the text aloud, while others may decide to read selected sections. It is important for the teacher not to impose a round-robin form of reading but instead to encourage students to help each other during the reading process. The teacher moves among the groups, observing and providing assistance when needed or requested.

Step 5: Review and Revise the Map or Chart. The students work in cooperative groups to review the map or chart, making changes based on information obtained from the text. As the students work in cooperative groups and become more adept at the use of the strategies, the teacher shifts from the role of a mediator in teaching the strategies, to that of a facilitator, with the students taking major responsibility for using the strategies and mediating their own learning. For example, as Hermán and his group worked on the unit "Great Rivers of the World," they decided that their map should be expanded to illustrate the important features of the various great rivers. Each member of the group agreed to research one of the rivers and incorporate information on the map. Figure 8.5 illustrates the group's findings as the students expanded their map. Clearly, the students in the group demonstrated the application of strategic knowledge as they assisted each other in broadening their content knowledge.

Step 6: Use the Map or Chart. The students use the map or chart as a tool for studying the content and writing essays in the same way they used the tool during interactive teaching.

The effectiveness of this model for students who are learning a second language and as a vehicle for English language development can be best demonstrated through a student's work. Hermán was a fourth grader, second language learner with learning disabilities. He had just been transitioned into English instruction. It was the beginning of the school year, and he had not participated in content area learning in English, nor had he written a story or essay in English. Although the social studies class was primarily taught in English, the teacher gave Hermán the choice to initially submit his work in Spanish. Figure 8.6 illustrates his writing skills in Spanish at that time. During the course of the semester, Hermán gradually shifted into English: "Miss, I want to say it in English, but I don't know how to write it down [in English]." In

FIGURE 8.5. Map Made by Hermán's Group for the Unit "Great Rivers of the World"

en las Montaños ay animales y Riyos
y ay muchos arboles y sacate y mucha
Matas y tamdien ay Piebras grandes
en dese en las Montañas ay
arboles grandes y én dese en
las Motañas ay lagos onde
ay Pescadus grandes

there are animals and rivers in the Mountains
and there are many trees and grass and many
Plants and also there are big Rocks
sometimes in the Mountains there are big trees
and sometimes in the Mountains there are lakes where
there are big fish

FIGURE 8.6. Hermán's Written Recall for the Chapter "Montañas Viejas y Nuevas" (Student and Typed Versions)

teaching Hermán, we encouraged him to use his group's map and to discuss what he wanted to say with a peer, then write down what he had just finished saying. "But [what] if I can't spell the words?" was his concern. We reminded him that it was more important to get his ideas down first and that he could fix his spelling later. Hermán's emerging literacy in English is demonstrated in Figure 8.7, an essay on one of the mountain regions of the world, which he wrote with the help of his group's map.

CONCLUSION

If we are to move language-minority students to conceptual learning that results in school success, then we need to design educational environments that not only model and provide opportunities for conceptual learning but also assist them in developing higher-level language and cognitive skills in English (Reyes, 1994). Interactive teaching and learning strategies, based on a model of interactive teaching and learning, provide such an environment. In our research and teaching, we have used these strategies with upper-elementary language-minority students, particularly those students who also demonstrate specific learning disabilities. We have found the strategies effective at increasing content learning and at increasing the effective use of the cognitive and metacognitive strategies associated with text comprehension and content learning (Bos & Anders, 1992b; Bos, Allen, & Scanlon, 1989; Bos & Reyes, 1989, December; Reyes, 1994). We encourage you to incorporate these strategies into your teaching routines as you build on the resources the students

The Himalayas

The Himalayas or in Asia.
an en Tha Himalayas dey
Had Tha biggst Mounton en
Tha Wolds

The animales
in the Himalayas
ders som animules
dat or cold yak
dey or ustto The
Pipul da of Nemad
sherps. Tha yak
Hav daro ledy Mit Mic
dey loc lac deyu Hav a
Musc.

ForMins
The PiPel of
cold sherpas.
deyform Pateros Rias sow Bins.

The Himalayas
The Himalayas are in Asia. And in the Himalayas they had the biggest mountain in the world.

The Animals in the Himalayas
There are some animals that are called yak. They are used to the people that are naimed sherpas. The yak have hard leather, meat, milk. They look like they have a mask.

Farming
The people are called sherpas. They farm potatoes, rice, and soy beans.

FIGURE 8.7. Hermán's Written Recall for the Chapter "Mountain Regions Today" (Student Version and Typed Version as Read by Student)

already bring to the classroom and as you provide opportunities for the students to have meaningful interactions with each other and with content while building their English language skills. Perhaps the best testimony to the effectiveness of this model was offered by Hermán, who said, "This [the learning strategy] is good. It helps me learn a lot. It helps me learn English, too."

REFERENCES

Anders, P. L., & Bos, C. S. (1986). Semantic feature analysis: An interactive strategy for vocabulary development and text comprehension. *Journal of Reading, 29,* 610–615.

Bos, C. S., Allen, A. A., & Scanlon, D. J. (1989). Vocabulary instruction and reading comprehension with bilingual learning disabled students. In S. McCormick & J. Zutell (Eds.), *Cognitive and social perspectives for literacy research and instruction* (Thirty-eighth yearbook of the National Reading Conference, pp. 173–180). Chicago: National Reading Conference.

Bos, C. S., & Anders, P. L. (1992b). Using interactive teaching and learning strategies to promote text comprehension and content learning for students with learning disabilities. *International Journal of Disability, Development, and Education, 39,* 225–238.

Bos, C. S., & Reyes, E. I. (1989, December). *Knowledge, use, and control of an interactive cognitive strategy for learning from content area texts.* Paper presented at the annual meeting of the National Reading Conference, Austin, TX.

Bos, C. S., & Reyes, E. I. (1996). Conversations with a Latina teacher about education for language-minority students with special needs. *Elementary School Journal, 96,* 343–352.

Carr, S. C., & Thompson, B. (1996). The effects of prior knowledge and schema activation strategies on the inferential reading comprehension of children with and without learning disabilities. *Learning Disabilities Quarterly, 9,* 48–61.

Chamot, A. U., & O'Malley, J. M. (1996). The cognitive academic language learning approach: A model for linguistically diverse classrooms. *Elementary School Journal, 96,* 259–274.

Collier, V. P. (1995, Fall). Acquiring a second language for school. *Directions in Language and Education, 1*(4).

Cummins, J. (1994). The acquisition of English as a second language. In K. Spagenbert-Urbschat & R. Pritchard (Eds.), *Kids come in all languages: Reading instruction for ESL students* (pp. 36–62). Newark, DE: International Reading Association.

Diaz, S., Moll, L. C., & Mehan, H. (1986). Sociocultural resources in instruction: A context-specific approach. In California State Department of Education (Ed.), *Beyond language: Social and cultural factors in schooling language minority students* (pp. 187–230). Los Angeles: California State University, Evaluation, Dissemination, and Assessment Center. (ERIC Document Reproduction Service No. ED 304 241).

Diaz, R. M., Neal, C. J., & Anaya-Williams, M. (1990). The social origins of self-regulations. In L. C. Moll (Ed.), *Vygotsky and education: Instructional implications and applications of sociohistorical psychology* (pp. 127–154). New York: Cambridge University Press.

Duran, B. J., Dugan, T., & Weffer, R. E. (1996, February). *Increasing teacher effectiveness with language minority students.* Paper presented at the conference of the American Association of Colleges for Teacher Education, Chicago.

Farnan, N., Flood, J., & Lapp, D. (1994). Comprehending through reading and writing: Six research-based instructional strategies. In K. Spagenbert-Urbschat & R. Pritchard (Eds.), *Kids come in all languages: Reading instruction for ESL students* (pp. 135–157). Newark, DE: International Reading Association.

Gersten, R. (1996). The language-minority student in transition: Contemporary instructional research. *Elementary School Journal, 96,* 217–220.

Hudson, P., Lignugaris-Kraft, & Miller, T. (1993). Using content enhancements to improve the performance of adolescents with learning disabilities in content classes. *Learning Disabilities Research & Practice, 8,* 106–126.

Jiménez, R. T., García, G. E., & Pearson, P. D. (1996). The reading strategies of bilingual Latina/o students who are successful English readers: Opportunities and obstacles. *Reading Research Quarterly, 31,* 90–112.

Johnson, D.,D., & Pearson, P. D. (1984). *Teaching reading vocabulary* (2nd ed.). New York: Holt, Rinehart & Winston.

Krashen, S. D. (1982). *Principles and practices in second language acquisition.* Oxford, England: Pergamon.

Moll, L. C., & Diaz, S. (1987). Change as the goal of educational research. *Anthropology and Education Quarterly, 18,* 300–311.

Ovando, C. J., (1993). Language diversity and education. In T. A. Bank & C. A. McGee Banks (Eds.), *Multicultural education: Issues and perspectives* (2nd ed., pp. 215–236). Boston: Allyn & Bacon.

Pearson, P. D., & Johnson, D. D. (1978). *Teaching reading comprehension.* New York: Holt, Rinehart & Winston.

Pressley, M., Brown, R., El-Dinary, P. B., & Afflerbach, P. (1995). The comprehension instruction that students need: Instruction fostering constructively responsive reading. *Learning Disabilities Research and Practice, 10,* 215–224.

Reyes, E. I. (1994). *Classroom discourse communicative competency of bilingual students with learning disabilities during content learning in three learning environments.* Unpublished doctoral dissertation, University of Arizona, Tucson.

Reyes, E. I., Duran, G. Z., & Bos, C. S. (1989). Language as a resource for mediating comprehension. In S. McCormick & J. Zutell (Eds.), *Cognitive and social perspectives for literacy research and instruction* (Thirty-eighth yearbook of the National Reading Conference, pp. 253–260). Chicago: National Reading Conference.

Reyes, M. L., & Molner, L. A. (1991). Instructional strategies for second language learners in the content areas. *Journal of Reading, 35,* 96–103.

Richard-Amato, P. A. (1996). *Making it happen: Interaction in the second language classroom, from theory to practice.* New York: Longman.

Scanlon, D. J., Duran, G. Z., Reyes, E. I., & Gallego, M. A. (1992). Interactive semantic mapping: An interactive approach to enhancing LD students' content area comprehension. *Learning Disabilities Research and Practice, 7,* 142–146.

Tikunoff, W. J. (1987). Mediation of instruction to obtain quality effectiveness. In S. H. Fradd & W. J. Tikunoff (Eds.), *Bilingual education and bilingual special education* (pp. 99–132). Boston: College Hill Press.

Voltz, D. L. (1995). Learning and cultural diversity in general and special education classes: Frameworks for success. *Multiple Voices for Ethnically Diverse Exceptional Learners, 1,* 1–13.

Vygotsky, L. S. (1978). *Mind in society.* Cambridge, MA: Harvard University Press.

PART III

Middle and High
School Grades

9

Literature-Based Cognitive Strategy Instruction for Middle School Latino Students

Robert T. Jiménez
Arturo Gámez
University of Illinois at Urbana-Champaign

In a provocative statement, Donaldo Macedo (1994) challenges teachers and others involved in the education of students from culturally and linguistically diverse communities:

> I am increasingly convinced that the U.S. educational system is not a failure. The failure that it generates represents its ultimate victory to the extent that large groups of people, including the so-called minorities, were never intended to be educated. (p. 36)

Macedo's challenge is not easy to dismiss, especially when one examines the literacy learning and educational opportunities available to Latino students. The U.S. Census reports that during the last decade, there has been a 30% increase in the number of persons who identify themselves as Latino, but the number of Latino teachers in the United States is less than 3% (de la Rosa, Maw, & Yzaguirre, 1990). Waggoner (1991) points out that approximately 35% of all Latino students discontinue their education before completing high school and that these dismal dropout rates are much higher in urban areas. In spite of the tremendous need for high-quality instructional programs for students from culturally and linguistically diverse backgrounds, only about 15% of the close to 10 million such students actually have access to English for speakers of other languages classes or bilingual education (National Education Association, 1990; Waggoner, 1994).

Without a doubt, much more could be done to improve the literacy learning of Latino students. Yet, even if a national commitment to such an endeavor were to emerge right now, it is not clear that concrete, practical information is available to teachers and others who see these students on a daily basis (Goldenberg, 1996).

The problem of an impoverished research and literature base is exacerbated for those who work with middle school students, because of the assumption that students at this level have already received necessary literacy instruction (García et al, 1995). This chapter reports one effort to learn about and improve the literacy instruction provided to Latino students.

We visited a middle school over a period of one school year during which we observed students and teachers, interviewed them, and taught the students for approximately two weeks. Information reported in this chapter is derived primarily from the two-week period that we worked directly with the students. The instruction we designed and delivered was characterized by the use of culturally relevant and familiar texts, a focus on comprehension, and the provision of opportunities to build reading fluency.

THE SCHOOL AND THE STUDENTS

To accomplish our task, we asked the bilingual program director of a large midwestern urban school district if we could work collaboratively with one or two teachers of Latino students. We explained that we were most interested in students who were experiencing difficulties with literacy learning. The bilingual program director introduced us to the principal of Swanson Middle School.[1] The principal invited us to observe seventh grade students in Ms. Holden's self-contained special education classroom. In the fall of 1994, the enrollment at Swanson Middle School consisted of 819 students, 407 of whom were Latino.

There were approximately 14 students in Ms. Holden's classroom, all of whom were Latino. The teaching assistant, Ms. Ramirez, who helped Ms. Holden was bilingual and occasionally spoke to the students in Spanish. We asked Ms. Holden if she could identify from three to five of her students who she believed were experiencing the most problems with reading and writing. She told us that all of her students performed at low levels in English language literacy, but she gave us the names of Adán, Sara, and Victor.

All three of these students had grown up in the United States. They had completed all of their schooling in the United States and spoke English fluently, according to their teacher and her teaching assistant. Yet, although these students were enrolled in grade 7, they were reading at about a third grade level in English, as determined by teacher judgment and standardized test scores. These students were not currently receiving any formal instruction in Spanish except for occasional comments made to them by the teaching assis-

---

[1] All names used are pseudonyms.

tant. All available test scores for each of the three students are included in the sections that follow.

Adán

Adán scored 77 out of a possible 223 on the Total Reading Battery for the Metropolitan Achievement Test (MAT), a group-administered English language test. Adán completed the test in February of 1994, which was approximately 7 months before this study began. He received a grade-equivalent score of 3.2 in English language reading. Adán was also tested individually by a bilingual psychologist using the Woodcock Spanish Psychoeducational Battery in September of 1995, about 4 months after data were collected for this study. He scored a grade-equivalent score of 4.6 on the Reading Achievement Cluster on this Spanish language test.

Adán's language abilities in Spanish and English were tested using the Receptive and Expressive One-Word Picture Vocabulary Tests (ROWPVT, EOWPVT-R). He scored a language age of 7 years 8 months (7-8) on the English version of ROWPVT, while in Spanish his score was considerably higher at 11-2. His English expressive vocabulary was estimated at 8-2, and his Spanish expressive vocabulary at 8-0. Adán's language proficiency scores exhibited depressed and uneven language development, a not uncommon occurrence for a language-minority student with a learning disability.

Adán began school in a bilingual general education preschool classroom and moved into a bilingual kindergarten class. After kindergarten, he was referred to what the district called a bilingual developmental first grade classroom. Children referred to these classrooms are considered to be at risk for referral to special education. Adán then completed first grade in a bilingual classroom, and he was referred for a psychological evaluation while in second grade. He began to receive special education services toward the end of grade 2 (March 1990). The psychologist determined that Adán suffered from significant weaknesses in oral language ability. English language reading was singled out as an area where Adán's performance was borderline. He has remained in a self-contained bilingual special education classroom ever since.

Sara

Sara's teacher stated that Sara had a very difficult time with reading. Sara herself described reading as her least-favorite subject. Sara's Total Reading Battery score on the Metropolitan Achievement Test was 67 out of a possible 223. Her grade-equivalent score was 3.0 (test date: February 1994). Sara also completed the Woodcock Achievement Battery in Spanish and scored a grade equivalent of 2.4 on the Reading Achievement Cluster (test date: May 1994). The psychologist who administered this test concluded that Sara was four years below current grade placement.

Sara received a receptive English language age score of 10-2 and an expressive English language age score of 9-6. Her receptive Spanish language age was 11-8, and her expressive Spanish language age was 6-6 (test date: May 1994). In other words, Sara's oral English and English language comprehension skills were a bit lower than would be expected for a student her age. Sara's Spanish language proficiency was stronger in the area of listening comprehension than in speaking—again, a not uncommon phenomenon for students from language-minority communities in the United States.

Sara began school in an all-English, general education kindergarten class. Like Adán, after kindergarten she was referred to what the district called a bilingual developmental first grade classroom. In fact, she was referred for a full evaluation while in this setting. Placement in special education was not recommended at that time. Sara continued in general bilingual classrooms during grades 2 and 3, at which time she was referred for another evaluation. She was diagnosed as having a reading and writing learning disability while in grade 3, and she was placed in a self-contained bilingual special education classroom the following year, during grade 4. She remained in a self-contained bilingual special education classroom from grade 4 until the completion of this study.

Victor

Victor's reading test scores were at about the same level as those of the other two students. He received a score of 69 out of a possible 223 on the Total Reading Battery of the Metropolitan Achievement Test. His grade-equivalent score in English reading was 3.1 (test date: February 1994). Victor's parents did not respond to requests for release of his special education evaluation records. It was, therefore, not possible to report his test scores of expressive and receptive Spanish and English language abilities, nor was it possible to report his Spanish language reading test scores.

Victor began school in a bilingual kindergarten. His teacher recommended that he repeat kindergarten, which he did in another bilingual kindergarten. He was referred for testing for possible placement in a special education classroom during his second year in kindergarten. He was then placed in a bilingual special education classroom for first grade, and he remained in a comparable setting during grades 2–6, until the time of this study.

OUR APPROACH

We visited Swanson Middle School over a period of one full school year. We visited on nine different occasions for a total of 17 school days. During our last visit, we were at the school for 8 days (Tuesday through Friday of each week).

On four separate occasions, we observed the three students in their classroom, during which time we targeted language arts activities. We observed the students for at least one hour during each visit. The activities included reading, writing, and an English language grammar exercise. We took extensive field notes during these observations; during three of the four visits, two observers took notes jointly. These observations spanned a period of three months.

We then met with the three students as a group. During that meeting, we showed the students five or six trade books and asked them to choose one. We asked them to read a short portion of their book silently. Next, we demonstrated the think-aloud procedure for them, and we asked them to try it as well. The think-aloud procedure is described in more depth on pages 158–160.

During later meetings, we interviewed each of the three students individually. We asked the students about their language-learning histories, their language preferences, and their school experiences. Prior to the interview, we had asked the students to select a text, either a book or a magazine from their classroom, that they felt comfortable reading. We then asked them to read the text a line at a time and to tell us what they thought about as they read (G. E. García, personal communication, January 10, 1995). We used this information, along with our observations, to begin to get a sense of the students as readers. We taped and later transcribed all of our interviews with the students. Our analysis of this information revealed that the students' word recognition and oral reading fluency were rudimentary (second or third grade level), and their knowledge and implementation of strategic reading processes was very limited.

After we completed the observations, interviews, and initial think-alouds, we arranged to spend eight school days at Swanson Middle School so that we could meet with the students for one full period a day during that time. This chapter focuses primarily on the instruction and interaction with the students that occurred during these eight days. We taped and transcribed all of our interactions with the students for later analysis.

DEVELOPING RAPPORT
WITH THE STUDENTS

Because we purposely chose to work with three students who did not have a history of success with literacy, we knew we would have to devote attention to winning their confidence and gaining their trust. This task, it turned out, was more difficult than we originally thought it would be (Bos & Vaughn, 1988). The students were not initially enthusiastic about the project. At our first group meeting, for example, I (the first author) informed the students that their involvement was voluntary and that it was their choice whether or not to participate. All of the students immediately stood up and asked to return to their classroom. I told them that it was their decision to make, but I asked them to first listen to what we had in mind. Fortunately for us, after hearing more about the project, they decided to continue.

We decided to begin by simply engaging the students in conversation. We asked about their families—brothers and sisters, moms and dads—we asked about their favorite foods, about special holidays and the menus for such events.

We then put four objects on the table. These were corn flour (*masa harina*), two ears of corn, and a package of tortillas. We purposely chose items that we were certain the students would recognize. We chose things that we knew were culturally familiar, and that we knew were mentioned or discussed in the texts that we planned to present to the students later. Because both of

Corn is found in a rancho. There are millions of them on the rancho. You have to help corn grow by giving it water. Once it grows you must clean it, wash it, cut it, and then take it to the store. Corn can be used to make masa. Masa is then used to make tortillas and tamales. Tamales are made on special days. Tamales are made during Christmas, birthdays, and 5 de Mayo. Many family members help make tamales, like moms, sisters, aunts, grandmothers, and cousins.

We did tamales de chile, dulce, carne de chivo, carne de marrano y a veces hacemos gorditas, tortillas, arroz y frijoles. Los elotes los siembran y les echan agua y despues los echaban a las tiendas para venderlos. El último día que mi familia hizo tamales fue el viernes que acaba de pasar. Mi prima le ayuda y también mi tía. Estas comidas se hacen cuando festejamos algún día especial como el día de las madres y los cumpleaños.

FIGURE 9.1. Student-Produced Language Experience Text

us (authors) were raised within close proximity to Swanson, we were familiar with the broader Latino community and its customs.

Our main concern during this phase of the work was to ensure that students would be able to engage in conversation. We wanted to be able to encourage, support, and gently push students to produce extended discourse. We were only moderately successful in eliciting quantities of student-produced language. Figure 9.1 displays the written text that was produced as a result of the students' conversation with us. In essence, we used the language-experience approach (Allen, 1968; Tierney, Readence, & Dishner, 1990). We typed the students' language into a computer and provided each of them with a printed copy, which we then used as the basis for teaching students the think-aloud procedure.

THE THINK-ALOUD PROCEDURE

We demonstrated the think-aloud procedure for the students, and we provided them with multiple opportunities to try the technique on their own (Ericsson & Simon, 1984; Wade, 1990). The think-aloud procedure consists of presenting a text to a participant, asking the participant to read each line of the text silently, and, finally, asking the participant to describe and explain in as much detail as possible what she or he is thinking about during and after each line of text has been read. My choice of language, as researcher, was predominantly Spanish. I chose Spanish to develop rapport with the students. The students, however, were encouraged to use whatever language they were most comfortable using.

We spent two days (two class periods) working with students on this technique The following is an example of how we modeled the procedure (R1 = first author, R2 = second author, and the other letters represent the names of students):

Text: Estas comidas se hacen cuando festejamos algún día especial como el día de las madres y los cumpleaños. [These dishes are prepared when we celebrate some special day, like Mother's Day or a birthday.]

R2: Esta frase me hace pensar en los días festivos como los cumpleaños y día de las madres. En estos días nuestra familia acostumbra reunirse y estar juntos. Especialmente en los cumpleaños siempre celebramos los cumpleaños de mi mamá, mi papá y mis hermanos. Y hacemos comida. Casi siempre mi mamá y mis hermanas son las que cocinan, hacen comidas como tamales, pozole, menudo, comidas típicas. También el día de las madres le hacemos una comida a mi mamá o celebramos el día de las madres y nos reunimos. Toda la familia se reune. Es lo que me hace pensar esta frase. [This sentence makes me think about holidays, like birthdays or Mother's Day. On those days it is our family custom to get together. This is especially true of birthdays; we always celebrate my mother's birthday, and my father's, and my brothers' and sisters'. And we make food. It is almost always my mother and my brothers who cook, who make food like tamales, pozole, menudo, typical foods. Also, on Mother's Day, we make a meal for my mother, or we celebrate Mother's Day and we get together. All of the family gets together. That is what this sentence makes me think about.]

The students initially had problems implementing the procedure, as the following examples drawn from Sara's transcripts testify. These examples also illustrate that by creating a text that reflected recognizable and culturally familiar information, we could persist in asking that students participate in the dialogue. The transcripts also bear witness that this is not easy work; it definitely requires persistence and ample amounts of time. Although our early comments may appear somewhat harsh when they are separated from their total communicative context, we were determined to do everything possible to actively engage these students in literacy learning. As indicated in the final example, our efforts appeared to pay off.

R1: What does it make you think about Sara?

S: Nothing.

R1: Well, think a little harder.

R1: Habla, habla, habla. Eres muy inteligente Sara, y lo puedes hacer. [Talk, talk, talk. You are very intelligent, Sara, and you can do it.]

S: I don't know about any.

R1: Te voy a seguir molestando hasta que me hables. [I'm going to keep bothering you until you talk to me.]

S: OK, I think of music and there are people sitting around and they are eating. And that's it.

R1: That's it. You did it, that's cool! You know how to do it! Thank you. Can you do that next time?

S: I'll try.

We found that use of both Spanish and English during this time was extremely helpful. We believed that by using both languages, we could provide opportunities for students to make use of their full linguistic repertoire. Of special interest to us was that the students seemed to appreciate the opportunity to use Spanish, and that its use may have improved rapport and student participation. In addition, we believed that by using both languages, we were able to encourage students to discuss their previous experiences. The following are some examples of how students used both languages:

R1: ¿Qué te pasó en Navidad? [What happened to you at Christmas?]

S: Comí tamales y different kinds of food. [I ate tamales and different kinds of food.]

V: Unos estan creciendo. Hay morados, allá where I live. Hay unos "woods" you go walking a lot y hay bien hartos elotes. You can grab thousands of them. [Some are growing. There are purple ones, over there where I live. There are some woods. You can go walking a lot and there are lots and lots of ears of corn.]

R1: What's leather?

S: It's like . . .

A: Como piel de animal. [Like animal skin.]

USE OF CULTURALLY RELEVANT TEXT
AND DEMONSTRATION OF
SELECTED READING STRATEGIES

After we finished our initial efforts to demonstrate the think-aloud procedure, we introduced the students to trade books that contained what we considered culturally relevant text (Au, 1993; Harris, 1993). As much as possible, we tried to provide students with text that was also culturally recognizable—that is, mention was made of events or information that was within their experience. We put together a thematic strand of literature that we selected to build on and take advantage of the initial work we did in building the students' prior knowledge and making connections with their community experience. We used three books for this purpose: *A Quetzalcóatl Tale of Corn* (Parke & Panik, 1992), *The Day It Snowed Tortillas* (Hayes, 1985), and *Aztec, Inca & Maya* (Baquedano, 1993). All three of these books included stories or expository text that involved corn, corn flour, tortillas, and many other food items commonly used in Mexican cuisine.

We emphasized three cognitive and metacognitive strategies during the reading of all three texts. These were (a) *approaching unknown vocabulary,* which included using context, looking for cognate relationships, and making sure students could approximate pronunciations of words; (b) *asking questions,* which was often accompanied by overt comprehension monitoring; and (c) *making inferences,* which involved the integration of their prior knowledge with information found in print. These strategies have been identified and shown to be present in the think-aloud protocols of successful bilingual Latino readers of English (Jiménez, García, & Pearson, 1995, 1996). One example of our approach to presenting and teaching each of these strategies follows:

Approaching Unknown Vocabulary

R1: You know that word in Spanish, so we can use a Spanish clue to help us figure out what it means. Victor, what does *espectacular* mean?

V: That it's useful?

R1: It's something very . . .

S: Special?

R1: Special, you got it! I like this. So [for] something very special, you can say wonderful, maravilloso. The Spanish clue helped us with *spectacular* because that is exactly the same in English and Spanish. Have you guys heard that word on the radio, *spectacular*? [The researcher writes this on the blackboard.] That's English, and here's Spanish, *espectacular*. The only difference between English and Spanish is that we put an *e* in the front in Spanish. That's exactly the same word. It almost sounds exactly the same, only a little bit different. But when you guys can do this, you're taking advantage of your bilingualism and you're using what you already know to help you understand. OK? I think it's really cool when Latino kids do that. That makes a lot of sense to me.

Asking Questions

S: Quetzalcóatl wanted very much to help the people that he loved.

R1: OK. What's your question now? What kind of question would you ask yourself? He wants very much to help the people that he loves, so you wonder, well . . .

S: Is it gonna happen or not?

Making Inferences

S: "The people of the Earth will starve unless they get food," said Quetzalcóatl.

R1: What does that mean, "The people of the Earth will starve"?

S: I don't know. Well, they don't have any food. They will starve.

R1: Starve means what?

S: They don't have food. They don't eat food.

R1: What happens if you don't eat?

S: You die.

R1: Exactly. So that's what it makes you think about. See, you're using what you know. You're integrating it with what you're reading here. You know that if people don't eat, they're going to die. They will starve. That's making an *inference*, OK? Putting together what you know with what you read.

BUILDING READING FLUENCY

Our classroom observations and individual student interviews revealed that all three students were experiencing major difficulties with word recognition and reading fluency. As a result, we decided to work with the students on these abilities, with the goal of helping them achieve what Samuels (1988) calls automaticity.

It was our belief that this work needed to be embedded within an overall context of meaningful, culturally relevant text, student-generated discourse, and instruction designed to promote comprehension. We always asked students to first read text silently. We then, on occasion, asked individual students to read orally. We viewed the building of reading fluency as one means of helping students more carefully monitor their reading comprehension.

We did not continually interrupt students' oral reading every time they had difficulty pronouncing a word. Instead, we waited until they stopped because they were unable to pronounce a word, or until they got to the end of a sentence. If students demonstrated difficulty with word recognition or overall fluency in reading (i.e., overly slow or choppy reading with meaning-altering miscues), then we asked them to orally reread specific phrases. At times, we asked them to do this two to three times. We took care not to embarrass students, by occasionally asking the other students present to read chorally with the group. The purpose of rereading was focused squarely on the larger goal of comprehension. Whenever students were asked to reread any portion of the text, we made sure that they then reread silently the problematic section within its larger context.

We explicitly emphasized that reading fluency was a means to comprehension, not an end in itself. We explained to the students that a consequence of poor reading fluency is an inability to understand. By the seventh and eighth day, we noticed that students appeared to be experiencing fewer problems with word recognition. The following is an example produced on the third day of working with the students:

V: The people began the children cried and Quetzalcóatl and those who had been . . . ? [Text: "The people begged, the children cried, and Quetzalcóatl, the feathered serpent, heard their sadness."]

R1: OK, read it again a little bit faster.

V: The people began, the children cried, and Quetzalcóatl, the feathered serpent heard their sentence.

R1: OK, read it again.

V: The people began, the children . . . [student pauses]

R1: Does that make sense, "The people began"?

V: No.

R1: What's that word? The people what?

S: *Begun.*

R1: Look at it [carefully].

S: *Began.*

R1: Is that *began*?

S: No.

V: *Begged.*

R1: You got it, what is the meaning of *begged*?

V: They were begging for something. The people begged, the children cried, and Quetzalcóatl, the feathered serpent, heard their sadness.

PROMISING RESULTS

By the end of our time working with the students, we began to notice some encouraging changes in their statements about reading. Sara made a statement that appeared to reflect added confidence in her ability to read and in her desire to read. Statements made by all three students also reflected increased metacognitive knowledge about themselves as readers and about useful strategies for increasing comprehension of text (Baker & Brown, 1984). These statements occurred during the last two days of our involvement with them:

R1: Yesterday, Sara was telling me what she used to think about reading.

S: I didn't like it.

R1: What was it that you didn't like?

S: [It was] hard.

R1: Hard. It was very hard for you to read, OK. How about now?

S: I kind of like it.

R1: How come?

S: Because it makes a little more sense, sort of. And I can read better.

We found that encouraging students to reflect on the activity of reading was also an excellent opportunity to review important information concerning cognitive and metacognitive reading strategies. The following two examples indicate that these three students began to discuss reading in ways similar to more experienced or successful readers (Jiménez et al, 1995; 1996). We found their statements very encouraging:

R1: What do you think you need to do to become a really good reader?

A: Read a lot.

R1: Yeah, read a lot.

R1: What else do you have to do when you're reading?

S: Picture things in your head.

R1: Yeah, you have to picture things in your head and what else?

S: Try and look for clues for words you don't know.

R1: Look for clues.

S: Try the words out in Spanish.

R1: Try it in Spanish, yeah. That's really smart. What else Victor, what do you do to become a good reader? These are good answers because the first time I talked to you guys . . .

V: Imagine it and ask yourself questions.

R1: How about you Victor? What's the difference between someone who is a good reader and someone who isn't? What do good readers do?

V: [They make] pictures in their head.

S: They ask questions.

R1: They ask questions, they make pictures in their head, and they do what?

V: Mix what we know . . .

R1: Mix what they know with what they're reading about. Mix it together and they understand.

CONCLUSION

Based on our experience, we believe that an emphasis on comprehension, use of culturally relevant texts, and instruction in—and practice of—reading fluency has strong potential for promoting and fostering the reading abilities of Latino students who are performing at low levels of literacy in the middle school grades.

Our earlier classroom observations and individual student interviews provided evidence that for all intents and purposes, the students we worked with were reading and comprehending at quite rudimentary levels. Toward the end of this project, there were indications of changes in their motivation to read and in their ability to verbalize important information about reading strategies. We believe that this preliminary work provides encouragement for those working with Latino students who are performing at low levels of literacy. These students are too often viewed simply as at risk for school failure when, in fact, they may possess large, untapped potential for success in literacy.

We also strove to provide concrete examples of where to start and what to do with middle school students who are experiencing these kinds of problems. Instruction—defined broadly as interaction with and among students, information that is provided in the form of demonstrations, and focused attention on and practice of specific strategies and other literate behaviors—still appears to be a crucial element necessary for the academic success of Latino students (Reyes, 1992).

For us, the most exciting aspect of this work was that these students were willing and eager to work hard and to participate in activities designed to improve their reading comprehension. Instruction, however, had to make sense to them. Macedo's (1994) challenge to provide Latino students with a worthwhile education may, at least in part, be met by literacy instruction that emphasizes culturally relevant, quality literature and that focuses heavily on comprehension-enhancing strategies.

REFERENCES

Allen, R. V. (1968). How a language experience program works. In E. C. Vilscek (Ed.), *A decade of innovations: Approaches to beginning reading.* Newark, DE: International Reading Association.

Au, K. H. (1993). *Literacy instruction in multicultural settings.* Fort Worth, TX: Harcourt Brace Jovanovich.

Baker, L., & Brown, A. L. (1984). Metacognitive skills and reading. In P. D. Pearson (Ed.), *Handbook of reading research* (pp. 353–394). New York: Longman.

Bos, C. S., & Vaughn, S. (1988). *Strategies for teaching students with learning and behavioral problems.* Needham Heights, MA: Allyn and Bacon.

de la Rosa, D., Maw, C. E., & Yzaguirre, R. (1990). *Hispanic education: A statistical portrait, 1990.* Washington, DC: Policy Analysis Center, Office of Research, Advocacy, and Legislation, National Council of La Raza.

Ericsson, K. A., & Simon, H. A. (1984). *Protocol analysis: Verbal reports as data.* Cambridge, MA: MIT Press.

García, G. E., Stephens, D. L., Koenke, K. R., Harris, V. J., Pearson, P. D., Jiménez, R. T., & Janisch, C. (1995). *Reading instruction and educational opportunity at the middle school level.* (Tech. Rep. 622). Urbana-Champaign, IL: University of Illinois, Center for the Study of Reading.

Goldenberg, C. (1996). The education of language minority children: Where are we and where do we need to go? *The Elementary School Journal.*

Harris, V. J. (1993). *Teaching multicultural literature.* Norwood, MA: Cristopher-Gordon.

Jiménez, R. T., García, G. E., & Pearson, P. D. (1995). Three children, two languages, and strategic reading: Case studies in bilingual/monolingual reading. *American Educational Research Journal, 32*(1), 31–61.

Jiménez, R. T., García, G. E., & Pearson, P. D. (1996). The reading strategies of Latina/o students who are successful English readers: Opportunities and obstacles. *Reading Research Quarterly, 31*(1), 90–112.

Macedo, D. (1994). *Literacies of power.* Boulder, CO: Westview.

National Education Association, (1990). *Federal education funding: The cost of excellence.* Washington, DC: National Education Association.

Reyes, M. de la Luz (1992). Challenging venerable assumptions: Literacy instruction for linguistically different students. *Harvard Educational Review, 62*(4), 427–446.

Samuels, S. J. (1988). Decoding and automaticity: Helping poor readers become automatic at word recognition. *The Reading Teacher, 41*(8), 756–760.

Tierney, R. J., Readence, J. E., & Dishner, E. K. (1990). *Reading strategies and practices* (3rd ed.). Boston: Allyn and Bacon.

Wade, S. E. (1990). Using think alouds to assess comprehension. *The Reading Teacher, 43*(7), 442–453.

Waggoner, D. (1991). *Undereducation in America: The demography of high school dropouts.* New York: Auburn House.

Waggoner, D. (1994). Language-minority school-age population now totals 9.9 million. *NABE News, 18*(1), 1, 24–26.

CHILDREN'S BOOKS

Baquedano, E. (1993). *Aztec, Inca & Maya.* New York: Alfred A. Knopf.

Hayes, J. (1985). *The day it snowed tortillas: Tales from Spanish New Mexico.* Santa Fe, NM: Mariposa.

Parke, M., & Panik, S. (1992). A Quetzalcóatl tale of corn. Carthage, IL: Fearon Teacher Aids, Simon & Schuster Supplementary Education Group.

ACKNOWLEDGMENTS

The authors would like to thank the teachers, children, principal, and bilingual program director of Swanson Middle School for their help, support, and encouragement during this project. We would also like to thank Georgia Earnest García, Daniel Thompson, and Richard C. Anderson for helpful comments on earlier drafts of this chapter. This work was supported in part by a grant from the Division of Innovation and Development, Office of Special Education Programs, U.S. Department of Education, No. H023A40035. An earlier version of this chapter appeared in "Literature-Based Cognitive Strategy Instruction for Middle School Latina/o Students" by R. T. Jiménez and A. Gámez, 1996, *Journal of Adolescent and Adult Literacy, 40*(2), pp. 84–91. Copyright by the International Reading Association. All rights reserved.

10

Instructional Strategies and Techniques for Middle School Students Who Are Learning English

Anne Graves
San Diego State University

G arcia (1993a) projects that by the year 2030 approximately 70% of the students in California will speak a language other than English as their primary language. In one local middle school in San Diego, as many as 52 languages are spoken, including many African and Asian languages. Teachers all over the nation, at some point, will encounter students who are learning English as a second or third language (Fitzgerald, 1995). Reports indicate that many students who are learning English as a second language are at risk for school failure and at risk for dropping out. In some urban areas, as many as 50% of students drop out before high school (see Rumberger, 1995). Rumberger (1995) has found some evidence, however, that school climate and students' academic success in school can help lower the number of dropouts in middle school. Because those at risk for failure in middle school are typically those at risk for dropping out, the preparation of teachers for the linguistic diversity they face is critically important (Baca & Cervantes, 1989; Banks, 1991; Gay, 1993; Gersten, Jiménez, & Brengelman, 1994).

Specifically, students who reach middle school without the ability to listen, read, write, interpret, and study with proficiency in English are likely to encounter extraordinary challenges (Garcia, 1993b). Middle school teachers often find students who need a wide range of academic skill development as well as content knowledge and English language development (ELD). The following represent four of the types of students I have observed in middle school here in Southern California:

- *Student 1.* Huong is a sixth grader who speaks mostly Vietnamese and very little English. She lives in a large Vietnamese community. She has been in English-only classes since she came to the United States four years ago but has learned almost no English. Her family members do not speak English and do not read or write. At times, Huong is sullen and withdrawn.

- *Student 2.* Socorro is an eighth grader who was born in Mexico. She moved to Southern California in the fourth grade. She was a good student in Mexico and learned to read and write quite well in Spanish. When beginning her time in school in the United States, she was placed in English-only classrooms. In her classes she understands English and can complete most assignments; however, her grades have remained around the C level, and she often appears to misunderstand key vocabulary and key reading comprehension and writing tasks.

- *Student 3.* Pon is a sixth grader in a very diverse middle school. His first language was Khmer (Cambodian). He is a nonreader in English and struggles with even the simplest words. His spoken English is quite limited when he interacts with students and the teacher in class. He has behavior problems in school. He often defies his teachers and engages in antisocial behaviors (fighting, stealing, etc.).

- *Student 4.* Pablo is a seventh grader who sits quietly in social studies class, as if he understands everything. He reads English and comprehends at about a fourth grade level, but he speaks with a heavy accent. His spelling is extremely poor, with errors similar to patterns he uses when speaking English. He has difficulty using recognizable structures in his sentences or in his paragraphs. Spanish was his first language, and he was taught in bilingual classes until the third grade. His transition to English has been weakest in writing.

These students have various content area, academic, and ELD issues that often present dilemmas for middle school teachers. All of these issues require what has been referred to as language-sensitive instruction. Language-sensitive instruction includes a simultaneous focus on developing (a) English language, (b) content area knowledge, and (c) academic proficiency (Echevarria & Graves, 1997). This chapter includes the findings of research on and observations of language-sensitive instruction in science, social studies, math, and English. The organizational framework for this chapter is as follows: (a) provision of explicit structures, frameworks, scaffolds, and strategies; (b) techniques to improve comprehension and transfer; (c) mediation and feedback; and (d) respect for and responsiveness to diversity. Each section contains specific descriptions of lessons and classrooms.

PROVISION OF EXPLICIT
STRUCTURES, FRAMEWORKS,
SCAFFOLDS, AND STRATEGIES

While the teacher provides comprehensible and meaningful content, students may also benefit from explicit structures for improving academic proficiency and English language (Gaffney & Anderson, 1991). One such explicit structure is ensuring adequate background knowledge in each unit or chapter in the book by planning activities that both trigger existing knowledge and build new knowledge (Cummins, 1989; Krashen, 1985). Another such explicit framework includes both the identification of academic and language challenges and the design of explicit instruction to address those challenges (Figueroa, 1989). To accomplish this, a content area teacher may develop a long-term plan to teach various skills and strategies over time. For part of the instructional time, a teacher may include explicit instruction on key vocabulary and academic strategies (Chamot & O'Malley, 1994; Saville-Troike, 1984; Short, 1994). Much emphasis has also been placed on the importance of vocabulary building as part of the instruction in content areas (Jiménez, Garcia, & Pearson, 1995; Short, 1993), as well as explicit strategy instruction for improving academic proficiency (Chamot & O'Malley, 1994). Vocabulary instruction will be discussed in the comprehension and transfer section of this chapter. Explicit strategy instruction in reading and explicit strategy instruction in writing will be discussed later in this section.

Adequate Background Knowledge

Considerable convergence of theories and research from many different perspectives in the field of education indicates that teachers are likely to facilitate learning if they use the relevant experiences of their learners during instruction (Allen, 1989; Lim & Watson, 1993; Moll, 1988; Palincsar, 1986; Vygotsky, 1978). Most models of instruction advise that relevance be established near the beginning as well as throughout the lesson (Cloud, 1993; Faltis & Hudelson, 1994). Using connections and associations from the lives of students serves the dual purpose of bringing the learners consciously and actively to the task at hand and validating their own life experiences (King, 1990; Franklin & Thompson, 1994). This is likely to lower anxiety and promote motivation (Cadzen, 1992; Faltis & Arias, 1993). It is also likely to maximize the amount students learn, by helping them hook new knowledge to already existing knowledge.

For example, Henderson and Landesman (1992), in their study of mathematics and middle school students of Mexican descent, found marked improvement in student performance when they were involved in elaborate self-generated projects in which groups of students formed construction companies. The construction companies were named by the students, roles within the groups were assigned by the students, and goods were purchased by

Phase 1:

Brainstorm with whole group

Phase 2:

Provide direct experiences,
read sources, watch videos, and provide
information-gathering opportunities

Phase 3:

Provide a forum for using background knowledge
and for adding knowledge gained

FIGURE 10.1. Phases for Providing Adequate Background Knowledge

students from a "school warehouse." Each company was allotted $1.5 million and was responsible for paying workers and for the construction of a bridge. Literally every math skill taught in middle school was encountered during the project. Students learned adult responsibilities, such as check writing, accounting, paying taxes, and making a budget. They saw real purposes for math and were able to apply all of the background knowledge they had in completing projects.

Another way of tapping relevant background knowledge is by creating a brainstorming session for the topic at hand. Once students generate examples of their personal associations with a topic, those types of examples can be used to continue to establish relevance. For example, a seventh grade science teacher I observed (October 1995) presented, in phases, a month-long unit on marine biology (see Figure 10.1). In phase 1, she began the focus on oceans by asking students to brainstorm about their own relevant experiences. Students who lived near the ocean were asked to talk about what they had observed, and the comments were written on the overhead projector by the teacher and then copied and distributed.

In phase 2, the teacher provided opportunities for students to develop knowledge of and experiences with the ocean by planning a field trip to a marine biology center by the ocean. When students returned to school after the trip, they were again asked to talk about what they had observed, and the comments were written on acetate by the teacher and copied for all to peruse. Students also watched videotapes, the teacher read a few books, and the students found library books themselves about ocean life.

In phase 3, students chose an ocean animal about which they would each write notes on cards, compose a report, draw a picture, and make a map. One student chose the sea turtle. He found a few books on sea turtles in the library, wrote notes on cards, used the information to create a final report on the computer, drew a picture of a sea turtle, and made a map of places in the world where sea turtles are most prevalent.

I was able to observe the classroom on one of the final days of the marine biology unit. The students were putting the finishing touches on their projects and presenting them. The students, who were largely English language learners, seemed to particularly enjoy drawing and coloring their animals and making the maps. They each presented their animal report to the class and chose a spot for it to be displayed in the class.

Teaching Reading Strategies in Content Area Classes

To illustrate the type of strategy instruction that can benefit students, I will report my observations of three content area teachers who taught reading strategies explicitly. First, in the context of teaching a unit on coastal American Indian tribes (November 1994), a sixth grade ELD teacher I observed taught about finding main ideas as a part of the unit. Similarly, a seventh grade science teacher I observed taught about comparison and contrast as part of a unit on ecosystems (February 1995). An eighth grade history teacher taught about using a time line for note taking and learning while beginning a unit on the colonial period (September 1994).

The sixth grade teacher (November 1994) began the unit on American Indian tribes by showing recreated pictures of coastal tribes and pictures of recovered artifacts. He also read some information about various tribes. As a part of the teacher's effort to explicitly teach reading while continuing to cover content, the teacher established an instructional agenda based on an informal assessment of students. The teacher decided to use about 15 minutes a day as a time to specifically develop reading in the context of history.

Over the four days that I observed him, he focused on main ideas for about 10 to 15 minutes each day. Typically at the beginning of the period, he would put on the overhead projector a simple paragraph about an American Indian tribe and then hand a copy of the paragraph to all of the students (see Figure 10.2). He used the overhead projector and handouts as a way of providing visual representations to students. On the first day of his work on main ideas, he said, "A main idea tells what the whole paragraph is about. It does not tell what part of the paragraph is about, but it tells what the whole paragraph is about. Watch me as I read this paragraph and decide what the whole paragraph is about." He then presented a self-regulation component by telling students to ask themselves if they had found the main idea. "Ask yourself, 'do I know the main idea?' If you do, make a check at the bottom; if not, go back and reread." This metacognitive step was added by the teacher, based on my research demonstrating its effectiveness (Graves, 1986).

On subsequent days, he had the students find main ideas with him and on their own until they started to develop great confidence and competence. With each passing day, the looks on their faces indicated that they were pleased with their own success. The teacher said that he had learned through the years that students who were taught explicitly and then provided with a range of

Find the main idea:

The Chumash once flourished on the Southern Coast of California. They traveled back and forth between the mainland and the Channel Islands, which are just off the coast. They fished and grew crops for food. The artifacts which remain behind let us know that the most important animal to the Chumash was the dolphin. They made many picture stories, in caves and on rocks, that include dolphins. War with the Spanish conquistadors and others caused the decline of these great people.

FIGURE 10.2. Paragraph on the Chumash: Finding the Main Idea

practice opportunities learned faster and were able to use the skill throughout the year.

In another set of observations (February 1995), I watched an eighth grade science teacher teach a unit on ecosystems by having students construct fresh-water and salt-water aquariums. Students wrote reports about the two kinds of aquariums before they were built, and they were integrally involved in the planning and construction of each. The aquariums were completed over the course of a month, and students then wrote about their observations and for-mulated hypotheses as to why changes had occurred.

The teacher combined these types of activities with daily mini-lessons in reading to proactively provide strategies to increase comprehension. For ex-ample, she developed a series of 15- to 20-minute segments of instruction on appropriate strategies to use when students were asked to compare. On the first day of the series of lessons, the teacher said, "Watch, I will show you a way to compare two items." She then provided a visual organizer by drawing two overlapping circles on the board. "Let's compare the sea horse to the oc-topus." Next, she held up a picture of each animal and taped each picture in the outside portion of each appropriate circle. The teacher then asked stu-dents to describe each animal, and she made notes under the pictures in each circle. One student said that a sea horse is a fish and has a head like a horse. She then asked, "How are they alike?" She wrote what students said in the overlapping part of the circle. Students said that both animals live in the ocean, females of both animals lay eggs, and both animals live all over the world. After this initial example, she said, "Now, in your groups, compare the fresh-water ecosystem to the salt-water ecosystem." The students had a large Venn dia-gram drawn on poster board at each table, and each circle of the diagram had a picture of one of the ecosystems taped above it. The students appeared to transfer the knowledge rapidly and were learning something they could con-tinue to use whenever they saw the word *compare.*

In the previous two examples, I observed teachers using the overhead projector, the board, and handouts of various kinds to provide students with many visual representations during instruction. In another example (September 1994), I observed a history teacher who also used many demonstrations and visual images, such as maps, globes, graphs, charts, and time lines. In his effort to teach the students how to maximize comprehensible input while reading, he demonstrated making a time line. To provide explicit instruction for students, he started the unit by making a time line of his own life, from birth to that day. He drew a line on the board and began to write the major events of his life in order; he called it a personal time line. The teacher next assisted students in constructing their own personal time lines, and he posted them on the bulletin board. In the last 20 minutes of class, the teacher asked the students to open their books to the chapter on the early colonial period. As they read through the chapter, the teacher made a historical time line beginning with the settlement in Jamestown, and ending with the settlement at Plymouth Rock. Students were given a blank time line, and they filled it in along with the teacher. Throughout the year, with each new chapter, students were given a blank time line and asked to fill it in according to the information presented in the book.

Teaching Writing Strategies in Content Area Classes

Research in the past 10 years has yielded valuable information about teaching writing to students who are struggling in school (Englert & Mariage, 1992; Peyton, Jones, Vincent, & Greenblatt, 1994; Ruiz, 1995a; Ruiz, 1995b). Because good writers are thought to engage in a recursive or circular process during composing (Graves, Semmel, & Gerber, 1994), students can be required to engage in five basic steps in secondary course work. These steps are prewriting (or planning), composing, revising, editing, and completing a final draft (see Figure 10.3). The circle representing writing-as-a-process has arrows pointing each way, indicating that a writer may take any number of courses in composing. For example, she may begin with planning and composing, go back to planning during revising, begin composing again, and then go back to revising and editing before completing the final draft.

Writers' Workshop (WW), which was developed largely by Donald Graves (1983), typically consists of journal writing, prewriting activities for narrative or expository compositions, the five stages described as writing-as-a-process, and sharing and publishing final drafts. WW appears to be a viable approach for elementary students (see DuCharme, Earl, & Poplin, 1989). WW has also been successful for students who are learning English and for students who are having problems in school (Bos, 1988; Englert et al, 1995; Peyton et al., 1994; Ruiz, 1995a; Ruiz, 1995b; Zaragoza & Vaughn, 1993). Peyton and her colleagues (1994) reported findings of the positive effects of WW up through sixth grade.

Several teachers I observed who were particularly effective with students learning English were using WW. However, each of these teachers made it a point to teach strategies and skills explicitly as a supplement to WW, and

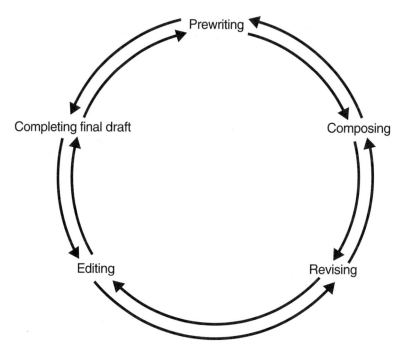

FIGURE 10.3. Writing-as-a-Process

researchers support that choice (Chamot & O'Malley, 1994; Englert & Mariage, 1992; Gersten & Jiménez, 1994; Graves & Montague, 1991; Graves, Montague, & Wong, 1990).

Quick writes or journal writing at the beginning of each class day or at the beginning of each unit appear to be critical for the development of writing in secondary students. For example, one seventh grade math teacher I observed (May 1994) required various types of prewriting and background knowledge checks throughout the year. Each student had a journal that remained at school and was turned in daily. Almost every day, the teacher required a quick write activity for three minutes, in which time students were to write their thoughts and feelings about the math homework. At times, students were also asked to write their reactions and thoughts after cooperative group activities and problem-solving assignments. At other times, students were asked to do a three-minute quick write about the ways in which the concept they were currently learning could be applied to their lives. Sometimes students were asked to share their writings in small groups, and sometimes the teacher read the writings to the class, but typically the teacher did not disclose the names of the authors of the writings. Each week the teacher collected the journals, read the entries the students had written, and commented on the entries, to create a written interaction with each student. The teacher not only became acquainted with the students but also created an opportunity for language development, even in math class.

An example of explicit strategy instruction in writing was provided in an eighth grade English class I observed (January 1994). About half of the students needed ELD and academic improvement. After overtly teaching the students each step of the writing process, the teacher used different colors of paper for the various stages of writing. Planning was done on yellow paper; the first draft was composed on orange paper; revising was completed on the orange sheet by marking through content; editing was also completed on the orange sheet by marking through and correcting various forms of spelling and punctuation; and the final draft was completed on the computer or on white paper. The English teacher had students engage in this process at least twice a month. Students learned to begin the writing process by simply expressing ideas.

Another sixth grade social studies teacher (January 1994) decided to devote at least 20 of her 50 minutes per class to *Writers' Workshop*. She would sometimes devote the whole period to writing, and other times she would devote only 20 minutes. One day she told me about her sense of the way she divided the time for writing each week. She said that students actually write for about one-third of the time; they share their work, either in presenting, revising, or editing it, one-third of the time; and they listen to minilessons or take part in teacher-directed learning or prewriting one-third of the time (see Figure 10.4). She didn't necessarily do all three activities each day, but she usually spent at least one hour each week on writing.

For example, during a unit on the California gold rush, students were asked to pretend they lived at the time of the gold rush and to write a story about their adventures. The teacher told students they would have 20 minutes each day during the week to complete the assignment. She chose the narrative genre for students because they were invariably more comfortable with story structure than with any other type of writing, and when writing in a new language it was important for them to be comfortable with the genre. Story writing also seemed to make history come alive for the students. She led students in a brainstorming activity to help them get started. Students created their own webs, or outlines, of their story and wrote a first draft.

For students who were floundering on narrative story structure, she used the story grammar cueing system developed by Graves et al. (1990). This cueing system was essentially a list of the story grammar parts (setting, characters, problem, resolution, ending), and students were instructed to think about these parts as they wrote and as they revised their stories (Graves & Hague, 1993; Graves & Montague, 1991). This system served as a metacognitive, or self-regulation, system for students, requiring them to reflect on their steps.

If students wanted to illustrate their stories, they were encouraged to do so. The next day, students formed peer pairs and made corrections and changes in their stories. In peer revision, students provided each other with abundant feedback. They had a revision format, which was provided by the teacher during several minilessons: (a) Does the story make sense? (b) What do I like about the story? (c) Does the story have characters, a setting, a problem, a resolution, and an ending? (d) Have capitals, overall appearance, punctuation, and spelling all been checked? It took students a while to answer each of these

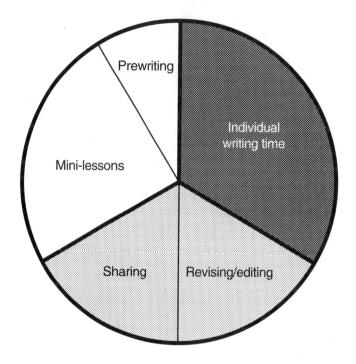

FIGURE 10.4. Writing Instruction Time Management

questions about each story. They seemed to rush through it and may have needed a bit more facilitation from the teacher to make sure each step was accomplished. At the end of the week, the students wrote final drafts on the computer and created a class book, which was sent to another sixth grade class as a gift.

In another set of observations (November 1994), a seventh grade English teacher learned that his students were struggling with a format for the expression of expository material, so he decided to teach report writing using a think-aloud modeling procedure. First, he read some materials to students about the tradition of Thanksgiving in the colonial period and, using the overhead projector, modeled the process of taking notes as he read. After the reading and note taking, he reviewed the five-paragraph essay format and provided students with a handout that specified an introductory paragraph, three supporting paragraphs, and a concluding paragraph (see Figure 10.5). He then modeled outlining the essay while thinking aloud about what he might want to write. He encouraged comments and suggestions from students as he constructed his outline on the overhead projector, consulting with students about the accuracy and logic of the outline.

Finally, he again used the overhead projector and actually wrote the report on Thanksgiving, encouraging student participation. Days later, he had stu-

Five Paragraph Essay

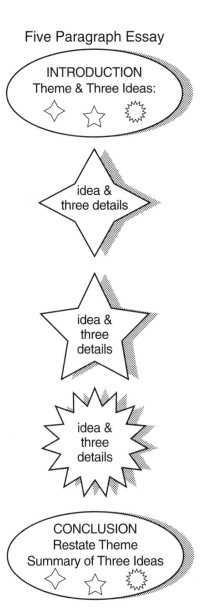

FIGURE 10.5. Five-Paragraph Essay

dents work together in groups to write another report—this time about various famous people in colonial history, such as Pocahontas, John Smith, and Miles Standish. Given 20 minutes each day, over the course of a week each group (a) shared the reading and note taking on orange paper on day 1, (b) prepared an outline on pink paper on day 2, (c) prepared a first draft on yellow paper on day 3, (d) edited the rough draft on day 4, and (e) entered a final draft into the computer on day 5. On day 6, the groups shared their reports with the rest of the class.

TECHNIQUES TO IMPROVE
COMPREHENSION AND TRANSFER

Peyton et al. (1994) found that the students in their study who were encouraged to write in their native language for journal time (about 10 minutes a day) gained comfort in school and improved their English skills faster than those who did not have native language opportunities. Though most teachers do not speak languages other than English, Lucas and Katz (1994) point out that many resources in the community and in the school itself are often available to teachers if they pursue them. Other students, parents, volunteers from the community, paraprofessionals, and other teachers can play major or minor roles in the classroom to facilitate some native language support for students.

In another study, Hornberger and Micheau (1993) and Perez (1993) found that students performed better when teachers went over key vocabulary in social studies classes in both English and Spanish to help students access knowledge and skills from their native language. In one lesson on the Pilgrims and Thanksgiving (Hornberger & Micheau, 1993), the teacher conducted a discussion in which she wrote the key words on the board in both English and Spanish (e.g., Thanksgiving—Día de Gracias). Jiménez, Pearson, and García (1995) also indicate that assistance for students in retrieving words they know in one language may faciliate progress in the new language.

Pease-Alvarez and Winsler (1994) provided a case study of a limited-Spanish-speaking science teacher who spoke some Spanish with his pupils to demonstrate the value he placed on their first language. He not only used the opportunity to learn Spanish but also served as a role model to demonstrate the kinds of questions to ask and the challenges that arise when one learns a new language. Though his knowledge of Spanish was quite limited, he sought help from students in using Spanish properly. He regularly labeled all of the scientific terms using both Spanish and English, and each day began with a Spanish translation of the key vocabulary and the topic at hand.

One seventh grade English teacher I observed attempted to help students access vocabulary knowledge by writing a key word or words on the board, accompanied by pictures or examples. Each day the teacher would say, "¿Qué es estos?" or "¿Cómo se dice en Español?" These simple phrases elicited the Spanish words, so that students could determine if the new vocabulary was related to Spanish or if cognates existed. It also allowed students to continue their language development in the first language. In one lesson on poetry, the words were *alliteration* and *rhyme*. The Spanish words were *aliteracíon* and *rima*. The teacher wrote the word *rhyme* on the board first, thinking that conceptually students would know the meaning but might be unfamiliar with the word in English. In answering the question posed by the teacher, the students immediately responded *rima,* and the looks on their faces and the head nodding indicated that they understood the word. The teacher said, "We see rhyming in this poem; I'll show you two words that rhyme—*love* and *dove.* Now you find two more words that rhyme."

For the word *alliteration,* however, the teacher knew that students might not know the meaning of the word and might not know the word in Spanish. When the teacher asked about this word, some of the students looked to each other and shrugged their shoulders. The teacher used one of the new hand-held computers to retrieve the word in Spanish and wrote *aliteración* on the board. The teacher told me that these computers translate in up to 20 languages and are invaluable tools for teachers working with students learning English.

As the teacher began to define each of the words, she was careful to use concise and consistent language. The teacher said, "*Alliteration*—words in a row with the same beginning letter sound. Listen: 'slippery slimy slivering snake' is alliteration. Now listen: 'happy lovable dog' is not alliteration. Why? Yes, because these are not words in a row with the same beginning letter sound." The teacher was careful to provide examples and nonexamples for students, to clarify the concept. The teacher was also careful to use consistent wording. The teacher was careful *not* to use the phrase "same beginning letter sound" one time and "similar beginning alphabet" another time (Gersten, Taylor, and Graves, 1997).

Jiménez, García, and Pearson (1995) point out that good bilingual readers tend to be very focused on increasing vocabulary knowledge. Particularly with new vocabulary, researchers have found that "less is more" (Gersten & Jiménez, 1994). When a teacher chooses vocabulary sparingly but teaches in great depth with abundant application, that vocabulary is more likely to be retained. For example, I observed (January 1996) a sixth grade math ELD class teacher who taught the vocabulary word *sort* as part of a unit on graphing. The word *sort* was critical in many word problems. To teach the word, she brought a number of kitchen items, all spoons and spatulas, from home that day, along with two buckets. She began the lesson by telling the students that they would sort coupons from the newspaper, and that they could use the coupons at the grocery store.

"First," she said, "let's learn what the word *sort* means." She wrote the word *sort* on the board and said, "Watch. I am going to sort these. Let's see . . . this is a spoon so this goes here in bucket 1. . . . This is a spatula so this goes here in bucket 2. . . . This is a. . . ." She became playful after a few examples and said, "This is a spoon so it goes in bucket 2. . . . Oops, no it goes in bucket 1 with the other spoons." She demonstrated the concept *sort* without actually defining it in words, but she was thinking aloud as she sorted to make the process overt for students. She also provided both examples and nonexamples of correct sorting, to clarify the concept. Following her demonstration, she asked the students to try to sort on their own. She gave each student an envelope with grocery store coupons in it. Each envelope had three coupons worth 25 cents and three coupons worth 50 cents. She asked the students to sort the coupons in piles on their desks. She monitored their work and occasionally commented, "Yes, you know how to sort." Note that the teacher spent about 10 minutes on one vocabulary word, rather than taking the more traditional approach of writing five words on the board and defining each one at the beginning of the lesson. The teacher taught *sort* in a way that made it comprehensible to all students, by using demonstrations, modeling, thinking aloud, and visual representations.

Effective teacher interactions are characterized by slower speech rate and gestures, clear enunciation, controlled vocabulary, use of cognates, and limited use of idiomatic expressions. Consistent wording without the use of synonyms is critically important for efficient language development. In a longitudinal study of second language learners, Gersten and Jiménez (1994) found that teachers who spoke clearly and precisely without references to reading materials and cultural information foreign to the students at hand were most successful.

MEDIATION AND FEEDBACK

Goldenberg (1992–93) and Echevarria (1995) have presented research suggesting the use of an interactive form of mediation and feedback called instructional conversations (IC). With IC, students engage in extended conversations with the teacher and with themselves to enhance language development. Using this approach, teachers will often say, "Tell me more about . . ." and "What do you mean by . . . ," and they will restate student comments by beginning, "In other words. . . ." Of course, the goal of the teacher is to create a safe environment for students to freely contribute and express ideas without fear of failure.

For example, I observed one sixth grade ELD teacher who used what may be called a modified instructional conversations approach. During a social studies lesson on community resources (September 1995), the teacher began with a map of his own neighborhood. He showed students where he lived, shopped, went to the doctor, and so on. He gave students a blank map and asked them to talk to their neighbors about their own neighborhoods. In a discussion, the teacher asked for students to speak up about the places in their own neighborhoods. Students could hardly wait to answer. As students began to speak, one said, "A park." The teacher asked, "What type of park?" As the student answered, the teacher asked, "How far is it from your house?" and continued to ask questions requiring the student to elaborate. The teacher included a similar format each day for 15 to 20 minutes to enhance the language and thinking of the students.

One point of contention among researchers and practitioners is when to provide corrective feedback. Whole-language and writing-as-a-process approaches often prohibit error correction, particularly in the beginning of reading and writing development. It is commonly believed that as students progress, they will begin to notice correct forms and begin to use them spontaneously. Reyes (1992) claims that this practice is not always best for the learners. Her research indicated that students who were not corrected did not progress and were often left farther and farther behind. These conclusions lend support to the perfect-final-copy requirement within the Writers' Workshop. Many teachers insist that students continually rewrite their work until everything is "perfect," hence insisting on self-correction.

To minimize anxiety, however, error correction during practice must be approached cautiously by teachers (Flores, Rueda, & Porter, 1986). Particularly, students who have experienced school failure or who are learning to speak English for speakers of other languages often need much encouragement, and they need to be told when they have responded correctly. For example, teachers are advised to approach error correction indirectly. If Marisa says, "When animals move from place to place, they midrate," then the teacher says, "Did you say 'migrate,' Marisa? [With emphasis on the *gr*.] That's right, Marisa, when animals move from place to place they migrate, good." The teacher then writes the word on the board once again. The teacher responds positively to the content, which is correct, and models the correct pronunciation of the word by stating it herself. In another example, I observed a sixth grade ELD class in which a student described a close-up picture to his teacher. He said, "It looks more big." The teacher responded indirectly and said, "Yes, it looks bigger." The student realized that the response was a correction and said, "Yes, it looks bigger." The student seemed to appreciate the information.

Reyes (1992) and Short (1994) have reported positive results from some direct teaching of vocabulary, academic strategies, and English language followed by teacher monitoring and correction of errors in a nonthreatening way. In the direct feedback approach, the teacher models the correct response and asks the student to repeat it or copy it. Then the teacher asks a similar question that requires the information. Even for a student who is first learning English, if the student writes *bruder* in his or her journal a few times in reference to a brother, the teacher can write the correct word above it in the journal and ask the student to spell it correctly the next time. At the same time, the teacher may want to compliment the student on his or her work and enjoy the content or point out correctly spelled words.

RESPONSIVENESS TO CULTURAL
AND PERSONAL DIVERSITY

Moll (1988) writes extensively about the value of the "funds" of knowledge that students bring to the classroom. These funds of knowledge can be tapped through daily journal writings. The knowledge gained regarding students' lives can then be incorporated into lessons and content for course work (Gonzalez et al., 1993). For example, in an ELD class, the teacher planned a unit entitled "¡Viva San Diego!" Each student was to pick an area of the city they wanted to learn more about, such as Balboa Park or San Diego State University. Students were to do research to learn as much as they could about the area they selected and then prepare a report or project. Students were encouraged to involve parents and family members in gathering information.

Alternative Grouping Strategies

Partner sharing and cooperative grouping are also important activities in which students can participate and feel valued (Schunk & Hanson, 1985; Slavin, 1987). One strength of these activities is the random nature of partner sharing and cooperative groups; students of different cultural and academic backgrounds must work together. Other strengths are that teachers can at times pair individuals with different strengths, so that students can learn from each other. Also, these kinds of activities can guarantee an equal opportunity for all to participate actively.

Partner sharing increases comfort and active involvement. The teacher who says, "Think about this word and talk to each other about what you think it means," affords quiet students and students who are struggling with English the opportunity to consistently answer questions and participate.

Cooperative groups give students opportunities to share among themselves, and they promote problem solving (Slavin, 1990). The teachers I observed typically structured cooperative group activities so that students knew exactly what was expected, how much time they had to complete a task, and what role each member of the group should play. In a history lesson entitled "Looking at the Revolution from Different Points of View" (Short, 1993), after various lesson components, the teacher divided students into cooperative groups and gave them an assignment to consider the point of view of various cultural groups in America and whether these groups would have wanted the Revolutionary War to take place. In so doing, the teacher assigned six groups: Native Americans, African Americans, Spanish settlers, French settlers, English settlers, and Loyalists. Students in each cooperative group decided how these cultural groups felt about the potential war. In the study reported by Short (1993), the group of students who were designated as Native American representatives reported pro-independence attitudes, because they thought that independence would also allow them to make their own laws and be free again. In this example, the students were able to think the way Native Americans in the 18th century may have thought, without letting the actual occurrences of history affect their answers.

Personal Relationships with Students

All of my observations indicate, not surprisingly, that teachers who seem to know each of their students and who take an active interest in them are the most successful. One sixth grade ELD teacher was also the faculty advisor for the Homework Club. The Homework Club met every day at lunchtime and was really just an invitation to students to come into her room to eat lunch. She played music that students chose on her boom box, helped them with their homework, and just talked to them if they wanted. She created a safe atmosphere of fun. She had also invited all of their parents to attend, and she stayed in close contact with parents in general.

ROLES FOR FAMILY
AND COMMUNITY MEMBERS

The celebration of cultural and linguistic diversity in the schools is not likely to feel real to parents and community members until there is a comfortable, warm place created for families of all students (Baca & Cervantes, 1989; Chang, 1992; Gonzalez et al.,1993; Lynch & Hanson, 1993; Scarcella & Chin, 1993). Along with learning about the cultures of all students in a class, establishing relationships with parents and family members and inviting them to serve in meaningful capacities in the classroom is highly recommended (Ogbu, 1992). Parents and family members can also be regular volunteers and can be encouraged to play any role, no matter how small, in the classroom. For example, volunteers could read a story to students or work with a small group. They could help students with a science project or participate in a field trip. When parents or community members have special skills that the teacher does not have, they can perform the function of teacher. For example, one teacher invited the father of Hassan to speak to the class about ocean animals, because he worked on a fishing boat. Hassan assisted his father with his English, and they worked together to present fish stories and pictures to the class.

SUMMARY AND CONCLUSIONS

In this chapter I provided examples of (a) explicit structures, frameworks, scaffolds, and strategies; (b) techniques to improve comprehension and transfer; (c) mediation and feedback; and (d) respect for and responsiveness to cultural and personal diversity. Having observed for extended periods in approximately 20 middle school classrooms in which the teacher was conducting some form of ELD, I have provided scenarios and examples of what appear to be sound practice.

REFERENCES

Allen, V. G., (1989). Literature as a support to language acquisition. In P. Rigg & V. G. Allen (Eds.), *When they don't all speak English* (pp. 55–64). Urbana, IL: National Council of Teachers of English.

Baca, L., & Cervantes, H., (1989). *The bilingual special education interface.* Columbus, OH: Merrill.

Banks, J. A. (1991). A curriculum for empowerment, action, and change. In C. E. Sleeter (Ed.). *Empowerment through multicultural education* (pp. 125–141). Albany, NY: State University of New York.

Bos, C. (1988). Process-oriented writing: Instructional implications for mildly handicapped students. *Exceptional Children, 54,* 521–527.

Cadzen, C. B. (1992). *Language minority education in the United States: Implications of the Ramirez report* (Educational Practice Report No. 3). Santa Cruz, CA: National Center for Research on Cultural Diversity and Second Language Learning.

Chamot, A. U., & O'Malley, J. M. (1994). *The CALLA handbook: Implementing the cognitive academic language learning approach.* Reading, MA: Addison-Wesley.

Chang, J. M. (1992). Current programs serving Chinese-American students in learning disabilities resource issues. In *Proceedings of the Third National Research Symposium on Limited English Proficient Issues: Focus on Middle and High School Issues* (pp 713–736). Washington, DC: U.S. Department of Education, Office of Bilingual Education and Minority Language Affairs.

Cloud, N. (1993). Language, culture and disability: Implications for instruction and teacher preparation. *Teacher Education and Special Education, 16,* 60–72.

Cummins, J. (1989). A theoretical framework for bilingual special education. *Exceptional Children, 56,* 111–128.

DuCharme, C., Earl, J., & Poplin, M. (1989). The author model: The constructivist view of the writing process. *Learning Disability Quarterly, 12,* 237–242.

Echevarria, J. (1995). Interactive reading instruction: A comparison of proximal and distal effects of instructional conversations. *Exceptional Children, 61,* 536–552.

Echevarria, J., & Graves, A. (1997). *Sheltered content instruction: Teaching English language learners with diverse abilities.* Boston: Allyn and Bacon.

Englert, C. S., Garmon, A., Mariage, T., Rozendal, M., Tarrant, K., & Urba, J. (1995). The early literacy project: Connecting across the literacy curriculum. *Learning Disability Quarterly, 18,* 253–277.

Englert, C. S., & Mariage, T. V. (1992). Shared understandings: Structuring the writing experience through dialogue. In D. Carnine & E. Kameenui (Eds.), *Higher order thinking* (pp. 107–136). Austin, TX: Pro-Ed.

Faltis, C. J., & Arias, M. B. (1993). Speakers of languages other than English in the secondary school: Accomplishments and struggles. *Peabody Journal of Education: Trends in Bilingual Education at the Secondary School Level, 69*(1), 6–29.

Faltis, C. J., & Hudelson, S. (1994). Learning English as an additional language in K–12 schools. *TESOL Quarterly, 28*(3), 457–468.

Figueroa, R. A. (1989). Psychological testing of linguistic-minority students: Knowledge gaps and regulations. *Exceptional Children, 56*(2), 111–119.

Fitzgerald, J. (1995). English as a second language learners' cognitive reading processes: A review of research in the United States. *Review of Educational Research, 65*(2),145–190.

Flores, B., Rueda, R., & Porter, B. (1986). Examining assumptions and instructional practices related to the acquisition of literacy with bilingual special education students. In A. Willig & H. Greenberg (Eds.), *Bilingualism and learning disabilities* (pp. 149–165). New York: American Library.

Franklin, E., & Thompson, J. (1994). Describing students' collected works: Understanding American Indian children. *TESOL Quarterly, 28*(3),489–506.

Gaffney, J. S., & Anderson, R. C. (1991). Two-tiered scaffolding: Congruent processes of teaching and learning. In E. H. Hiebert (Ed.), *Literacy for a diverse society* (pp. 184–198). New York: Teachers College Press.

García, E. (1993a). *Education of linguistically and culturally diverse students: Effective instructional practices* (Educational Practice Report No. 1). Santa Cruz, CA: National Center for Research on Cultural Diversity and Second Language Learning.

García, E. (1993b). Project THEME: Collaboration for school improvement at the middle school for language minority students. In *Proceedings of the Third National Research Sym-*

posium on Limited English Proficient Issues: Focus on Middle and High School Issues (pp. 323–350). Washington, DC: U.S. Department of Education, Office of Bilingual Education and Minority Language Affairs.

Gay, G. (1993). Building cultural bridges: A bold proposal for teacher education. *Education and Urban Society, 25,* 285–299.

Gersten, R., Brengelman, S., & Jiménez, R. (1994). Effective instruction for culturally and linguistically diverse students: A reconceptualization. *Focus on Exceptional Children, 27,* 1–16.

Gersten, R., & Jiménez, R. (1994). A delicate balance: Enhancing literature instruction for students of English as a second language. *The Reading Teacher, 47,* 438–449.

Gersten, R., Taylor, R., & Graves, A. (1997). Direct instruction and diversity. In R. Stevens (Ed.), *Teaching in America: Essays in Honor of Barak Rosenshine.* Columbus, OH: Merrill Ed./Prentice-Hall.

Goldenberg, C. (1992–93). Instructional conversations: Promoting comprehension through discussion. *The Reading Teacher, 46,* 316–326.

Gonzalez, N., Moll, L. C., Floyd-Tenery, M., Rivera, A., Rendon, P., Gonzales, R., & Amonti, C. (1993). *Teacher research on funds of knowledge: Learning from households* (Educational Practice Report No. 6). Santa Cruz, CA: National Center for Research on Cultural Diversity and Second Language Learning.

Graves, A., & Hauge, R. (1993). Using cues and prompts to improve story writing. *Teaching Exceptional Children, 25*(4), 38–41.

Graves, A., & Montague, M. (1991). Using story grammar cueing to improve the writing of students with learning disabilities. *Learning Disabilities Research and Practice, 6,* 246–251.

Graves, A., Montague, M., & Wong, Y. (1990). The effects of procedural facilitation on story composition of learning disabled students. *Learning Disabilities Research, 5*(4), 88–93.

Graves, A., Semmel, M., & Gerber, M. (1994). The effects of story prompts on the narrative production of students with and without learning disabilities. *Learning Disability Quarterly, 17,* 154–164.

Graves, A. W. (1986). The effects of direct instruction and metacomprehension training on finding main ideas. *Learning Disabilities Research, 1*(2), 90–100.

Graves, D. (1983). *Writing: Teachers and children at work.* Portsmouth, NH: Heinemann.

Henderson, R. W., & Landesman, E. M. (1992). *Mathematics and middle school students of Mexican descent: The effects of thematically integrated instruction* (Research Report No. 5). Santa Cruz, CA: National Center for Research on Cultural Diversity and Second Language Learning.

Hornberger, N., & Micheau, C. (1993). Getting far enough to like it: Biliteracy in the middle school. *Peabody Journal of Education: Trends in Bilingual Education at the Secondary School Level, 69,* 54–81.

Jiménez, R., García, & Pearson. (1995). Three children, two languages, and strategic reading: Case studies in bilingual/monolingual reading. *American Educational Research Journal, 32,* 67-97.

King, A. (1990). Enhancing peer interaction and learning in the classroom through reciprocal questioning. *American Educational Research Journal, 27,* 664–687.

Krashen, S. D. (1985). *The input hypothesis: Issues and implications.* New York: Longman.

Lim, H-J. L., & Watson, D. (1993). Whole language content classes for second-language learners. *The Reading Teacher, 46,* 384–395.

Lucas, T., & Katz, A. (1994). Reframing the debate: The roles of native languages in English-only programs for language minority students. *TESOL Quarterly, 28,* 537–562.

Lynch, E. W., & Hanson, M. J. (1992). *Developing cross-cultural competence: A guide for working with young children and their families.* Baltimore, MD: Brookes.

Moll, L. C. (1988). Some key issues in teaching Latino students. *Language Arts, 65,* 465–472.

Ogbu, J. U. (1992). Understanding cultural diversity and learning. *Educational Researcher, 21*(8), 5–14.

Palincsar, A. S. (1986). The role of dialogue in providing scaffolded instruction [Special issue on learning strategies]. In J. Levin & M. Pressley (Eds.), *Educational Psychologist, 21,* 73–98.

Pease-Alvarez, L., & Winsler, A. (1994). Cuando el maestro no habla Espanol: Children's bilingual language practices in the classroom. *TESOL Quarterly, 28*(3), 507–536.

Perez, B. (1993). Biliteracy practices and issues in secondary schools. *Peabody Journal of Education: Trends in Bilingual Education at the Secondary School Level, 69*(1), 117–135.

Peyton, J. K., Jones, C., Vincent, A., & Greenblatt, L. (1994). Implementing writing workshop with ESOL students: Visions and realities. *TESOL Quarterly, 28*(3), 469–488.

Reyes, M. de la Luz (1992). Challenging venerable assumptions: Literacy instruction for linguistically different students. *Harvard Educational Review, 62*(4), 427–446.

Ruiz, N. T. (1995a). The social construction of ability and disability I: Profile types of Latino children identified as language learning disabled. *Journal of Learning Disabilities, 28,* 476–490.

Ruiz, N. T. (1995b). The social construction of ability and disability II: Optimal and at-risk lessons in a bilingual special education classroom. *Journal of Learning Disabilities, 28,* 491–502.

Rumberger, R. W. (1995). Dropping out of middle school: A multilevel analysis of students and schools. *American Educational Research Journal, 32,* 583–626.

Saville-Troike, M. (1984). What really matters in second language learning for academic achievement? *TESOL Quarterly, 18,* 117–131.

Scarcella, R., & Chin, K. (1993). *Literacy practices in two Korean-American communities* (Research Report No. 8). Santa Cruz, CA: National Center for Research on Cultural Diversity and Second Language Learning.

Schunk, D. H., & Hanson, A. R. (1985). Peer models: Influence on children's self-efficacy and achievement. *Journal of Educational Psychology, 77,* 313–322.

Short, D. (1993). *Integrating language and culture in middle school American history classes* (Educational Practice Report No. 8). Santa Cruz, CA: National Center for Research on Cultural Diversity and Second Language Learning.

Short, D. (1994). Expanding middle school horizons: Integrating language, culture, and social studies. *TESOL Quarterly, 28*(3), 581–608.

Slavin, R. E. (1987). Ability grouping and student achievement in elementary schools: A best-evidence synthesis. *Review of Educational Research, 60,* 471–500.

Slavin, R. E. (1990). *Cooperative learning.* Englewood Cliffs, NJ: Prentice-Hall.

Vygotsky, L. S. (1978). *Mind in society: The development of higher psychological processes.* Cambridge, MA: Harvard University Press.

Zaragoza, N., & Vaughn, S. (1993). The effects of process writing instruction on three 2nd-grade students with different achievement profiles. *Learning Disabilities Research and Practice, 7,* 184–193.

11

Effective Instruction for High School English Language Learners

Anna Uhl Chamot
The George Washington University

E nglish language learning (ELL) students in American schools need instructional support from all teachers (not just English for speakers of other languages or bilingual teachers) for an extended time period if they are to achieve academic success. This chapter suggests ways in which high school teachers can meet the needs of linguistically diverse students in their classes. While the instructional practices suggested are effective for all students, they are of particular importance for nonnative speakers of English. Teachers with linguistically diverse students in their classrooms need to both understand their students' linguistic and cultural background and adapt their instruction so that it meets their needs.

The first part of this chapter identifies some of the major academic needs of linguistically diverse ELL students. The second part reviews research on effective instructional practices for language-minority and other at-risk students. The chapter concludes with a description of an instructional framework that can be used by teachers of different subject areas to increase the academic achievement of linguistically diverse students in their classrooms.

ACADEMIC NEEDS

While the needs of linguistically diverse students are not limited to academics, the role of academic success in determining options and future careers is nevertheless significant. The major academic needs of linguistically diverse ELL students include language development, instructional time, subject matter knowledge and skills, learning strategies, and self-efficacy.

Language development is an essential component of all educational programs for both ELL and native English-speaking students. Language development is important for both social interaction and for its critical role in intellectual growth. Most native English-speaking children come to school with good social language skills, which serve as a foundation for building the academic language skills used for learning in school. By secondary school, most English-speaking students have developed a repertoire of academic language skills and functions, including the ability to read both narrative and expository text, understand and express new ideas and information, write in different genres and content subjects, and use language to inform, explain, analyze, classify, and evaluate what is being studied in school. The expectations of high school teachers are that their students will have already learned to use language functionally in different subject areas. Since adolescent ELL students are often strongest in social communication skills and weakest in academic language skills, they may need considerable assistance in developing academic language proficiency.

Instructional time is a second major academic need of ELL students. Evidence from a number of large-scale research studies indicates that most students need five to seven or even more years of schooling in English to reach even a moderate level of success in the academic curriculum (Collier, 1987, 1989, 1991, 1995; Cummins, 1984, 1992). Elementary school ELL students have the great advantage of time in which to develop both academic English skills and content knowledge. Secondary students do not have time on their side. Sixth grade middle school students, for example, have only three years in which to learn how to use English for academic purposes if they are to enter a college-bound course of study in high school. The available time period diminishes at each higher grade level. It is no wonder that so many high school ELL students give up on school and drop out, having to content themselves with low-level jobs or, worse, no jobs. Additional instructional time is needed by most secondary school students still developing English proficiency in academic language domains.

Subject matter knowledge and skills are a third major academic need for linguistically diverse secondary school students. High school teachers expect that most of their students will have already attained a reasonable degree of prior knowledge in the different subject areas of the curriculum. For example, teachers assume that students have some understanding of scientific phenomena and processes, that they have basic computation and problem-solving skills, that they have some concepts about people and life in other times and places, that they can read a map, and that they have experienced different types of literature.

Secondary school ELL students vary considerably in their academic level on entering American schools. Some have excellent educational backgrounds and may have attained a higher academic level in their native language than their native English-speaking classmates have reached in the American curriculum. Students with strong educational backgrounds in their native countries typically do well in subjects like mathematics and science, whose curricula share many features with mathematics and science curricula in other countries.

They may, however, encounter more difficulties in subjects like social studies and literature, both because they may not have studied American history or literature previously and because the academic language of these two subject areas is demanding.

In contrast to such academically strong ELL students are the many whose education in their native countries has been interrupted by wars and political unrest, or who have not had access to education beyond a rudimentary level. Many may not be literate in their native language and may have little understanding of how to be a student. Their knowledge frameworks are based almost exclusively on personal life experiences, many of which include traumatic events, such as separation from parents, civil unrest and danger, and sole responsibility for their own survival. Naturally, these students have more than academic needs, some of which are beyond the scope of most schools to provide. However, among the needs that the school should meet is assistance in learning the subject matter concepts and skills that will enable ELL students to participate successfully in grade-level content classrooms. It is not easy to teach the whole range of the elementary school curriculum in an accelerated fashion to secondary students whose prior education is limited. And even while ELL students are learning about science, mathematics, social studies, and language arts, their English-speaking peers are moving ahead in these same subjects, increasing the distance between them. No matter how rapidly ELL students with limited prior education progress, the target toward which they are aiming is always moving ahead (Secada, 1991; Thomas, 1992).

Learning strategies are a fourth academic need for ELL students. Depending on the level and type of their prior education, many linguistically diverse secondary students may not have developed learning strategies, or how-to-learn skills. In some cases, the learning strategies they are most familiar with are rote memorization strategies, which, while adequate for reciting information, are not useful in developing higher-order thinking skills for the academic curriculum. Although many native English-speaking students also lack effective learning strategies, the need for strategies is particularly acute for ELL students because of the amount of language and content they need to acquire before they can be successful in the academic mainstream classroom. Knowing how to learn more efficiently is thus an important academic need for linguistically diverse students.

Self-efficacy, or an individual's level of confidence in successfully completing a task, is closely associated with effective use of learning strategies (Zimmerman, 1990). Self-efficacy is at the root of self-esteem, motivation, and self-regulation (Bandura, 1986). Self-efficacious learners feel confident about solving a problem because they have developed an approach to problem solving that has worked in the past. They attribute their success mainly to their own efforts, they believe that their own abilities will improve as they learn more, and they recognize that errors are a part of learning. Students with low self-efficacy, on the other hand, believe themselves to have inherent low ability; they choose less-demanding tasks on which they will make few errors, and they do not try hard, because they believe that any effort will reveal their own lack of ability (Bandura, 1986).

ELL students may lack high self-efficacy for a number of reasons, including experiences of failure at school, segregation into remedial programs, negative attitudes of teachers and classmates, and their own and others' low expectations for their success. Linguistically diverse students need an educational context that fosters the development of self-efficacy through a combination of high expectations and instructional practices that provide them with the tools needed for high achievement.

The five academic needs identified here are but five among the many complex needs of high school ELL students. Recent research on effective educational practices with both language-minority and language-majority students provides both hope and concrete suggestions for changing instruction so that it can meet these particular academic needs more successfully. In the next section, I provide guidelines and descriptions of instructional practices that can benefit all students in high school classrooms and that are critical to the success of ELL students.

EFFECTIVE INSTRUCTIONAL PRACTICES

Effective instruction for linguistically diverse students has the same characteristics as effective instruction for native English-speaking students. However, additional instructional features are needed to meet the needs of ELL students, including contextual characteristics and teaching approaches that lead to higher levels of achievement for high school ELL students. The instructional practices I describe can be attributed to a social-cognitive model of learning, in which learners are perceived as thinkers and as partners with teachers, texts, and peers in the construction of knowledge. Effective instructional practices are discussed in these categories: school context, classroom setting and organization, curriculum, teaching practices, and assessment.

School Context

In effective programs, teachers and other school staff have positive attitudes toward students and expect students to be successful in meeting instructional objectives (Good & Brophy, 1986; Wilson & Corcoran, 1988). Students achieve more when their teachers perceive them as able and interested in learning (Onosko, 1992). Research has documented the impact of positive teacher attitudes and high expectations on student achievement for both majority- and minority-language students. Tikunoff and his colleagues (1985; 1991) found that the teacher's expression of high expectations for student success is a feature of effective bilingual and English for speakers of other languages (ESOL) classrooms. In another study of effective bilingual schools, Carter and Chatfield (1986) found that high expectations for student achievement were an important component. Similarly, Lucas, Henze, & Donato (1990) found a number of concrete ways in which high expectations can be communicated to language-minority students, including the hiring of language-minority professional staff in leadership positions, offering college-preparation classes accessible to ELL students, and providing college-counseling services for both students and their parents in their native language.

An effective school context for high school students provides a strong emphasis on academic achievement for all students, not just for high-ability students. This is of particular importance for language-minority students, who all too frequently are tracked into remedial or basics courses, such as general mathematics or general science (Garza Flores, 1991–92). Developing the academic competence of language-minority students through high expectations and a challenging curriculum is a main feature of effective programs (Chamot & Stewner-Manzanares, 1985; Lucas et al., 1990).

Effective programs actively recruit parent participation and find ways to make it possible for parents to be partners in their children's education (Cummins, 1986). Activities that promote parent-school collaboration include traditional ones such as back-to-school night and parent-teacher conferences, as well as parent workshops, family visits from teachers, and the involvement of parents in multicultural school events (Lucas et al., 1990). Information about school activities and student progress should be available in the parents' native language, and bilingual school personnel should serve as personal points of contact between language-minority parents and the school (Chamot & O'Malley, 1996). A program that demonstrates a real desire for parent involvement is willing to try any number of innovative approaches that show parents they are welcome and needed partners with the school in fostering their children's education.

A number of programmatic adjustments in the overall school context can assist the academic achievement of language-minority students. Three types of contextual adjustments that seem of critical importance are the provision of native language services, the extension of instructional opportunities, and the availability of alternatives to standardized achievement tests.

The importance of providing native language support to enhance academic achievement has been widely documented in numerous research studies (see, for example, Chamot & Stewner-Manzanares, 1985; Cummins, 1986; Diaz, Moll, & Mehan, 1986; Lucas et al., 1990; Ramirez, 1992; Tikunoff, 1985; Tikunoff et al., 1991; Wong Fillmore, Ammon, & McLaughlin, 1983). Native language support services can range from a full bilingual program in which content subject areas are taught to language-minority students in their native language, to programs in which the language support is provided through bilingual aides, tutors, counselors, or other school personnel. Whether a school provides more- or less-intensive native language support depends on numerous factors, including the linguistic characteristics of the language-minority population, parent desires, and availability of specialized teachers and appropriate instructional materials. Native language support is discussed further in the section on effective instruction.

A second modification of the school context to meet ELL student needs is the provision of additional instruction. Extended instructional opportunities include services like after-school and Saturday classes or tutoring, evening school, extension of the academic year, summer school, college-preparation classes, and other types of special instructional programs. A recent study of effective high schools for language-minority Spanish-speaking students found that the presence of a wide range of academic courses in both Spanish and English and opportunities for before- and after-school learning made it possible for these ELL students to achieve high academic goals (Lucas et al., 1990).

A third adjustment to the school context that can improve the academic achievement of ELL students is the use of alternative assessment measures rather than an exclusive reliance on standardized tests. Standardized achievement tests were designed for native English-speaking students, and their use even with the population for which they were developed and formed has had a negative impact on the quality of instructional programs, because programs tend to teach to the test, thus excluding important parts of the curriculum and higher-order thinking skills (Herman, 1992). Interest in alternative assessment for language-minority students has developed because educators realize that assessment should serve multiple purposes, such as monitoring student progress on a continuing basis, providing different types of information about student performance, assessing authentic learning activities, and making assessments of content rather than exclusively of linguistic elements (O'Malley, 1991). Specific guidelines for alternative assessment techniques are described in the section on effective instructional practices.

Classroom Setting and Organization

How a teacher organizes a class for learning purposes also has an impact on the level of student achievement. Probably the least-effective model is the teacher-as-lecturer, or transmission, model (Cummins, 1986). In this model, the teacher is the sole possessor of knowledge, which has to be transmitted to students. The weakness of this model is that it fails to acknowledge the important role of the knowledge that students bring to the classroom and the interactive nature of the learning process. A classroom organized so that students have active learning experiences is a more effective classroom for all students, including ELL students. Two related approaches to classroom organization that foster active learning are cooperative learning and learning communities.

In cooperative learning, students work in groups or teams to complete a learning task. While there are a number of models of cooperative learning, all provide multiple opportunities for students to engage in the active practice of language and content (Kagan, 1986). In cooperative learning, both language-majority and language-minority students of varying degrees of linguistic proficiency and content knowledge can work in a group setting that fosters mutual learning rather than competitiveness (Johnson, Johnson, Holubec, & Roy, 1994; Slavin, 1987). For ELL high school students, the benefits of cooperative learning include additional practice with academic English, the opportunity to use prior cultural and linguistic knowledge, and independent learning experiences (Chamot & O'Malley, 1989, 1994; McGroarty, 1992). Teachers who set up cooperative activities in which group members have differing levels of English proficiency make it possible for students to help each other understand and complete the task (Chamot, Dale, O'Malley, & Spanos, 1993; Cohen, 1986; Diaz et al., 1986).

Cooperative learning is enhanced in classrooms that are organized as learning communities. Teachers who create classroom learning communities recognize both the social and the intellectual aspects of learning. They stimulate discussions about authentic intellectual issues, make explicit relationships between school learning and real-world activities, and involve all students in active learning and thinking (Faltis & Hudelson, 1994; Prawat, 1992). A classroom learning community for language-minority students is exemplified by the Cheche Konnen project, in which "communities of authentic scientific practice" were studied in a number of classrooms of Haitian Creole-speaking students:

> In this context, science is organized as a socially embedded activity in which students transform their observations into findings through argumentation and persuasion, not simply through measurement and discovery. In contrast to conventional textbook or lab-driven school science, students pose their own questions, plan original research to explore their question, collect, analyze, and interpret data, build and argue theories, negotiate claims, evaluate and establish "facts," and so forth. (Warren, Rosebery, Conant, & Hudicourt-Barnes, 1992, p. 2)

This setup is in vivid contrast to a transmission model of classroom organization, in which the teacher and textbook provide predetermined information and activities designed for students to "master" content by memorizing and reciting information.

A classroom context conducive to learning can be created through the teacher's attitude of respect for individuals, her or his high expectations for all students, and an organization that reflects the teacher's understanding of learning as a process of construction and interaction rather than transmission.

Curriculum

In recent years a number of curriculum reform movements have generated a reappraisal of the traditional curriculum taught in schools, leading to the development of national standards in each subject area. Curriculum reforms in major content areas have important implications for educational programs for linguistically diverse students. A major theme is that less is more, meaning that the curriculum should not attempt to cover all aspects of knowledge, but rather discover underlying principles and develop the ability to think critically (Wiggins, 1989). The retreat from the educational goal of encyclopedic knowledge may seem at first glance to be a product of the information age's rapidly expanding knowledge base, which makes it evident that, in practical terms, there is no way that all major knowledge can possibly be addressed by the school curriculum. Wiggins (1989), however, reminds us that more than 2,000 years ago, Socrates taught that "wisdom matters more than knowledge"

(p. 58). In a time of proliferating information in all disciplines, it is wise to remind ourselves that no one person can really know everything. Instead, we should teach students that knowing how to think, having intellectual habits such as open-mindedness and a desire for truth, and having a knowledge base that provides an objective rather than a personal experience point of view will prepare them better for achieving success and self-fulfillment than will memorization of an enormous set of facts from the academic curriculum. In practice, this means that the content taught should represent major principles and unanswered questions rather than a collection of discrete bits of information to be memorized.

Curriculum reform is being proposed by educators and professional organizations as essential for meeting Goals 2000 (Bush, 1991) and national standards in major content areas. In science, for example, the American Association for the Advancement of Science has developed Project 2061, which identifies the major conceptual objectives for science education (Rutherford, 1992). Similarly, the National Science Teachers Association has published a content core of science objectives organized into major scientific themes to guide curriculum development (National Science Teachers Association, 1992). In mathematics education, the National Council of Teachers of Mathematics has issued guidelines that emphasize problem solving, reasoning, and communicating mathematically (National Council of Teachers of Mathematics, 1989). This represents a departure from previous approaches, which emphasized computation skills prior to problem-solving activities (Secada, 1991). In social studies, curricular reforms have called for a reduction of coverage and review in order to focus on major concepts in history and geography, and for the expansion of the social studies curriculum to include a multicultural perspective (Brophy, 1990; California State Department of Education, 1987). In language arts, major innovations in recent years focus on reading for meaning (Dole, Duffy, Roehler, & Pearson, 1991), the integration of language skills and the use of authentic texts for the development of literacy (Goodman, 1987), and a process-oriented rather than only a product-oriented approach to writing (Scardamalia & Bereiter, 1986). Together, these curriculum innovations are challenging traditional views of what ought to be taught in schools.

A theme running through proposals for curriculum reform that is especially relevant for ELL students is the emphasis on communication in each of the content areas. While the idea of language across the curriculum is not new, what is new is that different disciplines are calling for more communication about important concepts, more dialogue, and more use of language for higher-order thinking (Brophy, 1992). Students are expected to not only read and write in all subjects but also to discuss their understanding of the concepts they learn, explain processes and problem solutions, propose and evaluate alternative solutions, justify a point of view, and in general use a variety of academic language functions. Sizer (1992) goes even further in his recommendation for an integrated high school curriculum that would consist of three areas: mathematics and science; the arts; and history and philosophy. All teachers in these areas would be responsible for infusing language development into their particular discipline and teaching students how to learn.

Sizer's proposals for general education bear striking similarities to integrated language and content programs for language-minority students. In a content-ESOL curriculum, for example, appropriate topics from content subjects are integrated with language development so that students can acquire the academic language functions of school subjects (Brinton, Snow, & Wesche, 1989; Chamot & O'Malley, 1994, 1996; Snow, Met, & Genesee, 1989). In sheltered, or language-sensitive, classrooms, content teachers adapt their instructional techniques to the linguistic needs of ELL students (Brinton et al., 1992; McGroarty, 1992; Spanos, 1990). Tikunoff and his coworkers (1991) found that exemplary ESOL curricula focused on teaching content while simultaneously developing students' English language skills. Lucas and her colleagues (1990) also found that effective high schools for language-minority students were characterized by the provision of academic courses taught in the native language and/or sheltered content courses adapted to the needs of language-minority students. Collier (1995) recommends that secondary ELL students be taught language through academic content and that learning strategies instruction should be included to develop thinking skills and the ability to solve problems.

Effective programs for ELL students include multicultural content as well as authentic academic content so that the curriculum is both more relevant to linguistically diverse students and better able to enhance their appreciation of their own cultural identity and that of others (Gersten, 1996; Wong Fillmore & Meyer, 1992). The inclusion in the curriculum of students' own culture and, if possible, their native language facilitates learning from several different perspectives (Cummins, 1986; Krashen & Biber, 1988; Wong Fillmore et al., 1983). First, ELL students can provide insights into a variety of information sources and approaches to learning and thus expand the knowledge and understanding of all class members. Second, recognition of ELL students' prior background knowledge and experiences not only enriches class discussions for all students but also validates the importance of the unique understanding and experience that linguistically diverse students bring to their American classrooms.

Learning-strategies instruction in all subject areas of the curriculum can have a positive effect on the academic achievement of linguistically diverse students. A considerable body of research on learning-strategies instruction has been conducted in various subject areas, including reading, mathematics, writing, and science.

Strategies that improve reading comprehension include summarizing, imagery, question generation, questioning-answering, story grammar mapping, and the use of prior knowledge or schemata (Pressley & Associates, 1990; Wood, Woloshyn, & Willoughby, 1995). Similarly, students taught clusters of reading comprehension strategies have significantly improved their reading comprehension and retained the improvement over time (Palincsar & Brown, 1985,1986; Palincsar & Klenk, 1992). When students are given explicit instruction on strategies to use during the planning, composing, and revising phases of written composition, there are positive results in student improvement on writing assignments (El-Dinary, Brown, & Van Meter, 1995; Harris

& Graham, 1992). In mathematics, a number of studies have shown that students can benefit from instruction in strategies for basic math facts and, more importantly, for problem solving (Carpenter, Fennema, Peterson, Chiang, & Loef, 1989; Pressley & Associates, 1990). Learning-strategy instruction has also proved effective in areas such as science problem solving (Roth, 1990; Silver & Marshall, 1990) and in general information acquisition (Derry, 1990).

Although fewer studies have been conducted on learning-strategy instruction with second language learners, the evidence is beginning to indicate that strategies instruction can also be beneficial for these learners (Cohen & Aphek, 1981; Hosenfeld, Arnold, Kirchofer, Laciura, & Wilson, 1981; Rost & Ross, 1991; Thompson & Rubin, 1993; Wenden & Rubin, 1987).

For example, in the learning-strategy research that my colleagues and I have been conducting since the early 1980s, we have found that effective second language learners are mentally active and purposeful in their learning approach, and that many such learners can describe these mental processes. Better second language learners use a greater variety (though not necessarily a greater number) of strategies and use them more appropriately and flexibly than less effective learners (Chamot, 1993; Chamot & Küpper, 1989; Chamot, Barnhardt, El-Dinary, Carbonaro, & Robbins, 1993; Chamot, Robbins, & El-Dinary, 1993; Chamot, Dale, O'Malley, & Spanos, 1993; O'Malley & Chamot, 1990; O'Malley, Chamot, & Küpper, 1989; O'Malley, Chamot, Stewner-Manzanares, Küpper, & Russo, 1985). We have also been successful in teaching learning strategies to ESOL and other second language students and in providing teachers with learning-strategy instructional methods (Chamot, 1991, 1994; Chamot, Barnhardt, El-Dinary, Carbonaro, & Robbins, 1993; Chamot, Robbins, & El-Dinary, 1993; O'Malley & Chamot, 1990; O'Malley, Chamot, Stewner-Manzanares, Russo, & Küpper, 1985). Teaching learning strategies across the curriculum is valuable for all students and can provide ELL students with essential tools for successful learning.

In summary, an effective curriculum for language-minority secondary students should include all of the components of an effective curriculum for native English-speaking students, including language development in all subject areas, the integration of subject areas, and learning-strategies instruction for both academic language and content subjects. In addition, the curriculum should include courses that are linguistically and culturally sensitive to students' backgrounds, such as academic courses taught in students' native language, content-based ESOL, sheltered classes that adapt the instructional language, and advanced-level classes in students' native language.

Teaching Practices

The curriculum and classroom organization principles described previously carry with them a number of implications for instruction. Five teaching practices that support cognitive instruction are (a) use of students' prior knowledge, (b) teacher modeling, (c) scaffolded instruction, (d) interactive teaching, and (e) the teaching of metacognition and thinking skills.

Building instruction on students' prior knowledge is not a new idea in education, but it has assumed a central role in teaching as cognitive research on learning has identified the dramatic effect that prior knowledge has on learning new information and skills (Leinhardt, 1992). In reading, for example, a student's prior knowledge frameworks, or schemata, about the text topic interact with the text, allowing the student to construct new knowledge (Wilson & Anderson, 1986). When a student does not have or does not have access to a relevant schema, comprehension is impeded. In science, students frequently have misconceptions or naive explanations for science phenomena, and these misconceptions actually hinder their comprehension of new scientific information (Roth, 1990).

Nowhere is the role of prior knowledge more important than in second language educational contexts. Students who can access their prior knowledge through the language and culture most familiar to them can call on a rich array of schemata, whereas students who believe that they can use only that knowledge they have explicitly learned in the second language are limited in their access. A major rationale for bilingual education is the premise that conceptual development and processes such as reading and writing can be achieved most efficiently through students' native language, and that this knowledge and these skills are readily transferable to the second language, English (Cummins, 1986, 1992; Wong Fillmore & Meyer, 1992). However, ELL students may not always transfer native language concepts and skills to English learning contexts (O'Malley et al., 1989). Effective teachers of linguistically diverse students help their students identify and transfer their prior linguistic and cultural knowledge through instructional practices that value the native language and culture and provide support ranging from content courses in the native language to bilingual tutors and the use of the native language in student-student interactions (Lucas et al., 1990; Tikunoff, 1985; Tikunoff et al., 1991).

The teacher is a model for students in both obvious and subtle ways. Teachers of linguistically diverse students are language models as well as intellectual models, and they may also be role models for their students. The teacher should also model thoughtfulness and reflection by "showing appreciation for students' ideas and for alternative approaches if based on sound reasoning, by acknowledging the difficulty of acquiring knowledge, and by explaining how they think through problems" (Onosko, 1992, p. 40).

This latter aspect of teacher modeling is particularly useful for students to see how teachers think aloud to express their thoughts, attitudes, feelings, and learning strategies (Idol, Jones, & Mayer, 1991; Jones, Palincsar, Ogle, & Carr, 1987). Modeling of expert performance can show students the goal they are aiming for, and modeling problem-solving processes can show students the false starts and intuitions that underlie expert performance (Collins, 1991). Modeling processes like reading comprehension and writing is especially helpful and reassuring for students learning English for academic subjects, because the thinking involved and the interaction between reader or writer and text is made transparent (Chamot & O'Malley, 1994). Modeling does not always have to be done by the teacher. Peer modeling and modeling for younger or less proficient students can provide incentives for the student doing the modeling and demonstrate realistic goals for other students (Harris & Graham, 1992).

Modeling by itself, however, is not sufficient for effective instruction. Teachers must also plan the instruction so that students can experience successful learning and develop independent learning skills. This process has been referred to as scaffolding, using as an analogy the construction of a building where scaffolding initially supports the developing structure and is gradually removed as different parts of the building are completed. Initially, the teacher provides sufficient support so that the student can practice a number of component skills integratively, rather than practicing each skill separately. Gradually, the teacher removes the supports, so that students can practice independently (Idol et al., 1991; Jones et al., 1987). One aspect of scaffolded instruction that is particularly important in academic learning is that in addition to teacher explanations and support, it provides opportunities for students to confront and change misconceptions that they may have had about the topic or processes being learned (Idol et al., 1991).

Interactive teaching is a natural outgrowth of using students' prior knowledge, modeling, and scaffolding. Each of these instructional techniques calls for dialogue between teacher and students. Dialogic teaching goes back at least as far as Socrates and involves asking students open-ended questions that make them think beyond right or wrong answers, and then listening and responding to their answers in a nonjudgmental, truth-seeking fashion. Students use academic language and their content knowledge to respond to and participate in the class's ongoing intellectual investigation. In Sizer's (1992) high school model, teachers and students learn together by talking about their ideas and reasoning. Interactive or dialogic teaching was found to be an important component of exemplary ESOL (SAIP) programs and was facilitated by cooperative learning activities in which students had to talk to complete assigned tasks, and teachers focused on the concepts expressed by students, rather than on the language form of their utterances (Tikunoff et al., 1991). Lucas and her colleagues (1990) also found that in effective high schools for language-minority Spanish-speaking students, teachers "challenged students with difficult questions and problems. . . . Teachers did not talk down to limited-English-proficient students in 'foreigner talk,' but spoke clearly, with normal intonation, explaining difficult words and concepts as needed" (p. 328).

A fifth instructional practice that promotes academic achievement for all students and is of special importance for language-minority students is focusing on the development of metacognition and higher-order thinking skills. Unfortunately, some educators and theorists believe that higher-order thinking must be delayed until basic skills are developed. This belief is pervasive in all types of compensatory programs for at-risk students, including those for language minorities (Anderson & Pellicer, 1990; Pogrow, 1990; Secada, 1991; Wong Fillmore & Meyer, 1992). Even in some current approaches to second language instruction, teachers are advised to ask only lower-level questions (i.e., questions requiring yes or no answers, either-or questions, and what, when, where, and who questions) at the initial stages of language acquisition

(Krashen & Terrell, 1983). This view is challenged by the curriculum reform movements discussed earlier, as well as by individual researchers who point out that the target language-minority students are aiming for is constantly moving ahead, so that while language-minority and other minority students may be mired in repetitive, low-level instructional activities (such as mathematical computation), their majority peers are participating in instruction that focuses on high-level thinking and problem solving (Secada, 1991; Thomas, 1992). Pogrow (1992) summarizes the limitations of compensatory programs as follows:

> There is renewed interest among practitioners, policy makers, and researchers in developing the thinking skills of at-risk students. This interest is accelerated because of a growing realization that: (a) the drill and kill approach hasn't worked, and (b) even if this approach were able to raise basic test scores, that outcome, by itself, is insufficient to prepare students for a more sophisticated world of work. (p. 87)

Teachers of ELL students should also ask their students challenging questions and provide learning tasks that require higher-order thinking skills.

Striking differences in student levels of thinking, influenced by the instructional context, were identified by Diaz et al. (1986), who found that bilingual students successfully engaged in higher-level comprehension activities in Spanish reading but were relegated to lower-level phonics instruction in their English reading classes. By making English reading instruction more congruent with the type of instruction provided during Spanish reading—that is, by focusing on higher-level reading comprehension—the same students were able to perform at a significantly higher level of reading in English. Gersten (1996) reports similar differences between teachers who focus on lower-level skills in reading and those who encourage their students to think, to reason, and to justify their ideas.

This is only one example of the powerful effects of asking students to think and to talk about their own thinking. The development of metacognitive knowledge, or the understanding of one's own learning and thinking processes, is an important educational objective for all students. Teachers can encourage students to describe the conditions in which they learn most effectively, and they can share with students their own approaches to problem solving. Teachers need to convey to students that they should (a) think about and identify the problem or task to be solved or completed; (b) remember the strategies they have used in the past to solve or complete similar problems or tasks; (c) select the strategy that seems most useful for the problem or task; (d) use the strategy; (e) evaluate how well the strategy works, and change it if necessary; and (f) apply the strategy (with further modifications as necessary) to related problems or tasks. When students develop metacognitive knowledge about how they learn, they are able to regulate their own learning processes (Zimmerman, 1994). Developing and nurturing students' metacognitive knowledge about their own learning approaches and outcomes is an important characteristic of effective instruction for all students, and it is particularly important for ELL learners.

Assessment

As discussed earlier, sole reliance on formal assessment, such as standardized language proficiency and achievement tests, does a disservice to language-minority students. Standardized tests tend to be culturally inappropriate; they traditionally assess only lower-order recall of information, and, because they are administered only annually (or less frequently), they are difficult to use to diagnose student difficulties in time to make adjustments to instruction. A critical component of effective instruction for linguistically diverse students, therefore, lies in the ability of teachers to plan, conduct, analyze, and make diagnostic use of informal assessment.

Informal assessment calls on students to demonstrate their performance on academic tasks, rather than merely regurgitate information. Informal assessment is also continuous, capturing examples of students' abilities throughout the school year. Performance assessments can include writing samples, group projects, debates, treasure hunts, oral history projects, historical and contemporary role playing, job interview role playing, games, design competitions, science fairs, merit badges, student-run banks and stores, designing newspaper ads, and developing a class newspaper (Wiggins, 1989). In other words, performance assessments are authentic when they are virtually indistinguishable from classroom activities. This became evident to Shavelson, Baxter, and Pine (1992) during their study of effective performance assessment for science: "Finally, these alternatives are developed with recognition of the symmetry between testing and teaching. That is, a good assessment makes a good teaching activity, and a good teaching activity makes a good assessment" (p. 22).

Student responses to informal assessment can include checklists, learning logs, book reports, writing samples, explanations of problem solutions, science lab reports with diagrams, dialogue journals, self-evaluations of strategy use, and oral descriptions of the assessment activity, among others. The teacher's responsibility is to organize the student work samples so that they can be used in a systematic fashion to assess how well individual students are attaining the instructional goals of the program.

A systematic way to organize examples of student work is through student portfolios, in which teachers and students work collaboratively to select examples of quality student work at different moments in the academic year. The portfolio is more than just a collection of student work. A portfolio should also contain information from the teacher about how well the student has met specific instructional goals. This information may be on teacher rating scales or checklists, with which the teacher rates observed student performance or student products. Portfolios should be

> part of an integrative plan that enables teachers to judge student achievement, growth, and thinking processes. Portfolios enable the teacher to

communicate with students, other teachers, parents, and with administrators about the progress being made by students, and enable the teacher to point to specific representations of the student's work that illustrate this progress. (Chamot & O'Malley, 1994, p. 127)

In summary, the opportunities for realistic assessment of the actual performance of ELL students on different types of learning tasks are enhanced when multiple types of student work and teacher evaluation are collected, analyzed, and used to guide instructional decisions.

INSTRUCTIONAL FRAMEWORK

The previous section discussed a number of effective instructional practices for teachers of ELL students. Curriculum and instruction that have been shown to be effective with all students include content emphasizing depth over breadth, classroom organization features that develop independent learning, teaching that builds on students' prior knowledge and shows students how to be effective learners, a focus on thinking and higher-level cognitive skills, and the use of alternative measures to assess student knowledge and performance. Effective instruction for language-minority students includes these features and adds to them the use of students' native language and culture both as sources of prior knowledge and to mediate instruction so that it is accessible to students.

These principles of effective instruction for ELL students provide the framework of the instructional model for ELL students that I developed with J. Michael O'Malley. The Cognitive Academic Language Learning Approach (CALLA) is based on a cognitive model of learning and integrates content selected from major subject areas, the development of academic language and higher-order thinking skills, and instruction in learning strategies for both content and language (Chamot & O'Malley, 1987, 1989, 1994, 1996). Instructional practices recommended in CALLA include extensive use of students' prior conceptual and linguistic knowledge, cooperative learning, teacher modeling and scaffolding, an emphasis on interactive dialogue on thinking and learning strategies, and alternative assessment.

CALLA instruction is sequenced in five phases that are recursive rather than linear—that is, the teacher can move back to an earlier phase as necessary to clarify or add new elements to the lesson's topic. The five phases are preparation, presentation, practice, evaluation, and expansion. Some examples of the types of instructional activities for each phase follow.

The purpose of the preparation phase is to help students identify any prior knowledge about the lesson topic, relevant academic language, and learning strategies they already use for learning similar material. Teachers typically begin a new lesson or unit with the preparation phase, in which students identify their prior knowledge and experiences related to the lesson's topic, through discussion and brainstorming activities. This identification of prior knowledge is accompanied by vocabulary development for the topic. During the preparation phase, teachers also help students identify the learning strategies they generally use for similar topics. For example, in an ESOL class, a teacher might introduce a folktale by asking students to share folktales on similar themes from their own countries of origin.

Teachers then move to the presentation phase, in which explanation of new information and modeling of new skills take place. Material is presented in a variety of ways—including visual, auditory, kinesthetic, experiential, and interpersonal channels—to reach students with different learning styles. In a CALLA science class, for example, the teacher might demonstrate and ask students to describe an experimental process, illustrate characteristics of living things with real plants and animals, and model the learning strategies involved in making accurate scientific observations.

New learning strategies are presented in various ways, including teacher think-aloud modeling, using posters or other visual aids as an instructional focus, or calling attention to a student's spontaneous use of a strategy.

The presentation phase of CALLA instruction is followed by (and frequently intermingled with) the practice phase, in which the focus of the lesson turns to hands-on activities that enable students to try out for themselves the information and processes demonstrated during the presentation phase. Cooperative learning activities in this phase provide opportunities for students to discover applications of the new information and processes. For example, students might work in pairs or small groups to develop graphic organizers that illustrate cause-and-effect relationships in social studies, or to make a story map for a piece of literature. The results of work done in groups are then reported to the class as a whole, providing students with opportunities to use appropriate academic language. Similarly, students might work in groups to identify key concepts in a science or social studies text by using learning strategies such as predicting, selective attention, and making inferences.

In the evaluation phase of the lesson or unit, students are asked to reflect on and evaluate their own learning. This can take the form of class discussions, journal writing, or answering questions such as, What was easy for you in this unit? What was difficult? Why? How can you learn what was difficult? and, How do you feel about your class work this week? Teachers also assess student progress through observation, interviews, tests, and work portfolios.

In the expansion phase, students make connections between the topic of the current lesson and other subject areas and between what they are learning in school and their daily lives. For example, after studying the properties and uses of electricity, students can research the uses of electricity and the types of electric motors in their own homes. In this phase, students might also be asked to apply a learning strategy they have learned in one class to a different class, and then to report on the results.

The CALLA model emphasizes instruction that allows ELL students to experience a variety of ways to learn content, develop academic language, and practice learning strategies. CALLA is being implemented in a number of school districts nationwide. Evaluations report substantial gains in student achievement (Chamot, 1996; Galland, 1995; Mayberger, 1994; Perrin, 1992; Thomas, 1990, 1991, 1992).

CONCLUSION

This chapter began by identifying some of the major academic needs of secondary ELL students, which include language, instructional time, subject matter concepts, learning strategies, and self-efficacy. The next part reviewed research on program effectiveness and effective instructional practices and identified major characteristics of programs and instruction that have been successful in meeting these academic needs. This research indicates that instruction for ELL students needs to change in three major areas: linguistic and cultural support, instructional time, and teaching practices.

We know that learning is assisted when the student's native language and culture are incorporated in the classroom and when teachers make explicit the value of the transfer of conceptual knowledge and academic skills from the first language to English. The availability of academic courses in their native language provides high school students with the opportunity of continuing their conceptual development while they are learning English, rather than interrupting their cognitive growth, as is too often the case. At the very least, students should have access to bilingual counselors and tutors on a daily basis. Language support is also needed in English. Effective high school programs for language-minority students incorporate content into the ESOL class and infuse language development into content area classes. Providing an adequate level of language support in both the native language and in English should be a priority in improving educational practices for linguistically diverse students.

The second area in which change is both necessary and long overdue is instructional time. The research evidence continues to accumulate about the length of time needed for students who do not speak English natively to acquire the level of academic language necessary to be successful in the academic curriculum. For most high school ELL students, there is simply not enough time left in school to reach this level of academic language.

Possible solutions are to allow students to spend more time in high school to earn the credits needed for graduation and to extend the amount of instructional time available in secondary programs. Extending the school day and providing study clubs, night school, and Saturday school would provide additional instructional time for language-minority students. A required summer school program could prove especially beneficial not only by providing additional instruction but also by preventing the "summer forgetting" problem that teachers cite as the reason for spending approximately three months at the beginning of each new school year in review of the previous year's work. Year-round schools (which are currently being tried out in various parts of the country, including Florida, Illinois, and Utah) could be a practical solution to the amount of instructional time needed by ELL students to develop academic English language skills.

The third area in which change is still needed is in instructional practices for linguistically diverse students. The effective instructional practices described in this chapter are not yet widespread among teachers of ELL students. Changes are needed in curriculum, in classroom organization practices, in teaching procedures, and in assessment. Both teacher and student attitudes about abilities and achievement expectations need to change. Classrooms need to become learning communities with high academic expectations, where the prior knowledge that students bring from diverse linguistic and cultural backgrounds is not only valued but seen as essential in constructing new knowledge. Teachers need to share with students the secrets of efficient learning, by modeling learning strategies and providing extensive scaffolded strategy practice for all kinds of academic tasks. By helping students become better learners, teachers will be developing the sense of self-efficacy that students need to persevere with their educational endeavors.

These proposals can help make the achievement of national educational goals a reality for linguistically diverse students.

REFERENCES

Anderson, L. W., & Pellicer, L. O. (1990). Synthesis of research on compensatory and remedial education. *Educational Leadership, 48*(1), 10–16.

Bandura, A. (1986). *Social foundations of thought and action: A social-cognitive theory.* Englewood Cliffs, NJ: Prentice-Hall.

Bragaw, D. H. & Hartoonian, H. M. (1988). Social studies: The study of people in society. In R. S. Brandt (Ed.), *Content of the curriculum: 1988 ASLD yearbook,* 9–29. Alexandria, VA: Association for Supervision and Curriculum Development.

Brinton, D. M., Snow, M. A. & Wesche, M. B. (1989). *Content-based second language instuction.* Boston, MA: Newbury House.

Brophy, J. (1990). Teaching social studies for understanding and higher-order applications. *Elementary School Journal, 90,* 351–417.

Brophy, J. (1992). Probing the subtleties of subject-matter teaching. *Educational Leadership, 49*(7), 4–8.

Bush, G. (1991). *America 2000: An education strategy.* Washington, DC: U.S. Department of Education.

California State Department of Education (1987). *California history–social science framework.* Sacramento, CA: California State Board of Education.

Carpenter, T., Fennema, E., Peterson, P., Chiang, C., & Loef, M. (1989). Using knowledge of children's mathematics thinking in classroom teaching: An experimental study. *American Educational Research Journal 26,* 499–532.

Carter, T., & Chaffield, M. (1986). Effective bilingual schools: Implications for policy and practice. *American Journal of Education, 95,* 200–232.

Chamot, A. U. (1991). Cognitive instruction in the second language classroom: The role of learning strategies. In J. E. Alatis (Ed.), *Linguistics, language teaching and language acquisition: The interdependence of theory, practice and research.* Georgetown University Round Table on Languages and Linguistics 1990, pp. 496–513. Washington, DC: Georgetown University Press.

Chamot, A. U. (1993). Student responses to learning strategy instruction in the foreign language classroom. *Foreign Language Annals, 26*(3), 308–321.

Chamot, A. U. (1994). A model for learning strategy instruction in the foreign language classroom. In J. E. Alatis (Ed.), *Georgetown University round table on languages and linguistics 1994*, pp. 323–336. Washington, DC: Georgetown University Press.

Chamot, A. U. (1996). Implementing the Cognitive Academic Language Learning Approach: CALLA in Arlington, Virginia. *Bilingual Research Journal, 19*(2), 221–247.

Chamot, A. U., Barnhardt, S., El-Dinary, P. B., Carbonaro, G., & Robbins, J. (1993). *Teaching learning strategies in foreign language instruction and informal assessment of language skills.* Final report submitted to Center for International Education, U.S. Department of Education. (Available from ERIC Clearinghouse on Languages and Linguistics)

Chamot, A. U., Dale, M., O'Malley, J. M., & Spanos, G. A. (1993 Summer/Fall), Learning and problem solving strategies of ESL students. *Bilingual Research Quarterly, 16* (3 and 4), 1–38.

Chamot, A. U., & Küpper, L. (1989). Learning strategies in foreign language instruction. *Foreign Language Annals, 22*(1), 13–24.

Chamot, A. U., & O'Malley, J. M. (1987). The Cognitive Academic Language Learning Approach: A bridge to the mainstream. *TESOL Quarterly, 21*(2), 227–249.

Chamot, A. U., & O'Malley, J. M. (1989). The Cognitive Academic Language Learning Approach. In Rigg, P., & Allen, V. G. (Eds.), *When they don't all speak English: Integrating the ESL student into the regular classroom* (pp. 108–125). Urbana, IL: National Council of Teachers of English.

Chamot, A. U., & O'Malley, J. M. (1994). *The CALLA handbook: Implementing the Cognitive Academic Language Learning Approach.* Reading, MA: Addison-Wesley.

Chamot, A. U., & O'Malley, J. M. (1996). The Cognitive Academic Language Learning Approach: A model for linguistically diverse classrooms. *Elementary School Journal, 96*(3): 259–273.

Chamot, A. U., Robbins, J., & El-Dinary, P. B. (1993). *Learning strategies in Japanese foreign language instruction.* Final report submitted to Center for International Education, U.S. Department of Education. (Available from ERIC Clearinghouse on Languages and Linguistics)

Chamot, A. U., & Stewner-Manzanares, G. (1985). *Review, summary, and synthesis of literature on English as a second language.* McLean, VA: InterAmerica Research Associates.

Cohen, A. D., & Aphek, E. 1981. Easifying second language learning. *Studies in Second Language Learning, 3*, 221–236.

Cohen, E. G. (1986). *Designing groupwork: Strategies for the heterogeneous classroom.* New York and London: Teachers College Press.

Collier, V. P. (1987). Age and rate of acquisition of second language for academic purposes. *TESOL Quarterly, 21*(4), 617–641.

Collier, V. P. (1989). How long? A synthesis of research on academic achievement in a second language. *TESOL Quarterly, 23*(3), 509–531.

Collier, V. P. (1991). A synthesis of studies examining long-term language-minority student data on academic achievement. *Bilingual Research Quarterly, 16*(1–2).

Collier, V. P. (1995). Acquiring a second language for school. *Directions in Language and Education, 1*(4), 1–12. Washington, DC: National Clearinghouse for Bilingual Education.

Collins, A (1991). Cognitive apprenticeship and instructional technology. In L. Idol &
B. F. Jones (Eds.), *Educational values and cognitive instruction: Implications for reform* (pp.
121–138). Hillsdale, NJ: Erlbaum.

Cummins, J. (1984). *Bilingualism and special education: Issues in assessment and pedagogy.* San
Diego, CA: College Hill Press.

Cummins, J. (1986). Empowering minority students: A framework for intervention.
Harvard Educational Review, 56(1), 18–36.

Cummins, J. (1992). Language proficiency, bilingualism, and academic achievement. In
P. A. Richard-Amato & M. A. Snow (Eds.), *The multicultural classroom: Readings for
content-area teachers* (pp. 16–26). White Plains, NY: Longman.

Derry, S. J. (1990). Learning strategies for acquiring useful knowledge. In B. F. Jones &
L. Idol (Eds.), *Dimensions of thinking and cognitive instruction* (pp. 347–379). Hillsdale, NJ:
Erlbaum.

Diaz, E., Moll, L., & Mehan, H. (1986). *Bilingual communication skills in classroom context
processing.* Washington, DC: National Clearinghouse for Bilingual Education.

Dole, J. A., Duffy, G. G., Roehler, L. R., & Pearson, P. D. (1991). Moving from the old
to the new: Research on reaching comprehension instruction. *Review of Educational
Research, 61*(2), 239–264.

El-Dinary, P. B., Brown, R., & Van Meter, P. (1995). Strategy instruction for improving
writing. In E. Wood, V. E. Woloshyn, & T. Willoughby (Eds.), *Cognitive strategy
instruction for middle and high schools* (pp. 88–116). Cambridge, MA: Brookline Books.

Faltis, C., & Hudelson, S. (1994). Learning English as an additional language in K–12
schools. *TESOL Quarterly, 28*(3), 457–468.

Galland, P. A. (1995). *An evaluation of the Cognitive Academic Language Learning Approach
(CALLA) in the High Intensity Language Training (HILT) science program in Arlington
Public Schools.* Unpublished master's research paper, Georgetown University.

Garza Flores, H. (1991–92). Please do bother them. *Educational Leadership, 49*(4), 58–59.

Gersten, R. (1996). The double demands of teaching English language learners. *Educational Leadership, 53*(5), 18–22.

Good, T., & Brophy, J. (1986). School effects. In M. Wittrock (Ed.), *Handbook of research
on teaching* (3rd ed., pp. 570–602). New York: Macmillan.

Goodman, K. (1987). *What's whole in whole language?* Portsmouth, NH: Heinemann.

Harris, K. R., & Graham, S. (1992). *Helping young writers master the craft: Strategy instruction
and self-regulation in the writing process.* Cambridge, MA: Brookline Books.

Herman, J. L. (1992). What research tells us about good assessment. *Educational Leadership,
49*(8), 74–78.

Hosenfeld, C., Arnold, V., Kirchofer, J., Laciura, J., & Wilson, L. (1981). Second language reading: A curricular sequence for teaching reading strategies. *Foreign Language
Annals, 14*(5), 415–422.

Idol, L., Jones, B. F., & Mayer, R. E. (1991). Classroom instruction: The teaching of
thinking. In L. Idol & B. F. Jones (Eds.), *Educational values and cognitive instruction:
Implications for reform,* 65–119. Hillsdale, NJ: Erlbaum.

Johnson, D.W., Johnson, R.T., Holubec, E. J., & Roy, P. (1994). *The new circles of learning: Cooperation in the classroom and school.* Alexandria, VA: Association for Supervision
and Curriculum Development.

Jones, B. F., Palincsar, A. S., Ogle, D. S., & Carr, E. G. (1987). *Strategic teaching and learning: Cognitive instruction in the content areas.* Alexandria, VA: Association for Supervision
and Curriculum Development.

Kagan, S. (1986). Cooperative learning and sociocultural factors in schooling. In California State Department of Education, *Beyond language: Social and cultural factors in schooling language minority students* (pp. 231–298). Los Angeles: Evaluation, Dissemination, and Assessment Center, California State University.

Krashen, S., & Biber, D. (1988). *On course: Bilingual education's success in California.* Sacramento, CA: California Association for Bilingual Education.

Krashen, S. D., & Terrell, T. (1983). *The Natural Approach: Language acquisition in the classroom.* Hayward, CA: Alemany Press.

Leinhardt, G. (1992). What research on learning tells us about teaching. *Educational Leadership, 49*(7), 20–25.

Lucas, T., Henze, R., & Donato, R. (1990). Promoting the success of Latino language-minority students: An exploratory study of six high schools. *Harvard Educational Review, 60*(3), 315–340.

Mayberger, S. (1994). *Cognitive Academic Language Learning Approach (Project CALLA): Community School District 2 Special Alternative Instruction Program Interim evaluation report, 1993–94.* New York: Office of Educational Research.

McGroarty, M. (1992). Cooperative learning: The benefits for content-area teaching. In P. A. Richard-Amato & M. A. Snow (Eds.), *The multicultural classroom: Readings for content-area teachers* (pp. 58–69). White Plains, NY: Longman.

National Council of Teachers of Mathematics. (1989). *Curriculum and evaluation standards for school mathematics.* Reston, VA: National Council of Teachers of Mathematics.

National Science Teachers Association. (1992). *Scope, sequence, and coordination of secondary school science: Volume I—The content core: A guide for curriculum designers.* Washington, DC: National Science Teachers Association.

O'Malley, J. M. (1991). Looking for academic language proficiency: Comments on Damico's paper. Paper presented at the Second National Research Symposium on LEP Student Issues, Washington, DC.

O'Malley J. M., & Chamot, A. U. (1990). *Learning strategies in second language acquisition.* New York: Cambridge University Press.

O' Malley, J. M., Chamot, A. U., & Küpper, L. (1989). Listening comprehension strategies in second language acquisition. *Applied Linguistics, 10*(4), 418–437.

O'Malley, J. M., Chamot, A. U., Stewner-Manzanares, G., Küpper, L., & Russo, R. P. (1985). Learning strategies used by beginning and intermediate ESL students. *Language Learning, 35,* 21–46.

O'Malley, J. M., Chamot, A. U., Stewner-Manzanares, G., Russo, R. P., & Küpper, L. (1985). Learning strategy applications with students of English as a second language. *TESOL Quarterly, 19,* 285–296.

Onosko, J. J. (1992). Exploring the thinking of thoughtful teachers. *Educational Leadership, 49*(7), 40–43.

Palincsar, A. S., & Brown, A. L. (1985). Reciprocal teaching: Activities to promote "reading with your mind." In T. L. Harris & E. J. Cooper (Eds.), *Reading, thinking, and concept development: Strategies for the classroom* (pp. 147–160). New York: College Board.

Palincsar, A. S., & Brown, A. L. (1986). Interactive teaching to promote independent learning from text. *The Reading Teacher, 39*(2), 771–777.

Palincsar, A. S., and Klenk, L. (1992). Examining and influencing contexts for intentional literacy learning. In C. Collins & J. N. Mangieri (Eds.), *Teaching thinking: An agenda for the twenty-first century* (pp. 297–315). Hillsdale, NJ: Erlbaum.

Perrin, J. (1992). *Final evaluation report: Title VII project S.T.Y.L.E., 1991–1992—Boston, Massachusetts.* Arlington, MA: Public Affairs Research Institute.

Pogrow, S. (1990). Challenging at-risk students: Findings from the HOTS program. *Phi Delta Kappan, 71*, 389–397.

Pogrow, S. (1992). A validated approach to thinking development for at-risk populations. In C. Collins & J. N. Mangieri (Eds.), *Teaching thinking: An agenda for the twenty-first century* (pp. 87–101). Hillsdale, NJ: Erlbaum.

Prawat, R. S. (1992). From individual differences to learning communities—Our changing focus. *Educational Leadership, 49*(7), 9–13.

Pressley, M., & Associates. (1990). *Cognitive strategy instruction that really improves children's academic performance.* Cambridge, MA: Brookline Books.

Ramírez, J. D. (1992). Executive Summary. *Bilingual Research Journal, 16*, 1–62.

Rost, M., & Ross, S. (1991). Learner use of strategies in interaction: Typology and teachability. *Language Learning, 41*(2), 235–273.

Roth, K. J. (1990). Developing meaningful conceptual understanding in science. In B. F. Jones & L. Idol (Eds.), *Dimensions of thinking and cognitive instruction,* (pp. 139–175). Hillsdale, NJ: Erlbaum.

Rutherford, F. J. (1992). *Update Project 2061: Education for a changing future.* Washington, DC: American Association for the Advancement of Science.

Scardamalia, M., & Bereiter, C. (1986). Written composition. In M. Wittrock (Ed.), *Handbook of research on teaching* (3rd ed., pp. 778–803). New York: Macmillan.

Secada, W. G. (1991). Student diversity and mathematics education reform. In L. Idol & B. F. Jones (Eds.), *Educational values and cognitive instruction: Implications for reform* (pp. 297–332). Hillsdale, NJ: Erlbaum.

Shavelson, R. J., Baxter, G. P., & Pine, J. (1992). Performance assessments: Political rhetoric and measurement reality. *Educational Researcher, 21*(4), 22–27.

Silver, E. A., & Marshall S. P. (1990). Mathematical and scientific problem solving: Findings, issues, and instructional implications. In B. F. Jones & L. Idol (Eds.), *Dimensions of thinking and cognitive instruction* (pp. 265–290). Hillsdale, NJ: Erlbaum.

Sizer, T. R. (1992). *Horace's school: Redesigning the American high school.* Boston: Houghton-Mifflin.

Slavin, R. E. (1987). Cooperative learning and the cooperative school. *Educational Leadership, 45*(3), 7–13.

Snow, M. A., Met, M. & Genesee, F. (1989). A conceptual framework for the integration of language and content in second/foreign language instruction. *TESOL Quarterly, 23*: 201–217.

Spanos, G. (1990). On the integration of language and content instruction. *Annual Review of Applied Linguistics, 10*, 227–240.

Thomas, W. P. (1990). Evaluation of Title VII program: The Cognitive Academic Language Learning Approach (CALLA) for mathematics project, 1989–1990. Arlington, VA: Arlington Public Schools.

Thomas, W. P. (1991). Evaluation of Title VII program: The Cognitive Academic Language Learning Approach (CALLA) for mathematics project, 1990–1991. Arlington, VA: Arlington Public Schools.

Thomas, W. P. (1992, April). An analysis of the research methodology of the Ramirez study. Paper presented at the American Educational Research Association annual meeting, San Francisco, CA.

Thompson, I., & Rubin, J. (1993). *Improving listening comprehension in Russian.* Report to International Research and Studies Program, U.S. Department of Education, Washington, DC.

Tikunoff, W. J. (1985). *Applying significant bilingual instructional features in the classroom.* Washington, DC: National Clearinghouse for Bilingual Education.

Tikunoff, W. J., Ward, B. A., van Broekhuizen, L. D., Romero, M., Castaneda, L. V., Lucas, T., & Katz, A. (1991). *Executive summary: A descriptive study of significant features of exemplary special alternative instructional programs.* Los Alamitos, CA: Southwest Regional Educational Laboratory.

Warren, B., Rosebery, A. S., Conant, F. R., & Hudicourt-Barnes, J. (1992). Cheche Konnen: Case studies in scientific sense-making. *Focus on Diversity, 1*(1), 2–3.

Wenden, A., & Rubin, J. (Eds.). (1987). *Learner strategies in language learning.* Englewood Cliffs, NJ: Prentice-Hall.

Wiggins, G. (1989). The futility of trying to teach everything of importance. *Educational Leadership, 47*(3), 44–59.

Wilson, B. L., & Corcoran, T. B. (1988). *Successful secondary schools.* New York: Falmer Press.

Wilson, P. T., & Anderson, R. C. (1986). What they don't know will hurt them: The role of prior knowledge in comprehension. In J. Orasanu (Ed.), *Reading comprehension: From research to practice* (pp. 31–48). Hillsdale, NJ: Erlbaum.

Wong Fillmore, L., Ammon, P., & McLaughlin, B. (1983). *Learning English through bilingual instruction: Executive summary and conclusion.* Washington, DC: National Clearinghouse for Bilingual Education.

Wong Fillmore, L., & Meyer, L. M. (1992). The curriculum and linguistic minorities. In P. Jackson (Ed.), *Handbook of research on curriculum* (pp. 626–659). New York: Macmillan.

Wood, E., Woloshyn, V. E., & Willoughby, T. (Eds.). (1995). *Cognitive strategy instruction for middle and high schools.* Cambridge, MA: Brookline Books.

Zimmerman, B. J. (1990). Self-regulating academic learning and achievement: The emergence of a social cognitive perspective. *Educational Psychology Review, 2*(2), 173–200.

Zimmerman, B. J. (1994). Dimensions of academic self-regulation: A conceptual framework for education. In D. H. Schunk & B. J. Zimmerman (Eds.), *Self-regulation of learning and performance: Issues and educational applications.* Hillsdale, NJ: Erlbaum.

12

Preparing Text and Classroom Materials for English Language Learners

Curriculum Adaptations in Secondary School Settings

Jana Echevarria
California State University, Long Beach

One of the greatest challenges for middle school and high school teachers is making curriculum accessible to students who have a primary language other than English (Faltis, 1993; Fradd, 1987; Henze & Lucas, 1993; Minicucci, 1993; Short, 1989, 1994). Teachers cite the need for more-appropriate texts and materials for English language learners, who often find textbooks and secondary course work difficult semantically and syntactically (Lucas & Katz, 1994).

These curricular issues become more complex when we realize that many new immigrant students in secondary schools are underprepared for grade-level work because they enter school with few years of formal academic preparation (Short, 1994). Some students have only the most basic literacy skills yet are confronted with texts and activities that require much higher literacy levels. For students learning English, much of the curriculum and instruction they receive requires modification to ensure comprehension.

The previous two chapters were focused on instructional modifications that can be made to facilitate success for English language learners in middle school and high school. The purpose of this chapter is to delineate strategies and techniques for modifying and adapting curriculum in secondary schools.

The chapter is divided into the following five sections: (a) focusing on both subject matter knowledge and the academic skills necessary for effectively learning content material; (b) including language development and content vocabulary knowledge activities for students; (c) rewriting curriculum; (d) modifying assignments; and (e) demonstrating sensitivity to cultural and linguistic diversity through appropriate content adaptations. This chapter includes numerous examples of science, social studies, and math lessons adapted for English language learners in secondary classrooms. The students discussed in the chapter spoke a variety of languages and represented a variety of ethnicities.

FOCUSING ON BOTH
SUBJECT MATTER KNOWLEDGE
AND ACADEMIC SKILL DEVELOPMENT

In each subject area, there are at least two important curricular strands with which teachers must concern themselves. First, teachers determine the subject matter knowledge that students must gain (e.g., an understanding of the universe, water, air, plants, animals, and the human body) and how they will gain it. Second, teachers must examine the level of academic skills required of students for them to understand and learn the content material (Echevarria & Graves, 1998).

Subject Matter Knowledge: What to Cover?

Gonzales (1994) suggests developing an annual plan whereby teachers review the textbooks, state framework guides, curriculum guides, and teacher manuals for purposes of determining the essential content for a specific grade level or course. Planning involves examining the topics to be covered and then deciding on ways to link the critical concepts and ideas into meaningful, connected units that build on each other. Once the most important concepts have been determined, the nonessential details may be eliminated. Moreover, the broad range of students' academic needs can be addressed by using a planning pyramid (Schumm, Vaughn, & Leavell, 1994). In this process, planning is guided by the questions, What do I want *all* students to learn? What do I want *most* students to learn? and, What do I want *some* students to learn? These questions acknowledge that while all students can learn, not all students can realistically be expected to learn everything in content area textbooks.

This type of big-picture planning assists teachers in modifying existing curriculum to deliver cohesive lessons that build on one another, providing English language learners with continuity and reinforcement of major concepts and vocabulary. It also lends itself to thematic teaching and an interdisciplinary approach.

With thematic teaching, the teacher selects a concept or theme and weaves it across the curriculum. For example, in an American history course, the teacher analyzes the content for the entire course by constructing a time line spanning the academic year. The teacher then determines relevant information to be covered throughout the year, focusing on pieces of history that fit together with one another and historical linkages or patterns that render the material more understandable. A theme such as liberty or democracy is addressed in a variety of ways across lessons, linking the historical events together through the theme. For example, you could discuss with students the concept of liberty. Some students may have fled oppressive governments and can talk personally about liberty and freedom. Weave this concept or theme throughout discussions about historical events, such as the colonists leaving their homelands to settle in the New World because they believed they would have more freedom. Point out that the establishment of the colonies required labor, and that some workers' freedom was restricted or taken away completely, as in the case of Native Americans, indentured servants, and slaves brought from Africa. Further, when the English government denied liberties the colonists believed they were entitled to, the American Revolution began. Each event is viewed from the perspective of the theme, giving students a familiar concept they can tie the information to. A theme can also be carried across content areas, such as in interdisciplinary teaching.

Teaching from an interdisciplinary perspective is considered valuable for students learning English, because it can provide a bridge across subject areas. In observations of a sixth grade American history course in a coastal Southern California community where the students came from a variety of ethnic backgrounds, teachers developed a thematic social studies unit on coastal Native Americans. In this unit, students were simultaneously studying oceanography for science application, counting and keeping records of whales and dolphins for math application, reading the book *Island of the Blue Dolphins* (O'Dell, 1970) for literature infusion, and writing, in cooperative groups, a report on various coastal Native American tribes. Thus, knowledge and skills were developed around a theme in the areas of reading, writing, math, science, and social studies.

Subject Matter Knowledge: How Will It Be Covered?

Once the subject matter to be covered has been determined, teachers still frequently wrestle with ways to make content accessible to English language learners. Many of the textbooks used in classes for these students are written at a high reading level and in a style that is quite difficult for most students to comprehend, let alone students who are English language learners. In a study that assessed 69 sheltered classes and 26 cotaught classes (Goodwin, 1991), teachers expressed the need for materials and visual aids appropriate for instruction with English language learners.

Although recognizing that resources are often limited in schools, I suggest here a variety of ways that visuals can be used to enhance comprehension for English language learners and bring meaning to text. A wide range of photographs and drawings available on the market depict practically any object, process, or topic covered in secondary school curricular areas. As an alternative to purchasing commercially made materials, pictures may be drawn by the teacher or students, or they can be cut out of magazines. A simple yet effective method of providing visual clues for students is the consistent use of an overhead projector. As material and information are introduced, the overhead can be used to give visual information to students by jotting down words or sketching out what is being presented verbally. This way of giving continual visual clues helps students focus and retain information.

Demonstration can bring life to the text. In a class studying archeology, the teacher demonstrated the process by which objects become buried deep underground, by placing a quarter in a pie pan. He proceeded to blow dirt onto the quarter and covered it a bit. Then he put dried leaves on top, followed by a sprinkling of "rain." Finally, he put some sand on top, and the quarter was then underneath an inch or so of natural products. Although the process was described in the text, most students did not have the reading skills or English proficiency to understand it. The demonstration made a much greater impression on the students, and it was referred to later when discussing the earth's layers and other related topics.

Technology offers a multitude of options in this area, from something as simple as listening to a tape recording of Truman's announcement of the dropping of the atomic bomb to an interactive laser computer display. Videos, filmstrips, CD-ROM programs, and tape recordings are examples of visual supplementary materials.

Time lines are particularly useful in the social sciences. As the class progresses through U.S. history, mount a time line (perhaps on butcher paper) along the length of a wall, to visually represent each historical event as it relates to other events and periods in history. As an event is studied, make some visual representation on the time line and continue adding to it throughout the course of the year (see Figure 12.1).

Bulletin boards may be used as visual representations of lesson information, whether it be an example of business letter and friendly letter formats, or a three-dimensional paper model of stalactites and stalagmites, with labels.

Finally, most districts provide a list of resources for teacher use, to supplement the curriculum (see Figure 12.2 for examples of multicultural curriculum resources for teachers of grades 6–12). This can be a time-saver during planning activities. Options for supplementing the core curriculum are often included in these resource guides. Rather than the teacher researching topics and spending time looking for materials, some of the kinds of supplements teachers need are already listed. For example, on the topic of the War for Independence, the district resource guide may have suggestions for activities, such as a colonial newspaper; a list of relevant movies, such as "Crossing the Delaware" or "A Fireball in the Night"; and a list of reading selections, such as "Paul Revere's Ride," by Henry Wadsworth Longfellow, or "I'm Deborah Sampson: A Soldier in the War of the Revolution."

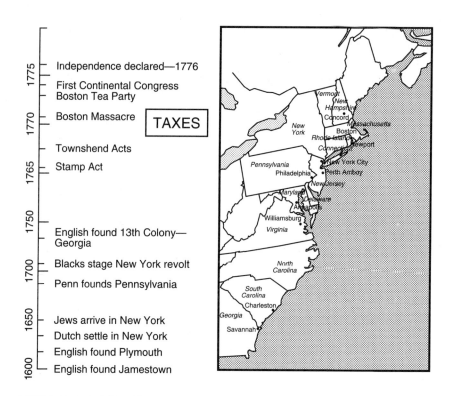

FIGURE 12.1. Social Studies Time Line

FIGURE 12.2. Multicultural Curriculum Resources for Teachers Grades 4–12

Multicultural Curriculum Resources for Teachers
Middle Grades (about 4–9)

Americans, Too!
> Workbook to use with grades 5–9, to teach a critical perspective on minority groups' histories.
>> Good Apple
>> P.O. Box 299
>> Carthage, IL 62321-0299

The Asian American Comic Book
> Stories illustrating common concerns different Asian American groups face, particularly racism and poverty.
>> Asian American Resource Workshop
>> 34 Oak Street, Third Floor
>> Boston, MA 02111
>> (617) 426-5313

Colonialism in the Americas
> Comic book format, provides an overview of how colonialism has worked historically and today, from perspectives of indigenous Americans.
>> VIDEA
>> 407-620 View Street
>> Victoria, B.C., Canada V8W 1J6
>> (604) 385-2333

FIGURE 12.2. *(Continued)*

A Curriculum Guide to Women's Studies for the Middle School
Twenty lesson plans, organized around the following topics: stereotyping, women in the past, women in today's world, taking charge of our lives. Publisher: Feminist Press, 1981.
Embers: Stories for a Changing World
Elementary basal reader, by Meyers, Banfield, and Colon. Stories focus on racism, sexism, and to some extent classism. Publisher: Feminist Press, 1983.
Multicultural Women's History and Curriculum Unit
Activities for integrating five women into elementary history or language arts curricula.
National Women's History Project
7783 Bell Road
Windsor, CA 95492
(707) 838-6000
Myth, Music and Dance of the American Indian
Teacher's resource book and cassette tape, featuring music and background information about music from several specific North American Indian tribes.
Ward-Brodt Music Co.
2200 West Beltline Highway
Madison, WI 53701
(800) 369-6255
Portraits of Mexican Americans, Portraits in Black, Portraits of Asian-Pacific Americans,
and *Portraits of Native Americans*
Workbooks about four American minority groups. Each book contains biographical/historical information followed by a variety of reproducible activity sheets that require thinking and more learning.
Good Apple
P.O. Box 299
Carthage, IL 62321-0299
United States and New York State History, Grade 7, Volumes 1–3
U.S. history for grades 7–8, reworked from a multicultural perspective; activities emphasize viewing situations from more than one viewpoint.
New York City Schools
Instructional Publications Sales
131 Livingston Street, R. 515
Brooklyn, NY 11201
(718) 935-3990

Multicultural Curriculum Resources for Teachers
High School (about 8–12)

The African American Experience
African American history textbook paralleling the approach in the *African American Baseline Essays.* Publisher: Globe, 1991.
African American Literature
Textbook with extensive collection of African American literature selections, organized by both historical period and genre. Publishers: Holt, Rinehart & Winston and Harcourt Brace Jovanovich, 1992.
Japanese American Journey
History of Japanese American people, biographies of famous Japanese Americans, three short stories.
JACP Inc.
P.O. Box 1587
San Mateo, CA 94401
(800) 874-2242
The Latino Experience in U.S. History
Text that looks at U.S. history through the eyes of Latino people; designed to supplement any U.S. history course or to be used for a Latino studies course. Publisher: Globe, 1994. Cost: $22.95 for student edition, $41.95 for teacher's resource manual.

(Continued on next page)

FIGURE 12.2. *(Continued)*

Making History
> Social studies curriculum guide that teaches skills for citizen participation and social change.
>> Education for Social Responsibility
>> 23 Garden Street
>> Cambridge, MA 02138
>> (617) 492-1764

Mexican American Literature
> Textbook for classroom use, organized chronologically; preceded by a history of Mexican Americans. Publisher: Harcourt Brace Jovanovich, 1990.

Multiculturalism in Mathematics, Science, and Technology
> Resource material to supplement math and science curriculum. Contains information about diverse people who have made important contributions, and suggestions for integrating this information into curriculum. Publisher: Addison-Wesley, 1992. Cost: $32.00

A People's History of the United States
> Text by Howard Zinn, on U.S. history. High school or college-level text. Publisher: Harper & Row, 1980.

The Power in Our Hands
> Collection of lesson plans by William Bigelow and Norman Diamond, for teaching about the history of labor and laborers in the United States.
>> Network of Educators on the Americans
>> 1118 22nd Street, NW
>> Washington, DC 20037
>> (202) 429-0137

Taking a Stand Against Racism and Facial Discrimination, Taking a Stand Against Sexism and Sex Discrimination, Homelessness in America, and *The African American Movement Today.*
> Books for kids on these issues. More informative, political, and critical than classroom materials usually are; also provide suggestions for what kids can begin to do about these issues.
>> Franklin Watts
>> 5450 N. Cumberland Avenue
>> Chicago, IL 60656
>> (800) 672-6672 or (312) 393-3300

Tapestry: A Multicultural Anthology
> Softcover anthology of U.S. literature, featuring the work of authors from many different ethnic backgrounds. Publisher: Globe.

Women in United States History
> Nine-volume set of booklets (about 50 pages per booklet) containing text and activity sheets, developing U.S. women's history. Can be used alone or along with a U.S. history textbook.
>> Upper Midwest Women's History Center
>> 6300 Walker Street
>> St. Louis Park, MN 55416

Selected Catalogs

Anti-Defamation League Catalog
> Books and AV materials for teaching students about prejudice and discrimination.
>> Anti-Defamation League of B'nai B'rith
>> 823 United Nations Plaza
>> New York, NY 10017

Bilingual Educational Services Catalog
> Children's books and other teaching materials in Spanish, Spanish-English teaching materials, and ESOL materials.
>> BES
>> 2514 South Grand Avenue
>> Los Angeles, CA 90007
>> (213) 749-6213

FIGURE 12.2. *(Continued)*

Globe Book Company Catalog
Of the major commercial textbook publishers, this one seems to have the best multicultural curriculum materials.
Globe Book Co.
4350 Equity Drive
Columbus, OH 43216
(800) 874-2242

JACP Catalog
For ordering books on Asian Americans; includes children's literature, Asian language and culture books, resource materials for adults, and so forth.
JACP Inc.
P.O. Box 1587
San Mateo, CA 94401
(800) 874-2242

Multicultural Literature for Children and Young Adults, 3rd ed.
Annotated bibliography (not catalog) for children's literature; excellent resource for building a multicultural children's literature library.
Publication Sales
Wisconsin Department of Public Instruction
P.O. Box 7841
Madison, WI 53707-7841
(800) 243-8782

Multicultural Publisher Exchange Catalog
Excellent source of books for various ages, by and about people of color.
Praxis Publications
P.O. Box 9869
Madison, WI 53715
(800) 558-2110

National Women's History Project Catalog
Source for resource material for integrating women into the curriculum.
National Women's History Project
7738 Bell Road
Windsor, CA 95492
(707) 838-6000

Network of Educators on Central America
Teaching resources on Central America and the Caribbean; also carries other multicultural materials.
NECA
1118 22nd Street, NW
Washington, DC 20037
(202) 429-0137

Social Studies School Service
Carries several useful multicultural curricula for social studies, although most material in the catalog is not multicultural.
Social Studies School Service
10200 Jefferson Boulevard, Room 29
Culver City, CA 90232-0802
(800) 421-4246

Women's Educational Equity Act Publishing Center
Resource material for integrating women into the curriculum; good source for math and science resources.
WEEA Publishing Center
Educational Development Center
55 Chapel Street, Suite 200
Newton, MA 02160
(800) 225-3088

Academic Skill Development

After determining the essential content knowledge and the planning of that content into teachable units, teachers need to establish the prerequisite or background academic skills needed for students to make sense of the content of the course. Short (1994) recommends that secondary teachers generate a list of objectives they wish to focus on for each lesson, using three categories: content skills (see previous section), language skills, and thinking/study skills.

Using this kind of planning, teachers analyze the skills required for students to successfully complete the lesson, and they pinpoint skills that need to be taught before students are expected to perform independently. This may entail allowing time to teach these skills (such as outlining or finding the main idea) or rethinking an objective that could be too difficult. For example, in a lesson on the Declaration of Independence, content skill objectives might be "Students will identify five main principles of the Declaration of Independence" and "Students will recognize at least two sources of ideas in the Declaration of Independence." Language skills objectives and thinking/study skills objectives are related to content objectives. For example, a language skills objective for the same lesson might be "Students will listen for the main idea of the reading." Recognizing the main idea may be a skill that needs to be taught or reviewed before the lesson is introduced. Examples of thinking/study skills objectives include "Using sentence strips, students will generate an outline of the Declaration of Independence" and "Students will classify subtopics for the outline" (Short, 1994).

A comprehensive and systematic approach for teaching prerequisite skills involves teachers conducting informal assessments of students in the class. Areas to be assessed might include reading comprehension, outlining, categorizing, map reading skills, and so forth. The informal assessment could consist of a multitask, teacher-made packet that appraises students' skill levels in a variety of areas. Once the informal assessment has been completed, teachers decide which of these skills will be most useful to the learners and which will be used most often in academic tasks related to the content area. Teachers then design a plan in which those skills are gradually taught throughout the year and practiced often. This is an adaptation of the curriculum, because it supplements standard content curriculum with knowledge and skills important to students' successful completion of science, social studies, literature, or math, based on individual need. For example, it is necessary in a literature class to assess which students need instruction and practice in finding the main idea of a passage. Many activities are based on the assumption that this skill has been mastered previously, which may not be true of all students.

Teachers need to follow through on the explicitly taught skills by encouraging students to use the correct forms they have learned. If the goal is to teach the main idea, instruction is given and students practice the skill. When the students are later asked to identify a main idea in the social studies text and it is misidentified, the teacher gives immediate corrective feedback and proceeds to give students practice in finding the main idea. The focus on form has in several instances tended not to undermine self-esteem but, on the contrary, to build superior skill use on the part of learners (Lightbrown & Spada, 1994; Reyes, 1992).

Building Background Knowledge and Experience

In addition to skill building, there may be a need to provide students with background experiences on which to build instruction. For example, before beginning a history unit on Reconstruction in the South, the teacher first determines the level of experience the students have with the concepts and content to be taught. Next, the teacher determines the experiences that need to be provided to equip students for understanding the content of the course (e.g., concepts of democracy and slavery, death and destruction caused by the war, etc.). This might involve discussions, pictures and projects in class at the introductory point of the unit, or it might involve videotapes, field trips, and library visits to become acquainted with the background information. Teachers must keep in mind that students may have incredibly diverse background experiences and understandings of the world; they must not assume that even the most common knowledge, such as geographic locations, the freedoms enjoyed in a democracy, or major historical events, are common to all students.

The teacher modifies the curriculum by providing students with requisite experiences as well as any other information that can be used to enhance and to formulate background knowledge. Also, the students are encouraged throughout this process to discuss and write about their own experiences relevant to the topic at hand. Making an explicit connection between their experiences and the information brings meaning to the subject matter.

SPECIFICALLY INCLUDING BOTH LANGUAGE DEVELOPMENT AND CONTENT VOCABULARY ACTIVITIES FOR STUDENTS

Activities that enhance language and vocabulary development in content areas are imperative supplements to the curriculum for several reasons. The primary reason is the strong relationship between knowledge of English vocabulary and academic achievement; to be most effective, vocabulary development needs to be closely related to subject matter (Saville-Troike, 1984). In addition, students learning English need to be adequately prepared for the content material that will be presented. Finally, English language learners need continued opportunities to develop English skills that can transfer to other courses and be used in their lives in the future (Henze & Lucas, 1993).

Language Development

Language development can be defined as curricular modifications that evoke talking, reading, and writing at the current English language level of the student. Although each of these areas is important, emphasis must be placed on creating opportunities for oral engagement, because there are surprisingly few opportunities in class for English language learners to practice and use the language they are expected to acquire (Arreaga-Mayer & Perdomo-Rivera, in press; Ramirez, 1992). Language development activities include pairs or small groups talking about issues or content, cooperative group writing projects, and cooperative group problem-solving activities.

In the social studies lesson about coastal plains Native Americans, for example, each cooperative group of four was asked to choose a Coastal Plains tribe, write a report, present it to the class, and illustrate it. The group had to first work out a plan for accomplishing all the tasks and assignments. The negotiations, discussions, and actions taken by the individual groups were socially relevant opportunities for language use and development.

In another example from the class studying archeology, before the demonstration already described was conducted, a student asked how things get buried deep underground. The teacher responded by telling the students to turn to a partner and come up with three hypotheses about how artifacts become buried so far underground. The activity took only a couple of minutes but provided students with an opportunity to practice using English language. Many teachers would be tempted to give a brief explanation themselves, unintentionally depriving students of an important aspect of instruction for English language learners.

Vocabulary Development

Content area courses in science, social studies, literature, and math are built on relevant vocabulary. Often, a lesson cannot be understood without knowledge of specific content-related vocabulary (Met, 1994).

One form of vocabulary development includes short, explicit segments of class time in which the teacher directly teaches key vocabulary. These five-minute segments consist of the teacher saying the vocabulary word, writing it on the board, asking students to say it and write it, and defining the term with pictures, demonstrations, and examples familiar to students. Vocabulary development may be an explicit part of the lesson's introduction, and it also may take place in context throughout the lesson.

Another way to reinforce vocabulary development is to form word banks. As vocabulary is introduced, words are written on butcher paper and posted around the room. These word banks become reference points for students to remember definitions and relationships between terms, and to model correct spelling.

REWRITING CURRICULUM

Most content area teachers are required to use texts that tend to be difficult for English language learners to read with comprehension. Short (1989) describes three ways of taking dense, difficult-to-read sections of text and making them more comprehensible. The three ways of adapting text are (a) graphically depicting the text, (b) outlining the text, and (c) actually rewriting sections of the

Agriculture—Farmers in the Middle Atlantic States grow many kinds of crops. In much of the region, the soil is fertile, or rich in the things plants need for growth. There is usually plenty of sunshine and rain. Each state has become famous for certain crops. New York is well known for apples. New Jersey tomatoes and blueberries, Delaware white sweet corn, Pennsylvania mushrooms, and Maryland grains are other well-known crops. Herds of dairy cattle and livestock for meat are also raised in the Middle Atlantic States. The region produces a great deal of food for the millions of people who live there.

Truck Farms—New Jersey is famous for its truck farms, which grow large amounts of many different vegetables for sale. *Truck farms* usually sell their products to businesses in a nearby city. New Jersey truck farms are the best known, but truck farms are found in all the Middle Atlantic States.

   Another way truck farmers sell their crops is at *farmers' markets* in cities. Sometimes a farmers' market is outside, on the street or in a city park. A market may be in a railroad station or in the lobby of a sky-scraper. At a farmers' market, city people and farmers can meet each other face-to-face.

Note. From "Adapting Materials for Content-Based Language Instruction" by D. Short, September 1989, *ERIC/CLL News Bulletin, 13*(1), pp. 1, 4–8. Reprinted by permission.

FIGURE 12.3. Original Text about the Middle Atlantic States

text. An original text about agriculture and truck farms in the Middle Atlantic States is referred to throughout this section (see Figure 12.3).

Graphically Depicting the Text

The literature across fields of study indicates consistently that student perfor-mance is often improved when the graphic depiction of text is possible (Clark & Paivio, 1991; Woolfolk, 1995) and when academic activities require deep processing. Graphic depiction can provide conceptual clarity to information that is difficult to grasp; it provides students with visual clues to supplement written or spoken words that may be hard to understand. English language learners typically have gaps in their vocabulary, and even a few unfamiliar words can render a topic or concept incomprehensible.

   This type of text modification appears to assist those for whom English is not a native language, but these modifications have also been demonstrated to improve the performances of students in general education and students with learning and behavior problems (Bos & Vaughn, 1994). Teachers of students learning English can use graphic organizers and visual displays effectively to supplement or replace portions of text that may be difficult to read. Visual or graphic adaptations include charts, graphs, Venn diagrams, maps, time lines, and clustering. Figure 12.4 shows a way that difficult-to-read text can be depicted graphically and, at the same time, used to teach students map skills and how to read a key (Short, 1989).

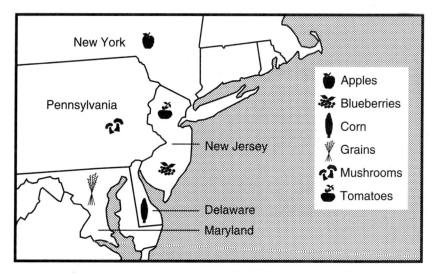

Note. From "Adapting Materials for Content-Based Language Instruction" by D. Short, September 1989, ERIC/CLL News Bulletin, 13(1), pp. 1, 4–8. Reprinted by permission.

FIGURE 12.4. Map Adaptation of Text about the Middle Atlantic States

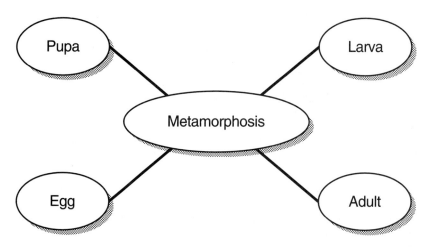

FIGURE 12.5. A Web Representing Metamorphosis

Another graphic adaptation is what is commonly referred to as a web, or cluster. This type of graphic adaptation is a useful tool in helping students organize their thoughts in a meaningful way, enabling them to recall information and recap the essence of a theme or topic. A web is among the simplest adaptations: Various aspects of a topic are written in a radiating pattern around an encircled word, the topic itself. For example, Figure 12.5 shows how a web

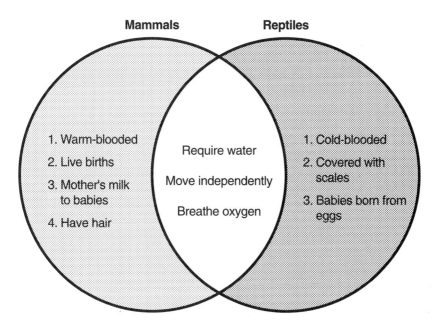

FIGURE 12.6. A Venn Diagram Comparison of Mammals to Reptiles

can be used when teaching a science lesson on metamorphosis. The encircled word represents the topic, metamorphosis, and the words radiating from the key word represent the stages of metamorphosis. Pictures may be used, in addition to the words, to add further clarity.

Venn diagrams are also examples of graphic organizers that can be used to modify text and reduce points to an easily observed, simple format. Venn diagrams have been borrowed from set theory in mathematics to demonstrate differences and similarities between situations, characters, or other selected aspects of a topic. The differences are listed in the large left- and right-hand circle portions. The similarities are listed in the intersection of the two circles. Figure 12.6 depicts a science lesson comparison of mammals to reptiles, with the intersection of the two circles representing characteristics that mammals and reptiles share, and the outer circles showing their unique characteristics.

Outlining the Text

Several types of outlining may be effective for summarizing and emphasizing important information in a text. Short (1989) shows how the original text about the Middle Atlantic States can be simplified by creating an outline (Figure 12.7). Such an outline can provide the support for a discussion or be used as a frame for note taking. The outline may also be presented graphically for further clarification.

Middle Atlantic States
I. Agriculture
   A. Many kinds of food crops
   B. State crops
      1. New York—apples
      2. New Jersey—tomatoes, blueberries
      3. Delaware—corn
      4. Pennsylvania—mushrooms
      5. Maryland—grains
   C. Cows for milk and meat
II. Truck Farms
   A. Many truck farms in New Jersey
   B. Sell vegetables to stores in a city
III. Farmers' Markets
   A. Farmers sell crops in the city
      1. On a street
      2. In a park
      3. In a train station
      4. In a building
   B. Farmers and city people meet

Note. From "Adapting Materials for Content-Based Language Instruction" by D. Short, September 1989, *ERIC/CLL News Bulletin, 13*(1), pp. 1, 4–8. Reprinted by permission.

FIGURE 12.7. Outline Adaptation of Text about the Middle Atlantic States

Rewriting Selected Sections of Text

Although time-consuming, rewriting text is an effective modification of curricular materials. Many English language learners in middle school and high school are not reading at the grade level for which the reading materials are intended. To assist student learning, written materials should be organized in small, sequential steps, avoiding long passages with dense groups of words. Short, simple sentences are preferable to long, complex ones. Here is an example of a complex sentence from a science text: "Electrons have negative electric charges and orbit around the core, nucleus, of an atom." A simple adaptation of this sentence is as follows: "Electrons have negative electric charges. They orbit around the atom. The core of the atom is called the nucleus."

In addition, rewritten paragraphs should include a topic sentence with several supporting details. The rewritten text should maintain a specific format to promote easier reading for information-seeking purposes. All sentences included in the rewritten text should be direct and relevant to the subject at hand. For example, the original text about the Middle Atlantic States (see Figure 12.3) is a series of sentences, some of which are not directly related to the topic. When the paragraph is rewritten, the format begins with a clear topic sentence, as follows: "Farmers grow many foods, or crops, in the Middle Atlantic States." The detail sentences follow with obvious support to the topic sentence (see Figure 12.8).

Agriculture in the Middle Atlantic States

Farmers grow many foods, or **crops,** in the Middle Atlantic States. The soil is good for plants. The plants have enough sunshine and rain to grow. Each state has one or two special crops:

New York—apples
New Jersey—tomatoes and blueberries
Delaware—corn
Pennsylvania—mushrooms
Maryland—grains

The farmers also raise cows. They get milk from some cows. They get meat from other cows.

New Jersey has many **truck farms.** The farmers grow a lot of vegetables. They bring the vegetables to the city by truck. They sell the vegetables to stores in the city.

Farmers also sell their crops at **farmers' markets.** Some markets are outside. They can be on streets or in city parks. Other markets are inside. They can be in train stations or in buildings. City people and farmers can meet each other at the markets.

Note. From "Adapting Materials for Content-Based Language Instruction" by D. Short, September 1989, *ERIC/CLL News Bulletin, 13*(1), pp. 1, 4–8. Reprinted by permission.

FIGURE 12.8. Rewritten Text about the Middle Atlantic States

There is no question that modifying and rewriting curriculum takes time, of which most teachers have precious little to spare. To maximize outcomes and minimize effort, a cooperative project among teachers is possible for accomplishing this goal. To cooperatively rewrite or modify curriculum, each teacher is assigned a number of chapters in the textbook to modify according to agreed-on guidelines, such as some combination of the methods just described. Then the modified chapters are collected, compiled, and distributed. This could be a within-grade-level project, a within-school project, or a district-level project. Another way to facilitate curricular modification is to get the students involved in rewriting texts and highlighting main ideas in texts as part of their assignments in the course. Students can be asked to rewrite a certain section of text, in their own words. This can be done individually, with a partner, in cooperative groups, or as a whole class, using specified guidelines for proper paragraph formation and consistency. Done another way, a language-experience approach could be used with the whole class or in small groups. With this approach, the students decide through discussion how to rewrite sections of the text, and the teacher writes what the students express. Over time, a text could be essentially rewritten by students into more comprehensible language.

An alternative to actually rewriting prose is to focus on the most salient aspects of the chapter by having students highlight main points of text during the lesson. For example, a middle school science teacher provided students with a photocopy of the chapter and had them highlight the main points with markers as she read the text aloud. Or students could be asked to focus on the topic sentence and two supporting details for each main idea throughout a section or a chapter. As is the case with rewriting, students could accomplish this individually, in small groups, or as a whole class. Students could also be asked to compare and contrast their individual highlighting and reach a consensus before submitting their highlighted section or chapter for a grade.

MODIFYING ASSIGNMENTS

If the student understands the information but is unable to express his or her knowledge in writing, allow alternative ways of expressing that knowledge. The student's language proficiency level must not be confused with his or her knowledge of the subject matter. Teachers are quite knowledgeable about a variety of topics, but if asked to explain a concept such as the three branches of the U.S. government in a language other than English, most would be unable to communicate the knowledge they possess. The same is true of English language learners—their language skills may restrict expression of their actual understanding of subject matter.

Alternative forms of expressing understanding include asking students to draw maps or pictorial representations, or to orally express their understanding through discussions in pairs or small groups.

Ask Students to Draw

Requiring students to draw maps or pictures can enhance learning and function as an alternative form of expression for students who are struggling with English. One high school science teacher asked students to draw a map of the water cycle. Students were learning about condensation and evaporation. Asking students to draw a map of the cycle of water was an alternative way to seek the knowledge that students had gained regarding the cycle. In a sheltered driver's education class, the teacher accepted labeled drawings in lieu of short written answers, which were difficult for some beginning speakers of English. In describing hydroplaning, one student drew a tire on a wet street and wrote the words "slippery, dangerous, hard to brake." The teacher accepted this alternative expression of the concept.

Discuss Material in Pairs and Small Groups

One middle school social studies teacher we observed paired students with stronger English language skills with those who had greater difficulties with the language. Whenever she asked a question for which there was more than one right answer, she asked students to turn to their partners and talk about the answer. In addition, this teacher created problem-solving activities and projects in which students were placed in four-person cooperative groups. In those groups, there were usually two English language learners who had stronger skills, and two who were not fluent. In one cooperative group assignment, students were asked to construct an Old West boomtown. Each group had access to wooden sticks, glue, colored paper, marking pens, crayons, and scissors. Students were to construct the towns based on their knowledge of the gold rush and the types of businesses that were likely to be present. These types of alternative group structures and alternative assignments were ideal for students who are struggling to learn English as well as content material.

Reduce the Length and Complexity of Assignments

Another way to modify assignments is to reduce their length and complexity. Have students answer only the even-numbered problems or questions; break down complex assignments into simpler, more meaningful parts. Multipart assignments can be overwhelming, and breaking down the assignment provides a model for students of how to systematically undertake assignments.

DEMONSTRATING SENSITIVITY TO CULTURAL AND LINGUISTIC DIVERSITY THROUGH APPROPRIATE CONTENT ADAPTATIONS

Culturally and linguistically appropriate curriculum is essential (Gaye, 1988, 1993). Culturally relevant literature is now available for most groups, and it has been established that the use of this literature can lead to increased success for students (Baca & Cervantes, 1989; Lynch & Hansen, 1992). In addition, student motivation is likely to be enhanced when modifications and adaptations of curricula include information about and examples from the cultural groups represented in the class (Banks, 1991).

A study with Latinos in their high school English classes (Trueba, 1990) provides an example of responsive teaching. English teachers modified the standard curriculum by giving students an assignment to conduct authentic research and write about their own lives and community. The students were more motivated, and the high quality of their work exceeded the teachers expectations.

Another example of responsive teaching can be seen in Short's (1994) description of adapted social studies lessons, which include significant amounts of information on the cultural diversity that existed at the time of the American Revolution. This is a way of illustrating to recent immigrant students that the United States has been a culturally diverse society since its inception. Of course, any books that emphasize the contributions of African Americans, Native Americans, European Americans, Asian Americans, Arab Americans, Jews, and Latinos throughout history are preferable. Other instances of responsive teaching include using current events familiar to students as examples when defining certain historical terminology, such as *protest*. Specifically, newspaper clippings (including pictures) from the events in Los Angeles after the first Rodney King verdict would be a modern example of the vocabulary word *protest* (Short, 1994). Adapting text materials in these ways exemplifies responsive teaching.

SUMMARY

This chapter has reviewed curricular adaptations that concern teaching content material to secondary students who are learning English. Teachers of science, social studies, literature, and math in middle school and high school face tremendous challenges—indeed, there are no easy answers. Teachers must guide students to listen, speak, read, and write in English while teaching them secondary curriculum. These two tasks are intertwined; curriculum adaptations provide an avenue for accomplishing these tasks more effectively.

Selecting the most critical content knowledge and using visuals to the maximum extent possible; determining the academic proficiency necessary for effectively learning the content; including language development and content vocabulary knowledge activities for students; rewriting curriculum; modifying assignments; and demonstrating sensitivity to cultural and linguistic diversity—all these techniques provide ways for content area teachers of English language learners to make existing texts and materials more relevant, meaningful, and comprehensible for their students.

REFERENCES

Arreaga-Mayer, C., & Perdomo-Rivera, C. (in press). Ecocultural analysis of instruction for at-risk language-minority students. *Elementary School Journal.*

Baca, L. M., & Cervantes, H. T. (1989). *The bilingual special education interface* (2nd ed.). Columbus, OH: Merrill.

Banks, J. A. (1991). A curriculum for empowerment, action, and change. In C. E. Sleeter (Ed.), *Empowerment through multicultural education* (pp.125–141). Albany, NY: State University of New York.

Bos, C., & Vaughn, S. (1994). *Strategies for teaching students with learning and behavior problems.* Needham Heights, MA: Allyn and Bacon.

Clark, J., & Paivio, A. (1991). Dual coding theory and education. *Educational Psychology Review, 3,* 149–210.

Echevarria, J., & Graves, A. (1998). *Sheltered content instruction: Teaching English-language learners with diverse abilities.* Boston: Allyn & Bacon.

Faltis, C. J. (1993). Critical issues in the use of sheltered content teaching in high school bilingual programs. *Peabody Journal of Education: Trends in Bilingual Education at the Secondary Level, 69*(1), 136–151.

Fradd, S. (1987). Accommodating the needs of limited English proficient students in regular classrooms. In S. Fradd & W. Tikunoff (Eds.), *Bilingual education and special education: A guide for administrators.* Boston: Little, Brown.

Gaye, G. (1988). Designing relevant curricula for diverse learners. *Education in Urban Societies, 20,* 327–340.

Gaye, G. (1993). Building cultural bridges: A bold proposal for teacher education, *Education in Urban Societies, 25,* 285–299.

Gonzales, L. (1994). *The sheltered instruction handbook.* Carlsbad, CA: Gonzales & Gonzales.

Goodwin, J. (1991). *Asian remedial plan: A study of sheltered and co-taught classes in new instructional model secondary schools.* (ERIC Document Reproduction Service No. 344 956)

Henze, R. C., & Lucas, T. (1993). Shaping instruction to promote the success of language minority students: An analysis of four high school classes. *Peabody Journal of Education: Trends in Bilingual Education at the Secondary Level, 69*(1), 54–81.

Lightbrown, P. M., & Spada, N. (1994). An innovative program for primary ESL students in Quebec. *TESOL Quarterly, 28*(3), 563–580.

Lucas, T., & Katz, A. (1994). Reframing the debate: The roles of native languages in English-only programs for language minority students. *TESOL Quarterly, 28*(3), 537–562.

Lynch, E. W., & Hansen, M. J. (1992). *Developing crosscultural competence: A guide for working with young children and their families.* Baltimore, MD: Brooks.

Met, M. (1994). Teaching content through a second language. In F. Genesee (Ed.), *Educating Second Language Children.* New York: Cambridge University Press.

Minicucci, C. (1993). Setting a research and policy agenda for the education of secondary students with limited English proficiency: Results of an invitational conference. *Peabody Journal of Education: Trends in Bilingual Education at the Secondary Level, 69*(1), 173–185.

O'Dell, S. (1970). *Island of the blue dolphins.* Boston: Houghton Mifflin.

Ramirez, J. D. (1992). Executive summary. *Bilingual Research Journal, 16,* 1–62.

Reyes, M. (1992). Challenging venerable assumptions: Literacy instruction for linguistically different students. *Harvard Educational Review, 62*(4), 427–446.

Saville-Troike, M. (1984). What really matters in second language learning for academic achievement? *TESOL Quarterly, 18,* 2.

Schumm, J., Vaughn, S., & Leavell, A. (1994). Planning pyramid: A framework for planning for diverse student needs during content area instruction. *The Reading Teacher, 47*(8), 608–615.

Short, D. (1989). Adapting materials for content-based language instruction. *ERIC/CLL News Bulletin, 13*(1), 1, 4–8.

Short, D. (1994). Expanding middle school horizons: Integrating language, culture, and social studies. *TESOL Quarterly, 28,* 581–608.

Trueba, H. (1990). Compassion and equity: Culture and English literacy for linguistic minority children. In H. Baptiste, H. Waxman, J. Walker de Felix & J. Anderson (Eds.), *Leadership, Equity, and School Effectiveness.* London: Sage Publications.

Woolfolk, A. (1995). *Educational Psychology.* Needham Heights, MA: Allyn and Bacon.

13

Productive Teaching of English Language Learners

What We Know and Still Need to Know

Sharon Vaughn
University of Texas, Austin

Russell Gersten
Eugene Research Institute
University of Oregon

S tudents who are learning English as a second language (i.e., English language learners) will represent the majority of students in California schools by the year 2030 (Garcia, 1993). Although the percentage of English language learners is climbing faster in California, Texas, and Florida than in other parts of the United States, every state will experience considerable increases in the number of these students. Even low-growth states, such as Illinois, Michigan, New Jersey, New York, Ohio, and Pennsylvania, will experience appreciable increases in the percentage of English language learners (Hodgkinson, 1995). By the year 2007, Latinos will overtake African Americans to become the largest ethnic minority group in the United States (Yzaguirre, 1995). For schools, the obvious implication of these demographic changes is that every teacher must be prepared to successfully teach students for whom English is not their primary language of communication.

The purpose of this book is to provide specific guidelines and instructional practices that teachers can use to enhance the academic outcomes and language proficiency of English language learners. Although many questions remain unanswered, the chapters in this book provide evidence that appropriate practices for English language learners are available and feasible for classroom implementation.

TRANSFORMING CLASSROOMS INTO LANGUAGE-LEARNING WORKSHOPS

Successful teachers of English language learners often think of their classrooms as language-learning workshops and provide structured and consistent opportunities for students to work on learning a second language. These opportunities can be organized so that students learn as much from each other as from the teacher (Bos & Reyes, 1996). If English language learners are to have adequate opportunities to learn a new language and grapple with concepts in the new language, it is essential that learning environments be established to provide instructional mediation and feedback (Arreaga-Mayer, chap. 5). Though difficult to achieve, the process of integrating language learning within the core curriculum is essential for successful language learning and content acquisition. In contrast, excessive questioning in which the teacher controls the conversation and students respond in one- or two-word answers does not result in the opportunities English language learners need to develop proficiency in English. Only by expressing more-complex ideas (i.e., structuring their thoughts into sentences and sequences of sentences) can English language learners successfully learn and integrate the structures of the new language. Unfortunately, a nonconversational recitation approach characterizes discourse in most classrooms (Moll, 1988; Oakes, 1986), even in those classrooms where the percentage of English language learners is high.

Use Peer Tutoring and Cooperative Learning to Actively Engage Students

Arreaga-Mayer (chap. 5) has identified several whole-class activities that teachers can implement to actively engage students in learning. One of the critical features of these activities is that they hold *all* students in the group accountable for learning. A second critical feature is that they require active responding on the part of the student. These activities are effective for heterogeneous groups of students and for pairs of students. They include ClassWide Peer Tutoring (CWPT) (Greenwood, Delquadri, & Cara, 1988), Student Teams and Achievement Divisions (STAD) (Slavin, 1978, 1988, 1991), and Numbered Heads Together (NHT) (Kagan, 1985, 1989–90). These activities are discussed in detail in chapter 5.

Alternative grouping practices that include partners, small groups, cooperative groups, and flexible groups provide opportunities for students to practice their language, share knowledge, and work together (Graves, chap. 10; Klingner & Vaughn, 1996). Teachers need to organize these groups to ensure that all students have a role, that instruction results in purposeful interaction between students, and that instruction includes procedures that hold students responsible for specific learning outcomes. A major benefit of CWPT and cooperative learning is that students can talk in both English and a native language in a nonthreatening environment, which greatly increases the chances of active student engagement.

Make Curriculum Accessible
to English Language Learners

An orienting premise of instruction for English language learners is to make curriculum concepts accessible to them (Echevarria, chap. 12; Fradd, 1987). To ensure accessibility, teachers must engage in a wide array of strategies that simultaneously work on (a) English language proficiency, (b) knowledge of complex content in content areas, and (c) comprehension (Echevarria & Graves, in preparation; Jiménez & Gámez, chap. 9; Klingner & Vaughn, 1996).

In Goodlad's (1993) discussion of the "moral imperative" for school reform, he noted that "parental satisfaction with a child's daily enjoyment of a humane, caring school can come to be enough, and it is much to be thankful for. But it is not enough" (p. 19). In fact, it may serve only as a way to set the stage for serious attempts at instructional interventions. This was precisely the case in the action research of Goldenberg and Sullivan (Goldenberg, 1996), who engaged in a collaborative project to improve reading achievement in a school where the school climate was excellent for English language learning, but reading achievement was dismal. Through the strategies discussed in Goldenberg's chapter in this book (chap. 1), they were able to help the school become not only a place where English language learners felt comfortable but also a place where students learned how to read. In essence, Goldenberg and Sullivan found that a blended model of reading instruction worked best. Students received structured instruction in learning the alphabetic principle, and the importance of reading as a meaning-based activity was always emphasized. The concerted schoolwide focus on literacy and the belief that English language learners could learn to read at grade-level standards were the major factors in the program's success.

Echevarria (chap. 12) provides a framework for secondary teachers to assist them in making the curriculum more accessible to English language learners. Within this framework, teachers are asked to seriously address basic orienting questions, such as, What material should I cover? How should I cover this material? What accommodations and adaptations should I make to ensure that English language learners have full access to the content? Echevarria suggests that teachers use the planning pyramid (Schumm, Vaughn, & Leavell, 1994) to assist with planning and instruction. In essence, teachers need to determine the principles or concepts that all students, regardless of English proficiency or ability to read the text, will learn.

At the secondary level, issues for English language learners shift from academic skills to content knowledge or subject matter knowledge. The issue of foundational academic skills, a primary focus in the elementary grades, is important at the secondary level primarily to the extent to which it enhances or impedes content knowledge learning (Echevarria, chap. 12; Graves, chap. 10). Because content learning is so important and reading problems so extensive, even for native English-speaking students, an emphasis in the secondary grades needs to be determining in a careful, systematic, and comprehensive way what *all* students should learn, regardless of the severity of their reading problems. Whereas in traditional models there may be an emphasis on providing secondary English language learners with a constant diet of basic skills instruction at the expense of content area instruction, more-contemporary models stress that even students with poor reading skills should have access to the same secondary content as students in the mainstream. English language learners may continue to have structured opportunities to develop and practice their fundamental reading skills (in the context of this secondary content), but other strategies (e.g., concept maps and CWPT) have to be used to ensure that reading difficulties do not preclude meaningful opportunities to learn and understand content area material.

INSTRUCTION FOR
ENGLISH LANGUAGE LEARNERS

Relate Home, Community, and Personal Experiences to What Students Are Learning in the Classroom

Increasingly, research demonstrates that learning is enhanced when new concepts are explicitly and clearly linked to the concrete experiences of students. Though this notion of connecting the child's interests, experiences, and community to the everyday learning experiences in the classroom may seem obvious, it is extremely difficult to integrate effectively.

Perhaps the best way to consider the link between a student's home/community experiences and school is to capitalize on what Moll (1988) refers to as the "funds" of knowledge that students bring to the classroom. If we consider that all students have unique and important experiences to share with us in the classroom, we approach students as individuals who can teach as well as learn from us and other students. In this conceptualization, students become class experts in particular areas, as well as sources of knowledge. Elba Reyes (Bos & Reyes, 1996) provided the following example of how she integrated a student's knowledge into the curriculum: "The teacher learned that one of her students was involved in a home business of making and selling tamales. This topic became the focal point for an integrated unit that involved math as it relates to measurement and money, social studies as it relates to setting up and managing a business, and literacy as students read and wrote about home businesses" (p. 350).

One obvious reason for failure to make these linkages is that teachers often lack adequate knowledge of students' experiences and of the communities and cultures from which these experiences are derived and can be interpreted. Teachers' understanding of this "information" can be increased through home visits, publicizing in the school the perspectives and values of community members, and, when possible, developing relationships with teachers from other countries (e.g., Mexico, Russia, Laos). English language learners can be encouraged to express these experiences and the worlds in which they live through academic activities such as Writers' Workshop (WW) (Gersten, 1996).

Many of the instructional techniques discussed in this book can encourage English language learners to make linkages between school and home and provide teachers with strategies to help make these linkages explicit. Integrating and linking home and school experiences can often be an awkward process, because cultural and social-class differences result in miscommunication. For example, Gersten found that teachers tended to minimize or redirect classroom discussions of troubling but nonetheless very real aspects of students' lives, such as poverty. Of course, the majority of these linkages will be positive, playing off concrete images of friendship, family trips, values, and personal interests in music, food, and dress, and they can be woven into classroom activities that help students' understandings of concepts like pride, anger, warmth, and memory.

Many of the strategies in this book are intended to build and support these linkages. For young children, the home-school connection is an essential means of assisting them in feeling that they are secure and their knowledge is valued (De León & Medina, chap. 2). They learn to appreciate that they are wanted and valued members of the classroom community and that their experiences are cherished. Developing these kinds of classrooms enhances opportunities for academic achievement. High expectations and systematic instruction that builds early literacy knowledge can occur more easily in classrooms where students feel that they are valued and their experiences are respected (Goldenberg & Gallimore, 1991). Connections between students' life experiences and school learning yield increased engagement and learning at the elementary and secondary levels (Graves, chap. 10).

Saunders, O'Brien, Lennon, and McLean (chap. 7) also refer to the importance of "drawing on students' personal experiences" for instructional purposes. They suggest that teachers can make adaptations in stories and activities to reflect these personal experiences. For example, after reading a story about a boy whose grandfather frequently told him stories, the teacher can integrate students' experiences by asking simple questions, such as What stories have you heard from someone in your family? or, What stories do you think you will want to remember to tell your grandchildren? Notice how generic these types of questions can be. They require no special training to ask, only a concerted effort to help children connect learning to their own experiences.

There are many subtle and not so subtle ways the school system, administrators, and teachers can convince students that they are a marginalized and unwelcome group. To prevent this, teachers need to actively build bridges between the children's experiences, families, and homes and the activities and expectations of the classroom. Connecting with students' backgrounds and experiences acknowledges their importance, thus linking them to the school community and learning.

Involve Parents in Their Child's Literacy Development

A common misconception throughout society is that parents of English language learners are either not interested in their child's schooling or too busy to be involved. On the contrary, they want to help and to be informed (Goldenberg, chap. 1). In fact, opinion polls and research demonstrate that educational achievement is one of the most important issues to Hispanics (De La Rosa & Maw, 1990). Parents are highly interested in doing what they know how to do, or are able to learn to do, to help their children.

Most Hispanic parents view their role as critical to their child's success in school (Goldenberg & Gallimore, 1991). When Hispanic parents are not involved, it is typically because they are unaware of the activities they should be involved in to help, or because they experience barriers to their participation (Harry, 1992; Klimes-Dougan, Lopez, Nelson, & Adelman, 1992). For example, in a study of Puerto Rican parents of children with disabilities, the lack of meaning of various special education procedures led to their withdrawal (Harry, 1992).

A study by Hughes (1995) illustrates some of the complexities in understanding parents' interest in being involved in the education of their children. Eighty Hispanic parents (40 parents of students with learning disabilities and 40 parents of average to high-achieving students) participated in a series of interviews and surveys. There were few differences between parent groups on the types of reading and writing activities the parents engaged in with their children at home. Activities that occurred with regularity included parents' reading books or stories to their children, parents' taking their children to the library, and parents' providing books and magazines for their children to use. When parents were asked what the schools could do to assist them in helping their children with reading and writing activities, parents most frequently stated that the schools and teachers needed to talk with them more. A Hispanic parent of a student with LD stated, "I think that it is very important to have meetings with the teachers every so often, to see how the child is progressing." In terms of barriers to assisting their children at home, the most common response was that the parents had difficulty with the English language. One parent said, "I do not speak much English. My pronunciation is bad. I do not like to go to the school if the people there speak to me in English."

The Hispanic parents in this study, like those in previous studies, valued their role in assisting with the education of their children. They often experienced barriers, primarily language related, that inhibited their communication and participation. However, they expressed high levels of interest in learning to do what would be helpful to enhance their children's reading and writing skills.

Use the Language of Acceptance

Students of all ages are able to detect when teachers are concerned about their welfare and are interested in them. When students perceive that teachers are personally interested in them and their learning, they are more engaged in learning. This may mean that teachers of young children use terms of endearment that are also used in the home and community (De León & Medina, chap. 2). With older students, it means taking extra time to ask about their progress or to follow up on a personal or family matter disclosed in class. Graves (chap. 10) reminds us of the importance of establishing a personal relationship with students and demonstrating interest in them. Teachers should know the "expertise" of all students in their classes and take advantage of that knowledge by giving all students the opportunity to be an expert on something.

Teachers have myriad ways to show acceptance of students in their classes. Looks of acceptance, warm greetings, genuine interest and concern for their welfare, and time spent to ensure understanding should be fundamental aspects of classroom culture. At all grades, teachers who are successful with English language learners are vigilant about finding students who are not fitting in, and then assisting them (Echevarria, chap. 12; Jiménez & Gámez, chap. 9).

This construct of the balance between acceptance and maintaining high reading standards is captured by Gersten (1996), who refers to respect for and responsiveness to cultural and personal diversity. This respect and responsiveness is often difficult to define, but English language learners, and other groups of students who are frequently marginalized, are aware of it when they receive it. As Palincsar (1996) reminds us, "The role of interpersonal relationships is central to understanding the successes and difficulties we encounter in teaching language-minority students" (p. 225).

Develop a Coherent Plan to Affect Change
in Outcomes for English Language Learners

To achieve success, schools must develop and stay focused on a systematic plan designed to enhance outcomes for English language learners (Goldenberg, chap. 1). It is probably impossible to overemphasize the importance of developing a plan, implementing it over several years, and evaluating outcomes in objective ways to determine the plan's success. Only then will schools be able to develop procedures for maintaining effective practices and modifying or discarding practices that are ineffective. Goldenberg (chap. 1) illustrates the difficulty of maintaining this focus in the context of typical school environments: "At our study school, as at many schools over the past decade, a steady downpour of initiatives and changes had fallen on school personnel, making it very difficult for teachers and administrators to maintain a consistent and coherent focus for their work." Their program was radically different in that literacy for English language learners remained the major focus for years.

In summary, while empirical studies of effective instructional practices and curriculum for English language learners are needed (Gersten, 1996), there is a knowledge base on which effective practices for English language learners can be determined (Gersten & Woodward, 1994). Saunders et al. (chap. 7) identify four fundamental theoretical premises that promote first and second language acquisition as well as academic achievement. These four Cs of instruction for English language learners are (a) challenge—providing ongoing opportunities for students to challenge each other, be challenged by the teacher and curriculum, and be engaged intellectually; (b) comprehensiveness—providing both skills and meaning instruction through teacher- and child-centered activities; (c) continuity—providing for smooth transitions in curriculum and instruction as students move through the grades; and (d) connections—building bridges between the student's knowledge and the academic curriculum.

REFERENCES

Bos, C. B., & Reyes, E. I. (1996). Conversations with a Latina teacher about education for language-minority students with special needs. *Elementary School Journal, 96*(3), 343–351.

De La Rosa, D., & Maw, C. (1990). *Hispanic education: A statistical portrait.* Washington, DC: National Council of La Raza.

Fradd, S. (1987). Accommodating the needs of limited English proficient students in regular classrooms. In S. Fradd & W. Tikunoff (Eds.), *Bilingual education and special education: A guide for administrators.* Boston: Little, Brown.

Garcia, E. (1993). *Education of linguistically and culturally diverse students: Effective instructional practices.* Santa Cruz, CA: National Center for Research on Cultural Diversity and Second Language Learning. (Educational Practice Report No. 1).

Gersten, R. (1996). Literacy instruction for language-minority students: the transition years. *The Elementary School Journal, 96*(3), 227–244.

Gersten, R., & Woodward, J. (1994). The language minority student and special education: Issues, themes, and paradoxes. *Exceptional Children, 60*(4), 310–322.

Goldenberg, C., & Gallimore, R. (1991). Local knowledge, research knowledge, and educational change: A case study of early Spanish reading improvement. *Educational Researcher, 20,* 2–14.

Harry, B. (1992). An ethnographic study of cross-cultural communication with Puerto Rican–American families in the special education system. *American Educational Research Journal, 29,* 471–494.

Hodgkinson, H. L. (1995). A demographer's view. In National Governors' Association, *What Governors Need to Know About Education Reform Perspectives* (pp. 53–56). Washington, DC: National Governors' Association.

Hughes, M. E. T. (1995). Parent involvement in literacy instruction: Perceptions and practices of Hispanic parents of children with learning disabilities. Unpublished doctoral dissertation, University of Miami.

Klimes-Dougan, B., Lopez, J. A., Nelson, P., & Adelman, H. S. (1992). Two studies of low income parents' involvement in schooling. *Urban Review, 24,* 185–202.

Klingner, J. K., & Vaughn, S. (1996). Reciprocal teaching of reading comprehension strategies for students with learning disabilities who use English as a second language. *Elementary School Journal, 96*(3), 275–293.

Moll, L. C. (1988). Some key issues in teaching Latino students. *Language Arts, 65,* 465–472.

Oakes, J. (1986). Tracking, inequality, and the rhetoric of school reform: Why schools don't change. *Journal of Education, 168,* 61–80.

Palincsar, A. S. (1996). Commentary: Language-minority students: Instructional issues in school cultures and classroom social systems. *Elementary School Journal, 96*(3), 221–226.

Schumm, J. S., Vaughn, S., & Leavell, A. G. (1994). Planning pyramid: A framework for planning for diverse student needs during content area instruction. *The Reading Teacher, 47*(8), 608–615.

Yzaguirre, R. (1995). In our nation's best interest: Achieving educational excellence for Latinos. In National Governors' Association, *What Governors Need to Know About Education Reform Perspectives* (pp. 119–122). Washington, DC: National Governors' Association.

Index